ETHNIC CONFLICT
IN WORLD POLITICS

D0280293

DILEMMAS IN WORLD POLITICS

Series Editor
George A. Lopez, University of Notre Dame

Dilemmas in World Politics offers teachers and students of international relations a series of quality books on critical issues, trends, and regions in international politics. Each text examines a "real world" dilemma and is structured to cover the historical, theoretical, practical, and projected dimensions of its subject.

EDITORIAL BOARD

FORTHCOMING TITLES

Deborah J. Gerner
**One Land, Two Peoples:
The Conflict over Palestine, second edition**

□ □ □

Gareth Porter and Janet Welsh Brown
Global Environmental Politics, second edition

□ □ □

Bruce E. Moon
International Trade in the 1990s

□ □ □

Karen Mingst and Margaret P. Karns
The United Nations in the Post–Cold War Era

ETHNIC CONFLICT IN WORLD POLITICS

■ ■ ■

Ted Robert Gurr

UNIVERSITY OF MARYLAND AT COLLEGE PARK

Barbara Harff

U.S. NAVAL ACADEMY

Westview Press

BOULDER □ SAN FRANCISCO □ OXFORD

Dilemmas in World Politics Series

Copyright © 1994 by Westview Press, Inc.

Published in 1994 in the United States of America by Westview Press, Inc., 5500 Central Avenue, Boulder, Colorado 80301-2877, and in the United Kingdom by Westview Press, 36 Lonsdale Road, Summertown, Oxford OX2 7EW

Library of Congress Cataloging-in-Publication Data
Gurr, Ted Robert, 1936–
    Ethnic conflict in world politics / Ted Robert Gurr and Barbara Harff.
        p.   cm. — (Dilemmas in world politics)
    Includes bibliographical references and index.
    ISBN 0-8133-1696-0. — ISBN 0-8133-1697-9 (pbk.)
    1. World politics—1989–   . 2. Ethnic relations—Political aspects.
3. Minorities.   I. Harff, Barbara, 1942–   . II. Title.
III. Series.
D860.G87   1994
305.8—dc20
                                                                                    94-10406
                                                                                    CIP

Printed and bound in the United States of America

The paper used in this publication meets the requirements of the American National Standard for Permanence of Paper for Printed Library Materials Z39.48-1984.

10   9   8   7   6   5   4   3   2   1

Contents

□ □ □

Tables and Illustrations

Photographs and Cartoons

□ □ □

Preface

In 1993, two years after the Cold War ended, twenty-two "hot" wars were still being fought around the world. Communal rivalries and ethnic challenges to states contributed to conflict in all but five of these episodes. About 25 million refugees were fleeing from communal conflict and repression, a number equivalent to the entire population of Canada. At least 4 million people reportedly had died as a direct or an indirect result of these conflicts, two hundred thousand of them in 1993 alone. The United Nations had thirteen peacekeeping operations under way, the most ever in its fifty-year history, and seven of these were aimed at separating the protagonists in communal conflicts.[1] This evidence does not signal "the end of history" but, rather, the early phase of a new era in world history, one that does not yet have a name. This book is an introduction to the new era of ethnic challenges to world order and security.

In the first chapter we use examples to illustrate the importance of ethnic conflict in the changing global system. In Chapter 2 we identify the main types of politically active ethnic groups, discuss their grievances and political strategies, and summarize the historical processes that explain why they have been and continue to be important actors in domestic and international politics.

In Chapters 3 and 4 we sketch the historical background and conflicts of four peoples. The Kurds in the Middle East and the Miskito Indians of Central America, the subjects of Chapter 3, are examples of groups whose members have a strong sense of communal interest and identity they want to protect by gaining political independence or autonomy. We chose to analyze the Kurds for two reasons. First, their nationalist aspirations continue to be a major challenge to regional stability in the Middle East. Second, Iraqi attacks on the Kurds in 1991 led to a precedent-setting collective response: The United Nations authorized for the first time the use of force to establish a protected zone for victimized people in a sovereign state. The Miskitos are not nationalists, nor have they suffered to the extent of the Kurds. Like most indigenous peoples, the Miskitos are mainly concerned with protecting their traditional lifeways, land, and resources. We selected them because unlike most other indigenous peoples, they rebelled against the Nicaraguan government, enabling themselves to take advantage of the U.S.-backed Contra war against the Sandinistas to secure greater autonomy.

The Chinese in Malaysia and the Turkish immigrants in Germany, described in Chapter 4, have been concerned mainly with protecting and improving their status in multiethnic societies. The low status and lack of citizenship rights of Turks in Germany typify the situation of many immigrants from poorer countries to developed Western societies. We are particularly interested in the Chinese in Malaysia because despite a history of insurgency in the 1950s and victimization in racial rioting in the 1960s, they have secured a power-sharing role in one of Asia's most successful examples of a modernizing, democratic state.

Chapter 5 begins with a review of some social science approaches to explaining communal conflict; we then propose a theoretical framework for analyzing the ways internal and international conditions lead ethnic groups into open conflict with states. This framework was developed and used by Barbara Harff in undergraduate courses. It takes a scientific approach, one that emphasizes precision and objectivity, which some readers may not find congenial. In Harff's experience it is pedagogically successful because it identifies for students the broad range of factors that need to be taken into account in case studies and helps overcome students' tendency to let preconceptions guide their selection and interpretation of evidence on value-laden topics.

We use the framework in Chapters 6 and 7 to compare the status and mobilization of the four groups analyzed in Chapters 3 and 4 and to assess some of the consequences of ethnic conflict. This leads us into a discussion of important policy issues such as how democracy affects ethnic conflict and whether countries' international economic and political status affects their treatment of minorities.

The eruption of new ethnic conflicts since the end of the Cold War and the persistence of old ones pose major legal, political, and humanitarian challenges to the international system. These challenges are identified in Chapter 1; international responses to them are the subjects of Chapters 8 and 9. We argue that an effective set of national and international policies of peacemaking in ethnic conflicts is rapidly emerging and that the political will to implement these policies consistently is needed most of all.

Ted Robert Gurr is largely responsible for the comparative analysis of ethnic groups in Chapters 1 and 2, the case studies of the Kurds and Miskitos in Chapter 3, the case study of the Turks in Germany, and the appendix. He also contributed the comparative analysis of the internal dynamics of ethnic conflict in Chapter 6 and the analysis of the international dimensions of conflicts involving the Miskitos and Turks in Germany in Chapter 7. Barbara Harff wrote the sections on the historical and international contexts of ethnic conflict in Chapters 1 and 2 and the analyses of the international system and its responses to ethnic conflict in Chapters 8 and 9. As noted earlier, she prepared the framework and methodological guidelines in Chapter 5. She also contributed the case study of the Chinese in Malaysia in Chapter 4 and the international analysis of the Kurds and the Chinese Malaysians in Chapter 7. We have both read and commented extensively on one another's sections. This book is, in other words, a fully collaborative effort.

We should like to acknowledge the support provided by the Interdisciplinary Program of Research on Root Causes of Human Rights Violations (known by its Dutch acronym, PIOOM) at the University of Leiden, the Netherlands, where we held appointments as visiting fellows during the first half of 1993. Ted Robert Gurr thanks Shin-wha Lee and the staff of the Minorities at Risk Project at the University of Maryland's Center for International Development and Conflict Management, who provided much of the source material for the case studies. Barbara Harff thanks the U.S. Naval Academy for giving her a semester's sabbatical to pursue this project. Far from least, we are indebted to Jennifer Knerr of Westview Press and to George Lopez, the series editor, for their sustained encouragement and advice.

Ted Robert Gurr
Barbara Harff

□ □ □

Acronyms

ALPROMISU	Alianza para el Progreso de Miskitos y Sumos (Alliance for the Progress of Miskitos and Sumus)
CIA	Central Intelligence Agency
CPM	Communist Party of Malaya
CSCE	Conference on Security and Cooperation in Europe
ILO	International Labor Organization
KDP	Kurdish Democratic Party (Iraq)
KDPI	Kurdish Democratic Party of Iran
MCA	Malaysian Chinese Association
MISURA	Miskitos, Sumus, and Ramas
MISURASATA	Miskitos, Sumus, Ramas, and Sandinistas United
NATO	North Atlantic Treaty Organization
NDP	National Democratische Partei, or National Democratic Party (Germany)
NEP	New Economic Policy
NGO	nongovernmental organization
OAU	Organization of African Unity
PKK	Partiya Karkaren Kurdistan, or Kurdish Worker's Party (Turkey)
PUK	Patriotic Union of Kurdistan (Iraq)
UNITA	União Nacional para a Indepêndencia Total de Angola (National Union for the Total Independence of Angola)
YATAMA	Yapti Tasbaya Masrika (Children of Mother Earth)

ONE

□ □ □

Ethnic Conflict
and the Changing World Order

Maps that show the world divided neatly into countries, each with its own boundaries and territory, convey a misleading image of people's political identities. Whereas most of the people who live within the boundaries of France think of themselves first and foremost as French, others—perhaps one-tenth of the population—think of themselves first as Bretons, Corsicans, Maghrebins, or members of other nationalities. Some may not strongly identify with France. If this is true of France, which has one of the oldest centralized governments in Europe, consider how many other competing ethnic identities may be found in newer countries, like Indonesia, Iraq, and Sudan.

This is the testimony of a young man whose life has been disrupted by ethnic conflict: Anselmo was a twenty-five-year-old Roman Catholic seminarian in the Indonesian province of East Timor who fled in 1988. "I am Timorese," he testified to the United Nations Sub-Commission on Human Rights later that year. "I had to abandon my country and my parents. I felt I could no longer bear to live there." When Anselmo was twelve the Indonesian army invaded East Timor, a region that had been governed by Portuguese colonial authorities since the sixteenth century. Four times between ages fifteen and twenty-five Anselmo was beaten and abused by soldiers for such infractions as walking past a military cemetery. Relatives were imprisoned because they were suspected of supporting the Timorese resistance, and some were tortured; two cousins were forced to serve the Indonesian army as porters and were later executed. Finally, when students and staff at St. Joseph's College, where Anselmo taught, were arrested and interrogated, he decided to flee. "My experience makes me fear reprisals against my family because of my testimony," he concluded, "and I therefore ask you to use every means you can to protect those of my family who have stayed in Timor and to promote the fundamental rights of the Timorese people."[1]

1

Individuals' feelings about their identity vary widely. Some people identify strongly with the state of which they are citizens, whereas others, like Anselmo, identify with their ethnic kindred. In this chapter we set the scene for the analysis of these kinds of identity-driven conflicts in world politics. First we sketch several contemporary examples, then we provide a global snapshot of the extent of **ethnopolitical conflict.** We then show how international factors, including changes in the world system, continue to reshape conflicts between **ethnic groups** and states.

CONTEMPORARY EXAMPLES OF ETHNOPOLITICAL CONFLICT

Since the 1960s increasing numbers of ethnic groups have begun to demand more rights and recognition, demands that are now recognized as the major source of domestic and international conflict in the post–Cold War world. (A listing of ethnic conflicts in 1993 is found in the Appendix.) The protagonists in the most intense ethnic conflicts want to establish their **autonomy** or independence, as was the case with the people of East Timor. Other ethnic conflicts arise from efforts by subordinate groups to improve their status within the existing boundaries of a state rather than to secede from it. For example, most black South Africans want majority control of state power. Turkish and other recent immigrants to Germany are worried about their security, seek greater economic opportunities, and hope to become citizens. Native peoples in the Americas want to protect what is left of their traditional lands and cultures from the corrosive influences of modern society. Here we consider some implications of both kinds of ethnic conflict.

The **civil wars** accompanying the dissolution of Yugoslavia into five new states show that subject people's demands for autonomy are seldom settled peacefully. After Slovenia, Croatia, and Bosnia declared independence in summer 1991, Serbia—the dominant partner in the old Yugoslavian federation—tried to reestablish its **hegemony** by promoting uprisings by Serbian **minorities** in the latter two states. These Serbs justified their actions by recounting Croat atrocities against Serbs during World War II. They devised brutal and often deadly policies called **ethnic cleansing,** which involved the murder or forced removal of Croatians, Bosnian Muslims, and other minorities from areas in which Serbs lived and prompted hundreds of thousands of refugees to flee to surrounding countries. In Serbia proper the government and local activists severely restricted the activities of Albanian and Hungarian minorities.

The Yugoslavian case also illustrates the international implications of ethnic conflict. Atrocities against Bosnian Muslims were widely publicized as a **genocide** in the making and prompted a flurry of responses by international and regional organizations that ranged from attempts to mediate the conflict to proposals for military **intervention** to protect those under Serbian attack. The Croat minority in Bosnia was encouraged by the newly independent Croatian government to take advantage of the unsettled situation to pursue autonomy.

By 1992 the appalling situation in Bosnia reminded many Europeans of the failure of appeasement policies to check Nazi expansionism in 1938. That recognition triggered different responses. A United Nations–sanctioned embargo on military supplies and fuel to Serbia was imposed but was not fully implemented. Many cease-fire agreements were negotiated by European mediators but were flagrantly violated. Eventually UN **peacekeeping** forces arrived, but they were only authorized to oversee the delivery of humanitarian assistance and could not intervene to halt the fighting. In fall 1993 the mediators reluctantly concluded that only the partitioning of Bosnia into Muslim, Serbian, and Croat regions would end the conflict—a solution that satisfied the victorious Serbs and Croats but not the victimized Bosnian Muslims.

Could more have been done? We believe the international community has an obligation to protect the rights of minorities, beginning with protecting the most basic rights to life and security from attack. From our point of view the civil wars and ethnic killings in the breakaway states of the former Yugoslavia should have been preempted by early and active international mediation that led to guaranteed independence and security for all newly emerging states in the region and to commitments from all parties to protect the rights of each state's ethnic peoples. But the international community is only gradually acquiring the legal principles, political will, and foresight to respond effectively to such conflicts. In this and Chapters 2–7 we illustrate why ethnic conflicts can become so bitter and so deadly; in Chapter 8 we look more closely at emerging international legal doctrines and strategies for responding to them.

One of the longest modern civil wars was waged by the people of the Ethiopian province of Eritrea, who supported a war of independence that lasted from the early 1960s until 1991. The Eritrean nationalists received some diplomatic and military support from Islamic states such as Egypt, whereas in the first decade of conflict the Imperial Ethiopian government relied heavily on military assistance from the United States. Even the military-led **revolution** that overthrew Emperor Haile Selassie in 1974 did not end ethnic conflict. Instead, the new Marxist military leaders of Ethiopia sought and received support from the Soviet Union to enable them to continue the war against Eritrea. By the end of the 1970s many other ethnic groups in Ethiopia were stimulated into rebellion by the Eritrean example. An alliance was eventually formed among Eritreans, Tigreans,

Oromo, and others that culminated in the rebels' triumphal capture of the Ethiopian capital, Addis Ababa, in May 1991.

Unlike the situation in Yugoslavia, there was no serious international effort to check the Ethiopian civil war. No major power recognized Eritrea as an independent state; international organizations regarded the conflict as an internal matter, and there was no media-inspired publicity of atrocities that might have prompted greater action. Only when famine threatened did the Ethiopian government allow humanitarian assistance to be provided, and then it prevented distribution of the aid in rebel-held areas.

Following thirty years of warfare, the moderate policies of the new revolutionary government allowed the possibility for a peaceful reconciliation. The government made and kept a commitment to hold referendums in 1993 to set up autonomous regional governments or, in the case of Eritrea, to allow full independence. The Eritrean referendum in April 1993 resulted in a 99.8 percent vote in favor of independence. Eritrean independence was accepted by the Ethiopian government, and the new state immediately received diplomatic recognition from the United States and many other countries. One new source of ethnic tension is already evident: Some Eritreans living in the Ethiopian capital are being forced to leave the country, and the Eritreans are threatening to expel Ethiopians. Without long-term material support and political encouragement from the international community, there is no surety of civil peace either in newly independent Eritrea or in what remains of Ethiopia.

Conflicts over group demands for better treatment within existing states and societies are seldom as deadly as the civil wars in Yugoslavia or Ethiopia; nor are they likely to have serious international repercussions. But they can be just as fateful for the people caught up in them, as the following example suggests. Kara (not her real name) is an attractive woman in her late twenties who works as an assistant manager of a resort hotel on Turkey's Aegean coast. She was born and raised in Germany by parents who had emigrated there as "guest workers." After Kara's graduation from secondary school, her parents accepted money from the West German government to return to Turkey. Kara also had to return, and, like her parents, she is prohibited from returning to Germany. Kara does not fear for her life or safety, but she is caught between two cultures: the German society in which she was raised and whose language she speaks fluently, and the Turkish society in which she must live and work. Her desk clerk, a man in his early twenties, has the same story and a similar problem: Turkish girls mock him as "the German" who speaks Turkish badly. Neither likes living in Turkey, and both have doubts about finding marriage partners.[2] Their lives would probably have been more satisfying, and their identities more secure, if they could have gained full citizenship and stayed in the country in which they grew up.

DEFINING AND MAPPING THE WORLD
OF ETHNIC GROUPS

Ethnic groups like the Timorese, the Eritreans, and the Turks in Germany are "psychological communities" whose members share a persisting sense of common interest and identity that is based on some combination of shared historical experience and valued cultural traits—beliefs, language, ways of life, a common homeland. They are often called **identity groups.** A few, like the Koreans and the Icelanders, have their own internationally recognized state or states. Most, however, do not have such recognition, and they must protect their identity and interests within existing states.

Many ethnic minorities coexist amicably with others within the boundaries of established states. The Swedish minority in Finland, for example, has its own cultural and local political institutions, which are guaranteed by a 1921 international agreement between Sweden and Finland. For seventy years the Swedish minority has had no serious disputes with the Finnish people or government. Since the 1960s the Netherlands has welcomed many immigrants from the Third World with little of the social tension or **discrimination** aimed at immigrants in Britain, France, and Germany. If peaceful relations prevail among peoples for a long time, their separate identities may eventually weaken. Irish-Americans were a distinctive minority in mid-nineteenth-century North America because of their immigrant origins, their concentration in poor neighborhoods and low-status occupations, and the prejudice most Anglo-Americans had toward them. After a century of upward mobility and political incorporation, Irish descent has little political or economic significance in Canada or the United States, although many Irish-Americans still honor their cultural origins.

The ethnic groups whose status is of greatest concern in international politics today are those that are the targets of discrimination and that have organized to take political action to promote or defend their interests. A recent study, directed by Ted Robert Gurr, of politically active national peoples and ethnic minorities throughout the world in the 1980s identified 233 sizable groups that were targets of discrimination or were organized for political assertiveness or both.[3] Most larger countries have at least one such ethnic group, and in countries like South Africa and Iraq they comprise more than half of the population. Taken together the groups involved more than 900 million people, or one sixth of the world's population. Figure 1.1 shows how these groups were distributed among the regions of the world in 1990. When the Soviet Union dissolved into fifteen independent republics at the end of 1991, the political demands of **ethnonationalists** like the Latvians, Ukrainians, and Armenians were

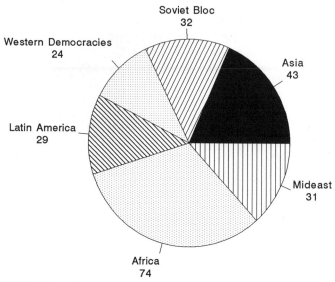

FIGURE 1.1   Politically active ethnic groups by region, 1990.

met. Since then, however, at least thirty additional ethnic groups in the new republics have begun to make political demands.

Nearly 80 percent of the politicized ethnic groups identified in 1990 lived with the consequences of historical or contemporary **economic discrimination** (147 groups) or **political discrimination** (168 groups) or both. Although a few ethnic minorities have some advantages, most are poor and are politically underrepresented compared with the majority groups in their societies. In many cases these inequalities are perpetuated by policies and practices that violate widely recognized standards of human rights.

Ethnic groups that are treated unequally resent and repeatedly attempt to improve their condition. More than 200 of the 233 peoples identified in the study organized politically at some time between 1945 and 1989 to defend or promote their collective interests against governments and other groups. In almost all cases they began with peaceful political protest that sometimes gave way to rioting and terrorism and, in at least eighty instances, escalated into guerrilla and civil wars. The most serious of these have been forty-nine **protracted communal conflicts** that have involved groups such as the Catholics of Northern Ireland, the people of East Timor, the Kurds and Palestinians, and the peoples of southern Sudan. Figure 1.2 shows the regions in which these conflicts occurred.

Protracted communal conflicts over the rights and demands of ethnic groups have caused more misery and loss of human life than has any other type of local, regional, or international conflict in the five decades

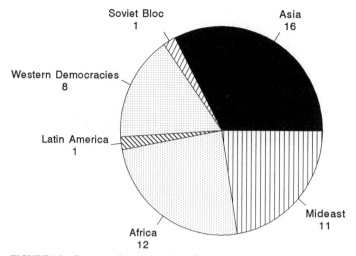

FIGURE 1.2   Protracted communal conflicts by region, 1945–1989.

since the end of World War II. They are also the source of most of the world's refugees: At the beginning of 1993, about 63 percent of the world's 42 million refugees were fleeing from ethnopolitical conflicts and repression. More than 9 million ethnic refugees had fled across international boundaries and were receiving assistance from host countries and international agencies. Another 17 million ethnic people had been displaced within their home countries. Many of the latter were in desperate need of assistance but were beyond the reach of relief agencies.[4] Figure 1.3 shows the number of refugees resulting from ethnopolitical conflict in each world region. The problem is especially severe in Africa south of the Sahara, where 16 million refugees make up 3 percent of the region's half a billion people.

THE CHANGING GLOBAL SYSTEM
AND ETHNIC CONFLICT

Ethnic conflict is not solely or even mainly a consequence of domestic politics. The potential for ethnic conflict, the issues at stake, and even the lines of **cleavage** between contending groups have been shaped and re-shaped by international factors. In this section we introduce three general issues to which we return later, especially in Chapters 7 and 8—the tension between the state system and ethnic identities, the impact the end of the Cold War has had on conflicts among nations and peoples, and the changing nature of international responses to ethnic conflict.

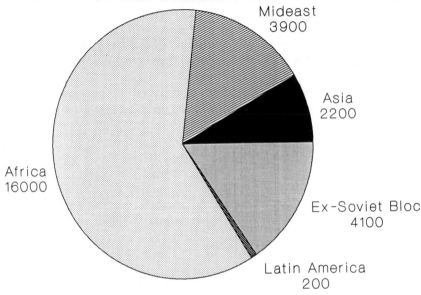

total: 26400

Mideast
3900

Asia
2200

Africa
16000

Ex-Soviet Bloc
4100

Latin America
200

FIGURE 1.3   Ethnopolitical refugees by world region of origin, 1993 (in thousands).

States or Peoples?

Historically, ethnic groups, nations, states, empires, and other forms of large-scale social organization—for example, Islam, Christendom—have coexisted, but since the seventeenth century the dominant form of social organization has been the **state system**—the organization of the world's people into a system of independent and territorial states, some of which controlled overseas colonial empires. The ascendance of the state system has meant that states are parties to the most deadly conflicts: wars between states, civil wars within states, and **genocides** and **politicides** by states.

Prevailing ideologies and political movements within the state system have dramatically influenced ethnic conflict. In the 1920s and 1930s anti-Semitic doctrines in Germany and other European countries promoted ethnic polarization. They competed with Communist doctrine in the Soviet Union, which emphasized the common interests of all Soviet peoples and minimized the significance of ethnic and nationalist identities. In the 1940s and 1950s anticolonialism emerged as a major form of resistance against European domination in Asia and Africa. For a short time nationalists were able to unite diverse ethnic groups in their efforts to replace colonial rule by European powers with their own independent states. By the early 1970s almost all European-ruled colonial territories had gained independence and become members of the state system. But tribal and ethnic consciousness soon reemerged in a number of states, such as the Congo immediately after its independence in 1970 and Nigeria a decade later. More recently we have seen a new kind of resistance to the state system that has affected every world region except Latin America: It is an accelerating wave of autonomy movements.

At times throughout the twentieth century ethnic peoples have coalesced across boundaries to join in common causes—for example, by joining pan-Islamic, **pan-Arab,** and **indigenous peoples'** movements. In the Arab world such movements have been short-lived and have been characterized by constantly shifting coalitions that resemble functional organizations. Despite paying lip service to equality of economic status, a shared religion, and the brotherhood of a common ancestry, Arabs have continued to fight fellow Arabs. Generally, a common ethnic background has been insufficient to cause peoples to subordinate the interests of states to a greater transnational identity or cause, even a limited one. This is especially true for peoples of countries with long-established boundaries who have developed identities beyond their immediate tribes and clans.

At present we witness two competing trends in human organization. At one extreme we see a reemergence of xenophobia in long-established countries—for example, the increase in exclusive ethnic identity that motivates antiforeign excesses in Germany, France, and Great Britain. No less extreme are movements that demand ethnic purity in formerly heterogeneous federations, such as Serbian nationalism in the former Yugoslavia. At the other end of the continuum are oppressive leaders who defend existing boundaries at all costs, despite historically justified claims by national peoples, such as Eritreans in Ethiopia and Kurds in Iraq, for internal autonomy or independence. Ironically, the new elites of former Asian and African colonies share with Saddam Hussein a willingness to fight to maintain existing boundaries and states, despite arbitrarily drawn borders that accommodated European interests but ignored demographic and cultural realities.

The End of the Cold War

The Cold War between the Soviet bloc and the U.S.-led Western alliance, for better or worse, created a sense of stability among most of the world population. Policymakers' calculations concerning conflict outcomes could be made with greater confidence in a more rigidly ordered world. The dissolution of the global system from a loose, bipolar world into an ethnically fragmented multipolar system has left in its wake a greater sense of insecurity among the leaders of the established states. This is what U.S. President Bill Clinton alluded to when he told a journalist, "I even made a crack the other day ... 'Gosh, I miss the Cold War.'" How does one deal with hostile warlords in Somalia and respond to ethnic and nationalist unrest in the Soviet successor states? Finding a workable framework for this new era and defining the role of the United States, Clinton added, "could take years."[5]

But events do not wait for policymakers to devise new frameworks. With the collapse of Soviet hegemony at the end of the Cold War, the citizens of the former Soviet Union and Eastern Europe are free to act upon communal rivalries with a vengeance. The demise of communism in the former Soviet Union has left a political and ideological vacuum that is yet to be filled. It was ideology that bound historically hostile peoples together; now old rivalries have reemerged, and neighbors have again become antagonists fighting for power, status, and control of adjacent territories. Communist citizens' place in society was predictable, and their economic welfare was guaranteed at a basic level. Communism in its ideal form also instilled a sense of collective responsibility and solidarity that overcame more parochial identities. The transformation of socialist society into a precapitalist society has led to a sense of alienation and isolation and an increased emphasis on narrow group interests and self-interests. This increased sense of isolation is being circumvented by a heightened ethnic awareness and a steady growth in intolerance toward members of other groups.

On the positive side, ethnic awareness in the former Soviet sphere may be the first step toward a new national identity that will unite different peoples. In Russia this would mean building a new sense of common interest and identity between the Russian majority and the Tatars, Ukrainians, Chechens, Volga Germans, and a multitude of other minorities who make up about one-fifth of the population. In times of economic stress, when peoples' first priority is economic survival, however, the chances of reestablishing a harmonious multiethnic state in the Russian Republic are greatly diminished, especially since it now seems so easy for regionally concentrated minorities to simply declare autonomy or independence. To further complicate Russia's problems, Russian and other ethnic refugees are entering the country in ever increasing numbers because of armed conflict and policies of exclusive nationalism in adjoining republics.

Enduring Conflicts, Changing International Responses

We cannot entirely blame the explosion of ethnic conflict in the 1990s on the end of the Cold War. Figure 1.4 shows that the number of global con-

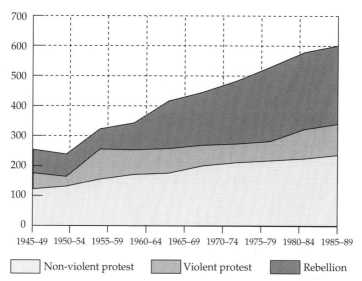

1945–49 1950–54 1955–59 1960–64 1965–69 1970–74 1975–79 1980–84 1985–89

Non-violent protest   Violent protest   Rebellion

FIGURE 1.4   Global trends in minority conflict, 1945–1989. This figure is based on an analysis of 233 groups in the Minorities at Risk study cited in note 3. The numbers do not represent numbers of events; rather, each group was scored for each five-year period on scales that registered the intensity of each type of conflict—nonviolent protest, violent protest, and rebellion. The figure was constructed by adding the scores for each type of conflict for each five-year period, then graphing them over time. The procedure and detailed trends are described in Gurr, *Minorities at Risk*, pp. 93–116.

flicts between minorities and states increased steadily from 1950 to 1989. The worldwide magnitude of ethnic rebellion, for example, increased nearly fourfold between the period 1950–1955 and the years 1985–1989. The question here is whether and how the international community—the United Nations, regional organizations, the major powers—has responded to these conflicts. We begin with two Third World examples.

In the 1970s the newly independent African states of Uganda and Equatorial Guinea experienced intense ethnopolitical conflict that had little relationship to the tensions produced by the Cold War. Dictators Macias Nguma of Equatorial Guinea (1968–1979) and Idi Amin of Uganda (1971–1979) each sought to consolidate power by killing thousands of their ethnic and political rivals. These horrifying events elicited no substantive response from the United Nations and few condemnations from individual states. Amin and Macias were virtually free to kill people they defined as enemies, in part because their countries were of little consequence to either the United States or the Soviet Union.

The consequences of colonialism were also a major impediment to decisive action. Colonial subjects in Africa and Asia had few rights, and many ethnic groups were trapped within artificial boundaries imposed by the departing colonial powers. Faced with challenges from peoples of different cultures and kinships, most leaders of newly independent Third World countries opted to accept existing boundaries, insisting on absolute sovereignty and the inviolability of territorial borders. This insistence on the right to conduct internal affairs without outside interference gave unscrupulous dictators like Macias and Amin freedom to commit atrocities against their subjects in the name of "nation-building."

If the United Nations and the superpowers were indifferent to ethnic conflict and mass murder in peripheral states of the Third World, could regional organizations have responded? Many such deadly episodes occurred in the member states of the Organization of African Unity (OAU, founded in 1963) and the Organization of the Islamic Conference (which represents all states that have significant Muslim populations). But these organizations have usually been politically divided and have had few resources; thus, they have seldom responded to ethnic warfare and severe human rights violations in member states. The OAU, for example, was limited by its charter to mediating conflicts between African states, not within them. In 1981 and 1982 the OAU made its first effort at active peacekeeping when it sent a multinational force to help de-escalate a civil war between communal rivals in Chad; the effort was largely a failure.[6]

The impotence of Third World regional organizations combined with the reluctance of the superpowers during the Cold War era to interfere in the internal affairs of states that had little impact on global competition virtually ensured that most ethnic conflicts would remain domestic affairs, even if they led to gross violations of human rights. Since 1991, however, the United Nations and the last remaining superpower, the United States, have taken more vigorous action against human rights violators and aggressive states.

The United Nations, established to create and preserve international peace, has had a mixed record as peacekeeper. During the Cold War it played a significant peacekeeping role by separating combatants in communal conflicts in the Congo, Cyprus, the Middle East, and Kashmir, but this occurred only because the superpowers agreed on the course of action. Since 1991, with encouragement from the U.S. government and other states, it has expanded its role. In Cambodia, for example, the United Nations mounted the biggest and most expensive peacekeeping operation in its history. Under a 1991 peace plan agreed to by warring Cambodian parties, an international force of twenty-two thousand police and military and administrative personnel was stationed in the country to help establish order and oversee the transition to an elected civilian government.

The effort was largely completed, and all military forces withdrawn, by October 1993. The outcomes of a similar effort in Somalia are far less certain.

The expanded role of the United States is illustrated by the dispatch of U.S. troops returning from the Gulf War to assist flood victims in Bangladesh in April and May 1991 and by the U.S.-led mobilization of reluctant states to intervene militarily in Iraq and Somalia in a renewed spirit of collective responsibility. In Europe, however, the world's second-most-powerful economic and military entity has been divided and paralyzed over the issue of whether and how to respond to escalating ethnic conflict in adjacent Eastern Europe. The North Atlantic Treaty Organization (NATO) is the only regional organization that has the military means to intervene forcefully in Bosnia. But U.S. and UN pressures have been insufficient to overcome the lack of political will among the leaders of NATO's European members.

Regional organizations in the Third World are also taking a more active role in response to internal conflicts. Their leaders are actively involved in drafting and arguing for extensions to the Human Rights Conventions that would allow for some exceptions to the rule of nonintervention. In the early 1990s, for example, the OAU established a new mechanism for conflict resolution and prevention that, in effect, redefined the OAU doctrine of noninterference in the affairs of member states. The OAU now monitors elections, makes periodic assessments of emerging conflict situations, and sends envoys to countries in which serious crises are brewing. In late 1993 the OAU sent an observation mission to Rwanda to reinforce a cease-fire in a civil war between rival communal groups, the Hutu and the Tutsi.

Nongovernmental organizations (NGOs) such as Amnesty International and International Alert, a London-based organization, also play a role by calling attention to ethnic conflict and repression. Activists have lobbied their respective governments and the United Nations to take active roles in supporting humanitarian efforts, have denounced various interventions, and have reported human rights violations to international agencies.

CONCLUSION

We have shown that the "explosion" of ethnopolitical conflicts since the end of the Cold War is, in fact, a continuation of a trend that began as early as the 1960s. It is a manifestation of the enduring tension between states that want to consolidate and expand their power and ethnic groups that want to defend and promote their collective identity and interests. The breakup of the USSR and power shifts elsewhere within the state system have opened up opportunities for ethnic groups to pursue their interests. Coincidentally, the CNN-led explosion of global news coverage has increased public awareness of the human dimension of these conflicts and thus has contributed to pressures on policymakers to take constructive action.

Recent developments send encouraging signals to those who are concerned about checking the rise of ethnopolitical conflict and human rights abuses such as ethnic cleansing. For the first time since World War II, the United Nations has begun to realize the vision of its founders: Since Boutros Boutros-Ghali became secretary-general in 1992, the United Nations has become more active as peacekeeper, intervenor, arbiter, and mediator in communal and regional conflicts. A consensus is emerging that the United Nations should establish minimum standards of global security through collective decisionmaking. Of course, the UN's ability to work for world security is directly dependent upon its ability to influence the outcome of emerging ethnic or nationalistic conflicts. The continuing caution apparent among most members over enhancing UN military capabilities signals those who stir up ethnic hatred that they may face a minor roadblock rather than a major obstacle.

The world of the 1990s mirrors in some respects the period following World War I, in which the collapse of the old order was followed by the birth of many new states, upsurges of ethnic violence and oppression, and the ascendancy of dictators and ideologies of exclusive nationalism. The pattern of conflicts in Bosnia, Serbia, the Caucasus, and Central Asia fits this scenario and signifies the beginning of challenging times.

TWO

□ □ □

The World of
Ethnopolitical Groups

F our important types of politically active ethnic groups coexist with modern states: ethnonationalists, indigenous peoples, **communal contenders,** and **ethnoclasses.** The basis for the typology can be explained briefly. We begin with a distinction between peoples who want separation or autonomy from the states that rule them (the first two types) and those who seek greater access or participation within existing states (the second two types). Ethnonationalists and indigenous peoples differ in their political history and specific objectives: Historically, ethnonationalists were usually independent and they want to (re)establish their own states, whereas indigenous peoples are mainly concerned with protecting their traditional lands, resources, and culture. Communal contenders and ethnoclasses face different situations and, therefore, pursue different objectives: Communal contenders are one among a number of culturally distinct groups in **plural societies** that compete for a share of political power, whereas ethnoclasses want equal rights and opportunities to overcome the effects of discrimination resulting from their immigrant and minority status.

We begin with a sketch of the global historical processes that caused these types of ethnic groups to become minorities in states that are dominated by other groups rather than becoming majorities in their own states. We then discuss each of the four types in more detail, including the traits that define them, their typical grievances and political strategies, and the international dimensions of their activities. We also discuss briefly the role of religion in ethnic conflicts.

THE WORLD HISTORICAL BACKGROUND
TO CONTEMPORARY ETHNIC CONFLICTS

Contemporary conflicts between ethnic groups and states are a part of the heritage of large historical processes: imperial conquest, colonial rule,

15

slavery, frontier settlement, and the international migration of labor. For example, every state that once established an empire did so at the expense of weaker and less fortunate peoples. Typically, European colonial agents exercised direct influence over the social, cultural, and political lives of their dominions. The same was true of most other peoples who established empires by conquest, including the Han Chinese, the Ottoman Turks, and the Amharas of the Ethiopian highlands.

Local economies were undermined by colonial rule. Through the introduction of economies that favored the dominant group, conquered peoples were forced into servitude, slavery, or dependency. Colonial rule also brought some benefits, especially to those who could supply the rulers with surplus food, minerals, or other valuable goods. The British and French colonial practice of relying on strategically located ethnic groups as clerks, soldiers, or middlemen in commerce often led to stratification of colonized people along ethnic lines.

The sense of a separate identity and grievances that result from imperial conquest and colonial rule can persist for many generations and provide the fuel for contemporary political movements. Burma (now called Myanmar), a former British colony, has been locked in ethnic conflict since independence in the late 1940s. The conflict began during World War II when nationalists within the Burman majority attacked the British colonial army, which was recruited largely from ethnic minorities such as the Karens, Chins, and Kachins. Thousands died in the ensuing struggles, and the conflicts between the minority peoples and the Burman state have yet to be resolved satisfactorily.

Ethnically divided and **stratified societies** were fertile ground for conflict when newly formed Asian and African states achieved independence from colonizers during the two decades following 1945. These new states were seldom ethnically homogeneous. Their borders were usually drawn arbitrarily to fit the political and administrative interests of the colonial powers. In some cases rival ethnic groups were forcibly merged into one new nation; other groups were divided among several states by European-imposed borders. Nationalists contending for political power in the new states often played ethnic groups against one another, thus polarizing them. Some ensuing conflicts eventually led to accommodations, which occurred following postindependence conflicts among the Hausa-Fulani, Yoruba, and Ibo peoples of Nigeria. Others have led to persistent and destabilizing violence, like the conflict between northerners and southerners in Sudan.

Another source of friction in colonial societies resulted from colonial policies that encouraged immigration of outsiders to work newly established plantations or to engage in commercial activities abhorred by the indigenous population. Most immigrants were neither assimilated nor incorporated into the indigenous social structure, leaving them politically and socially marginalized. During the nineteenth century thousands of Chinese and East Indians migrated to British Malaya. Malaya was eventually separated into two states, Singapore (largely Chinese) and Malaysia (half Malay, one-third Chinese, and one-tenth Indian); both states experienced ethnic tension between Malays and the descendants of immigrants. In Malaysia in 1969, resentment against Chinese domination of commerce exploded into violence that caused the deaths of more than two hundred people. Since that time, a program that gives special assistance to Malays has led to increased prosperity and a more equal distribution of wealth across ethnic lines, preventing (for now) further ethnic violence.

The previously mentioned policy of using immigrants and minorities to staff colonial bureaucracies often gave them privileged status in the host country and also provoked discriminatory measures against their descendants in the postindependence period. Again, the Chinese in Malaya provide an example. They readily adopted Western education, language, and styles and were resented by Malays for their privileged status and sometimes victimized by nationalist movements and state authorities.

In the Americas and Australia, Europeans settled in large numbers, with devastating consequences for indigenous peoples. Few of the latter were agriculturalists; most were hunters. Organized into nations, tribal federations, or bands (particularly in Australia), they thus competed with European settlers for use of the land. The victory of the settlers was accomplished through the slaughter, enslavement, forced **assimilation,** or forcible removal of indigenous peoples to reservations in remote and inhospitable areas. Thus, the migration of Europeans throughout the colonial period contributed to ethnic rebellions and mass slaughter and also to the displacement or genocide of indigenous peoples.

Another invidious European practice was the importation of Africans as slaves to provide labor for plantations. In some societies the descendants of slaves were eventually incorporated into the dominant society: Examples are found in Brazil, parts of the Caribbean, and Canada. In the United States, however, slaves liberated by the Emancipation Proclamation of 1863 were rarely given the opportunity to achieve higher status. In the rigid class structure of southern society following the Civil War, former slaves were free only of their chains.

In summary, each of the major historical processes left legacies of antagonisms and inequalities that fuel contemporary ethnic conflicts. Conquered peoples seek to regain their lost autonomy; indigenous peoples ask for restoration of their traditional lands; immigrant workers and the descendants of slaves demand full equality. Not all ethnic peoples with these kinds of heritages are pursuing political objectives today, but most have done so in the past or have the potential to do so in the future. It is

REGIONAL DISPUTES EXPLAINED

Regional disputes explained. By Jeff Danziger in *The Christian Science Monitor,* June 15, 1992. © 1992 TCSPS. Reprinted by permission.

essential, when one is trying to understand the passion and persistence with which ethnic groups pursue their objectives, to analyze the general historical processes and the particular experiences that have shaped each people's sense of identity and their grievances.

ETHNONATIONALISTS

Ethnonationalists are relatively large and regionally concentrated ethnic groups that live within the boundaries of one state or of several adjacent states; their modern political movements are directed toward achieving greater autonomy or independent statehood. Most have historical traditions of autonomy or independence that are used to justify these contemporary demands. In some instances autonomy was lost centuries ago, as was the case of the Corsicans and Bretons in France,[1] but it still motivates modern political movements. We have identified more than eighty such peoples that at some time since the 1940s have supported movements aimed at establishing greater political autonomy. Since the end of World War II thirty of these groups have fought protracted wars for national independence or for unification with kindred groups elsewhere.

Most people with nationalist aspirations live in the Third World, such as the southern Sudanese, the Palestinians and Kurds in the Middle East, and the Tibetans. They have fought some of the modern world's most persistent **wars of secession,** but few have won political independence.

Other ethnonationalists, including the Scots, Basques, French-Canadians, Slovenes, Latvians, and Armenians, live in developed European states. Their campaigns for greater autonomy have usually been pursued by nonviolent political means, although the terrorist campaigns of some Basque nationalists and some Armenians suggest that many have the potential for violence. Most ethnonationalists in European societies have gained significant concessions in the past few decades; many won independence in 1991 as a result of the breakup of the USSR and Yugoslavia.

Since 1991 more than a dozen new ethnonationalist movements have emerged within the boundaries of the Soviet and Yugoslav successor states. For example, 96,000 Muslim Abkhazians in the northwestern corner of the former Soviet republic of Georgia have fought successfully, with unofficial Russian assistance, to establish their own state. In October 1993 they decisively defeated the Georgian army and began to expel Georgian civilians from Abkhazia. To the east of Abkhazia, 164,000 Ossetians in northern Georgia want to be united in a new state with 402,000 Ossetians who live in an autonomous region in southern Russia.[2] The term **micronationalism** is often used to describe the independence movements of numerically small groups like these, although there is no minimum size required for statehood: Fifteen of the UN member states in 1990 had populations under 1 million, although none had fewer than 250,000 people.

Ethnonationalists usually have some kind of organized leadership and occupy substantial territory. Like the Ossetians, the Basques, who live in adjoining areas of France and Spain, and the Kurds, whose traditional homeland includes parts of five different states, more than half of ethnonationalist peoples straddle recognized international boundaries. Thus, political conflicts over autonomy are likely to have international repercussions. Wars for national independence attract military and political support from nearby states, stimulate similar movements in adjoining countries, and are the main source of international refugees. As a result, major powers and international organizations often attempt to contain nationalist wars by such policies as providing diplomatic support for negotiations, delivering humanitarian assistance, and—in some cases of particularly severe conflict—sending peacekeeping forces.

INDIGENOUS PEOPLES

Indigenous peoples are also concerned about autonomy issues but differ from ethnonationalists in other respects. They are the descendants of the original inhabitants of conquered or colonized regions. Before their conquest, most indigenous peoples lived close to the land as subsistence farmers, herders, or hunters, and many still do. Until recently few had large-scale political organizations or a strong sense of collective identity or purpose. Instead, in most countries indigenous people were divided among many separate clans or tribes that only gradually developed a larger group identity. Discrimination and exploitation by the more technologically advanced people who control them have been major causes of their growing sense of common identity and purpose.

The best-known indigenous groups are the native peoples of the Americas, substantial numbers of whom live in eighteen of the countries of mainland North and South America. In the aggregate, the 36 million native Americans (our 1990 estimate) comprise only 5 percent of the population of the Western Hemisphere, but in Bolivia, Guatemala, and Peru they make up about half of the population.

There are also many indigenous peoples in Asia. Half a dozen large and politically active indigenous tribes live in northeast India and the borderlands of Bangladesh, among them the Naga, Mizos, and Tripura. In Southeast Asia serious conflicts have developed over the political demands of indigenous peoples like the Cordillerans ("mountain people," a label provided by Europeans) in the Philippines, the Karen and Shan peoples of the Burman uplands, and the native Papuans of the Indonesian-controlled half of the island of New Guinea.

Because they live mainly in peripheral regions of modern states, these peoples—along with the Scandinavian Saami (who are called Lapps by outsiders), the Australian Aborigines, the cattle-herding Masai of East Africa, and others—have been called "peoples of the frontier." In the past they have faced severe political and economic pressures: Most were conquered and ruled without their consent, and almost all of these peoples have lost traditional lands and resources to settlers and developers. Similar themes are expressed repeatedly by their contemporary leaders: They want to protect their languages and ways of life from what their advocates call ethnocide—that is, the destruction of their culture—or cultural genocide, and they seek to regain as much control as possible over their lands and resources.

For centuries, traditional peoples resisted dominant groups through sporadic and uncoordinated uprisings and attempts to migrate to more remote regions. After the League of Nations was established in 1919, a number of North American tribes and the Maori of New Zealand began to petition it and other international bodies for recognition of their rights. Prior to the 1950s, however, only a handful of indigenous peoples secured significant political autonomy from Western-style governments. In New Zealand the Maori gained control of some traditional lands and obtained representation in the English settlers' parliament in 1867. As we describe in Chapter 3, the Miskito Indians of Nicaragua were recognized as constituting an autonomous state from 1860 to 1894. And the Kuna Indians of Panama gained local autonomy as the result of a rebellion in 1920.

By far the most important international development affecting indigenous peoples has been the global indigenous rights movement that was formed in the 1970s. The World Council of Indigenous Peoples (founded in 1975) is one of several influential nongovernmental bodies that has provided a forum for discussions, publicity, and planning of joint action among representatives of indigenous peoples from all parts of the world. At a May 1992 conference in Brazil, for example, the council issued an Indigenous People's Earth Charter that laid out a comprehensive set of cultural and environmental demands. Another such body is the UN Working Group on Indigenous Populations, which brings together two hundred indigenous representatives for annual meetings in Geneva. It has prepared a draft Universal Declaration of Indigenous Rights that should eventually become a part of **international law**.[3]

The indigenous people's movement has been highly influential in encouraging political activism among previously passive groups and in making presentations to international bodies. It has also directly or indirectly affected government policies toward indigenous peoples. The direct impact is a result of the fact that national officials responsible for developing such policies participate in the meetings cited in the previous paragraph; their own policy goals often change as a result. The indirect impact results from political actions inspired by the global movement. These have consisted mainly of forms of protest: publicity campaigns directed toward the media and national parliaments, demonstrations, blockades of access roads, and land occupations. The cumulative effect of protests has been to soften public and official resistance to indigenous demands in the countries in which they take place and to prompt similar protests, and obtain concessions, elsewhere. Another kind of indirect effect is seen in the work of other international organizations. In the late 1980s, for example, the International Labor Organization (ILO) substantially revised its standards for the treatment of indigenous and tribal peoples. Member states of the ILO were asked to give greater attention to the collective rights and interests of these peoples and to grant them a voice in decisionmaking about development plans that affected their homelands.[4]

COMMUNAL CONTENDERS

Communal contenders are ethnic groups whose main political aim is not to gain autonomy but is, rather, to share power in the central governments of modern states. Many communal contenders are found in African states as well as in some of the more established states in the Middle East and Asia—like Lebanon, Pakistan, and Malaysia. Each of these states governs a plural society, one that is made up of an assemblage of competing **ethnopolitical groups.** In Lebanon, for example, the main contenders historically have been Maronite Christians and the Druze, a distinct Muslim sect. The **Sunni Muslim** community has been a moderating force in the communal politics of Lebanon; since the 1970s the **Shi'i Muslim** minority has become a major political actor.

In Lebanon, as in other plural societies, the government's political power has been based on coalitions among the traditional or modern leaders of major ethnic groups. The balance of power between Christians and Muslims in the coalition was specified in Lebanon's National Pact, but in most states such arrangements have been informal and vulnerable to manipulation. Multiethnic coalitions are usually dominated by an advantaged group—like the Punjabis in Pakistan and the Malays in Malaysia—that uses a mix of concessions, cooptation, and sometimes repression to maintain its position. Such arrangements become unstable if and when one ethnic group's leader attempts to improve his or her relative position at the expense of others. If constitutional restraints and political guarantees are absent, and if other groups are unwilling to work out a new compromise, such conflicts can escalate into full-scale civil or revolutionary warfare. Recent examples of wars of secession caused by the failure to establish or maintain multiethnic coalitions have occurred in Lebanon, Sri Lanka, Sudan, Liberia, and Somalia. In some cases the ethnopolitical group that finds itself losing gives up hope of sharing power and shifts to a strategy of autonomy. This happened in Nigeria in 1967 when the Ibo-dominated Eastern Region proclaimed an independent Republic of Biafra and fought an unsuccessful war of secession.

War is not inevitable in such situations. By 1993 the white-dominated South African government had reluctantly but decisively accepted the right of other ethnic groups to participate in governance, raising expectations that the conflict can be settled without escalating into countrywide terrorism and civil war.

Conflicts engaging communal contenders are highly susceptible to international involvement. During the Cold War era the contenders sometimes became clients of the superpowers, as happened in Angola, for example. The southern Ovimbundu people, represented by an organization called the National Union for the Total Independence of Angola (UNITA), relied on military and political assistance from the United States and South Africa during a fifteen-year war against a coalition of their ethnic rivals, led by the Mbundu people, who held power in the capital of Luanda. Their rivals, in turn, were strongly supported by the Soviet and Cuban governments. Intense diplomatic efforts by the United Nations, the Organization of African Unity, and the United States throughout the 1980s attempted to defuse the conflict. An internationally brokered agreement among the rivals ended the fighting and led to a national election in 1992, but UNITA leaders rejected the results and were attacked by the government. By 1993 the country was again embroiled in a bitter and deadly civil war with little hope for a solution.

As some of these examples suggest, the distinction between ethnonationalists and communal contenders is not rigid. A communal group whose leaders at one time fought a breakaway war of secession may later be persuaded to join a governing coalition at the center. This illustrates one of the two most promising long-term strategies for accommodating the interests of large ethnopolitical minorities: to persuade communal leaders that it is in their interests to accept a share of power in the governing elite. The other, which can be used in combination with power sharing, is to grant communal groups regional autonomy within a federal political system.

ETHNOCLASSES

Ethnoclasses are ethnically or culturally distinct minorities who occupy distinct social strata and have specialized economic roles in the societies in which they now live. They are, in other words, ethnic groups who resemble classes. Most ethnoclasses in advanced industrial societies are composed of the descendants of slaves or immigrants who were brought in to do the hard and menial work the dominant groups would not perform. Examples include people of African descent in Britain and North America, the Turks in Germany, and Koreans in Japan. Upward mobility and policies of integration have eroded old ethnoclass barriers in most advanced industrial societies (although not in Japan), but members of these and similar groups are still disproportionately concentrated in occupations at or near the bottom of the economic and social hierarchy.

In Third World societies ethnoclasses also have immigrant origins, but their members are more likely to be economically advantaged merchants and professionals who are subject to political restrictions. Examples include the Chinese minorities in most Southeast Asian countries, the Lebanese communities in postcolonial Africa, and the Palestinians.[5] There are at least fifty politically active ethnoclasses in the world today, and more are likely to form as a result of the escalating movement of migrants and refugees from poor to rich countries.

The distinction between ethnoclasses and communal contenders is sometimes blurred. Ethnoclasses resemble communal contenders in the sense that they want to improve their status within an existing political system: They want greater economic opportunities, equal political rights, better public services. Some, such as the Muslim Maghrebins in France, the Koreans in Japan, and many African Americans, are also concerned about protecting and promoting their peoples' cultural traditions. Unlike most communal contenders, however, ethnoclasses are usually widely dispersed within a larger population. Even if they live in particular urban neighborhoods or rural villages, they rarely have a single territorial base or traditions of separate nationhood. Therefore, ethnoclasses virtually never use the language or demands of nationalists; instead, they are preoccupied with receiving more equitable or favorable treatment from the larger society.

The formation of ethnoclasses continues to be shaped by international factors. The transnational movement of immigrants and refugees fleeing poverty and violence is accelerating sharply, as we observed earlier. Most of these people are **visible minorities,** which means that they are subject to special, often discriminatory treatment in their host countries. Few are likely to return to their homelands. As their numbers increase, therefore, they are the source of growing tensions between sending and receiving countries as well as within receiving countries. Immigrant workers are also the focus of low-key, nonconflictual diplomacy between sending and receiving countries. The governments of France and of North African countries are engaged in ongoing consultations and agreements about the status and repatriation of Maghrebin workers in France, as are the governments of Germany and Turkey about those of Turkish workers.

We also need to mention **dominant minorities,** a distinctive type of ethnoclass that has historically been more common than it is at present. Dominant minorities are culturally distinct ruling groups like the Afrikaaners of South Africa and the Tutsi overlords who have governed the Hutu peasants of Burundi. Such minorities use the powers of the state to maintain political and economic advantages over subordinate majorities. Not all members of dominant minorities benefit equally. Some working-class white Afrikaaners, for example, are especially resentful of Blacks' demands for equality. Iraq provides another example: Its ruling elite consists of a small clique within the Sunni Muslim minority, most of whom come from Saddam Hussein's hometown of Tikrit.

One of the most widely shared values within the modern world, one that is ratified consistently in international agreements on human rights, is the principle that people of all ethnic and religious backgrounds within each society should enjoy equal economic and political opportunities. This principle has motivated political movements that work for greater equality among disadvantaged peoples throughout the world. It has pushed many governments to reduce discrimination against ethnoclasses and indigenous peoples and has contributed to the toppling of minority-dominated governments throughout the European colonized world, from

Algeria to Zanzibar. It also brings international pressures, both political and economic, to bear on the remaining handful of dominant minorities. Thus, countervailing international factors are at work on ethnoclasses. On the one hand, migration is creating new ethnoclasses; on the other, advantaged groups are being pressured to incorporate them on an equal basis with other classes and citizens.

POLITICALLY ACTIVE RELIGIOUS MINORITIES

The categories of ethnonationalists, indigenous peoples, communal contenders, and ethnoclasses enable us to compare and contrast most, but not quite all, politically active ethnic groups in the contemporary world. Much attention has been given in the past two decades to the resurgence of religious-based conflict, especially conflicts involving Muslims. The Protestants and Catholics of Northern Ireland are also examples of warring communal groups who define themselves in terms of religious beliefs.

It is important to recognize that many contemporary religious conflicts in and around the margins of the Islamic world arise from the reassertion of traditional Islamic values in opposition to the values and practices of secular governments. Most such conflicts occur between people with the same ethnic background, as, for example, in Jordan, Egypt, and Algeria. So-called fundamentalism is only likely to fuel ethnic conflict when the split between traditional Islamic and secular values coincides with ethnic divisions, as is the case in Sudan, where an Arab, traditional Islamic government in the north has attempted to impose an Islamic system of law and government on non-Muslim Africans in the south.

The general principle, exemplified by the situation in Sudan, is that religious differences create a special intensity in conflicts between peoples when a dominant group attempts to impose rules based on its religious beliefs on others. But our observations of the 233 ethnopolitical groups in the Minorities at Risk study (see Chapter 1, note 3) show that differences of religion are seldom the only or the most important cause of ethnic conflict. Instead, religious differences usually combine with or reinforce ethnic conflicts that are based on nationality and class differences. For example, the Palestinians' conflict with Israel is first and foremost a nationalist one whose intensity is reinforced by religious differences. Similarly, Northern Ireland's Catholics are motivated in part by their subordinate class status and in part by a nationalistic desire to be united with the Republic of Ireland. A shared religion provides some of the social cement that holds these groups together; in only a few contemporary societies do religious differences appear to be the primary source of conflicts with other groups. Of course, the relative significance of religious versus other factors in a particular conflict can change over time and can only be evaluated through detailed case studies.

CONCLUSION

We have defined and discussed four major types of politically active ethnic groups in the contemporary world. In Chapters 3 and 4 we present historical accounts of four peoples, one of each of these four types, whose status has been deeply affected by the interaction of internal and international political forces. The claims of ethnonationalists, who want greater autonomy or independence, pose the greatest dilemma for states and the international system; they are the source of some of the most deadly and protracted conflicts of the last half century. The history of the Kurdish people, detailed in Chapter 3, illustrates both the group type and the issues at stake. Communal contenders who seek a greater share of power in existing states usually pursue their objectives through conventional politics but sometimes become involved in revolutionary wars when their ambitions cannot be met through other means. The Chinese in Malaysia, whose history is surveyed in Chapter 4, provided the basis for a failed revolutionary movement in the 1950s; they now have a well-defined political and economic role within a multiethnic **democracy.**

The other two important types of politically active ethnic groups are indigenous peoples and ethnoclasses, whose demands and actions are seldom a major threat to regional or international security. Nonetheless, their status is of serious concern to the international community: Most are more disadvantaged and suffer greater discrimination than any other groups in their societies, and domestic conflicts over their status often have important spillover effects that require attention from regional and international organizations. These dilemmas are illustrated in our case study of the indigenous Miskitos of Nicaragua in Chapter 3 and in the account of Turks in Germany in Chapter 4, a group that typifies the growing numbers of ethnoclasses in Western societies.

THREE

□ □ □

The Pursuit of Autonomy:
The Kurds and Miskitos

E thnic groups become involved in political conflict for many reasons that are specific to a particular time, place, and political circumstance. Two underlying factors, however, are present in all instances. First, people become more sharply aware of their common identity. This may be triggered by attacks from other groups, by the appeals of their leaders, or by dramatic examples of political action undertaken by similar groups elsewhere. Second, people become increasingly resentful about their unjust and unequal status in comparison with other groups. The sense of resentment is usually based on inequalities and denial of people's rights and opportunities. The theoretical importance of these two factors is examined as part of the **model** presented in the second half of Chapter 5. The sketches in the present chapter and in Chapter 5 provide the information needed to gain an understanding of the historical and political circumstances that have shaped the identities and status of four peoples.

THE KURDS: A NATION WITHOUT A STATE

"Before I was born my whole family—my mum, my brothers and my grandfather—were put in prison by the Iraqi government. They put my family in prison because my father was a peshmerga—a fighter for the Kurds. The prison was in the south of Iraq, far away from our city of Halabjah in Kurdistan. ...

"I was born on the 19th [of] December 1976. My mother told me I was born in prison. ... In 1979, when the government gave up hope of catching my father, they let us out of prison on bail. We returned to our village ... four kilometers away from Halabjah.

"After a short time the government started to catch Kurdish families again and unfortunately they caught my grandfather and beat and tortured him so badly that half his body was paralysed. They tortured him to find out where my father was hiding. ... My mother and brothers and I had to leave our house ... to go to

live in the mountains of Kurdistan near where my father was. We had to move from place to place because the government kept shelling the area. When we got to school age at seven years my mother wanted to send us to school. There were no schools in the mountains so my mum had to send us to school in the Kurdish cities under the control of the Iraqi government. She put each of us three brothers in a different school and we had to change our names so the Iraqi government wouldn't know that we were the family of a peshmerga. ...

"In the summer holidays from school we lived with our parents in the mountains. ... Sometimes when we were in the mountains we hid from the bombs that the Iraqi government dropped, in tunnels. We took medicines, food and towels because sometimes we had to stay for some time in the tunnels. We made the towels wet to protect us from burns from chemical weapons. ...

"The government bulldozed our village and destroyed it in 1986. After the people had built it up, they came again in 1987 and destroyed it again. So my family had to move to the town of Halabjah. In March 1988 my brother and I were living in Halabjah with relatives. The Iraqi government destroyed Halabjah with chemical weapons. Over 5,000 Kurdish people were killed at Halabjah and thousands were injured. My brother and I were saved from death because a few hours before the bombing we had gone out of the town to a village. ...

"We had to go with thousands of other people towards the border with Iran. I walked with my grandmother and brother. ... When we got to Iran they took us to a camp and gave us a tent. At the camp we found our mother and grandfather. ... While we were in the camp the Iraqi government started to get its agents to put poison in the food and water in the camp. Because of that my father decided to sell everything and borrowed money from friends and found a way for us to leave Iran.

"I arrived in London on 17th September 1989 with my mum, dad and brothers."[1]

This personal account illustrates vividly the human dimension of the long and bitter conflict between Kurds and the Iraqi government. Its statements about policies and actions of the Iraqi government are consistent with information reported by many other sources. In 1975, during a lull in intermittent warfare with the Kurds, the Iraqi government initiated a policy of destroying Kurdish villages near the Turkish and Iranian borders and forcibly resettling their inhabitants. At least fifty villages were destroyed and tens of thousands of people—Kurdish sources say up to 300,000—were deported before the policy was reversed in 1976. In 1987 the policy was resumed on a much larger scale to discourage Kurds from supporting Iran during the last stages of the Iran-Iraq War: An estimated three thousand villages and hamlets were razed, and half a million Kurds were deported to detention camps. The government especially targeted villages and families that supported the guerrilla fighters known as *peshmergas* (literally, "those who face death"). It also began to use mustard

Kurdish refugees who fled from Iraqi army attacks, April 1991. Photo by Salah Aziz, Badlisy Center for Kurdish Studies, Tallahassee, Florida.

gas on civilian and combatant Kurds. Kurdish sources identify more than eighty such uses, the most deadly and best documented of which was the attack on the town of Halabja on March 16, 1988. Also in 1988 the Iraqi government began an operation, codenamed "Al-Anfal," during which 182,000 Kurdish civilians were arrested; police documents and videotapes captured in 1991 showed that many, perhaps most, became victims of mass executions.[2]

The conflict between Kurds and the Baghdad government flared up again in the aftermath of the 1990–1991 Gulf War, when U.S. President George Bush called on Iraqis to resist the regime of Iraqi President Saddam Hussein. Kurdish leaders interpreted this request as a promise of U.S. support, and in March 1991 they organized a widespread rebellion. It was crushed by Iraqi forces within a month, and the plight of a million or more Kurdish refugees fleeing toward neighboring Turkey and Iran prompted the U.S.-led coalition of governments opposed to Saddam Hussein to establish a protected zone in Iraqi Kurdistan in mid-April 1991. Coalition ground forces (withdrawn by mid-July) and long-term air cover from bases in Turkey made it possible to provide humanitarian assistance without risk of Iraqi government reprisals. A year later representatives of the estimated 3.4 million Kurds in the region established a democratically elected parliament and government and, in October 1992, declared a "federated state." The Iraqi government rejected the region's autonomy and blockaded deliveries of food and fuel through Iraq, forcing supplies to be trucked in from Turkey.

The 1991 rebellion of the Iraqi Kurds and the precedent-setting **humanitarian intervention** on their behalf by a UN-authorized international force must be understood within a larger historical and political context. We begin with a general overview and then focus in greater detail on the political status of Kurds in Turkey, Iran, and Iraq. It is important to recognize that the history of Kurdish society and politics is complex and is interpreted differently by Kurds than it is by the peoples who govern them. The points summarized in the rest of this section on Kurds are a synthesis of accounts by Kurdish writers and by outside observers, both scholars and journalists.[3]

The Kurdish People

The Kurds are a culturally distinct national group of 20 to 25 million people whose ancestors have lived for at least two thousand years in a four-hundred-mile arc of mountains and valleys that lie north and east of the Tigris-Euphrates River basin. Kurdistan, the term commonly used by outsiders since the nineteenth century to denote the region, is divided among contiguous areas of four Middle Eastern states: Turkey, Iran, Iraq, and Syria, as shown in Map 3.1. Estimates of the Kurdish population in the four countries vary widely; the 1990 figures shown in Table 3.1 are at the high end of the range.[4]

Many Kurds live beyond the boundaries shown in Map 3.1, as is evident from a comparison with Map 3.2. Map 3.2 shows that many Kurds, past and present, have lived beyond the periphery of Kurdistan in close association with Turks, Iranians, Azeris, Arabs, and others. This intermingling is partly a result of the Kurds' own expansion and migration and is partly a result of the resettlement policies of the governments and peoples with whom the Kurds have interacted for centuries.

The Basis of Kurdish Identity

The Kurds' identity is based on a number of shared traits: a common homeland and culture, a myth of common origin, a shared faith in Islam, similar languages, and a history of bitter conflict with outsiders. Kurds believe they are descended from the Medes, a people who were incorporated into the Persian Empire in the sixth century B.C. In fact, they are probably an amalgam of different peoples who gradually developed a common culture based on a life of seminomadic herding. Most Kurds

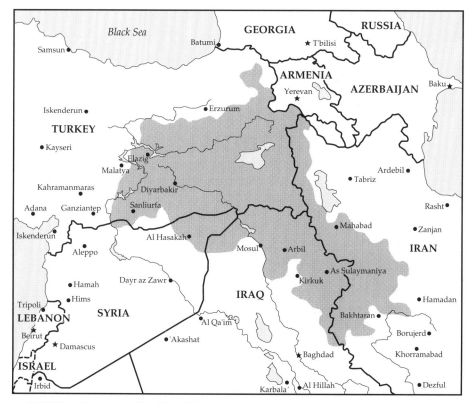

MAP 3.1 Contiguous Kurdish-inhabited areas in the 1990s. *Source:* Central Intelligence Agency.

speak dialects of Kurmanji, a language related to Persian; the dialectic differences between north and south Kurmanji make communication difficult. Records of the Kurds' history as a separate people date from their conversion to Islam in the ninth century A.D.; about three-fifths (estimates vary) are Sunni Muslims, one-tenth are Shi'is, and most others are followers of the Alevi and Yazid sects.[5]

Until the twentieth century most Kurds were mountain-dwelling pastoralists who followed a seasonal cycle of migration with their sheep to high summer pastures and then wintered in lower-lying villages. Like mountain clans and tribes elsewhere, they had a strong tradition of independence and of warfare and raids against outsiders. According to a folk saying, "Level the mountains, and in a day the Kurds would be no more." For more than one thousand years most Kurds resisted conquest by or assimilation with the three major peoples who surround them: the Ottoman Turks to the northwest, the Persians (Iranians) to the east, and the Arabs

TABLE 3.1   Estimates of Kurdish Population in Turkey, Iran, Iraq, and Syria

Country	Population	As % of Country's Population	As % of Kurdistan's Population
Turkey	13,650,000	24	53
Iran	6,600,000	12	26
Iraq	4,400,000	23	17
Syria	1,160,000	9	4
Totals	25,810,000		100

Source: Mehrdad R. Izady, *The Kurds: A Concise Handbook* (Washington, D.C.: Taylor and Francis, 1992), p. 117.

to the south and southwest. However, local Kurdish leaders—*aghas, mirs, begs, shaikhs*—often accepted the authority and fought in the service of the rulers of surrounding states.[6] Some became generals and senior officials in the governments of their conquerors, a pattern that continues to the present.

The Political History of Kurdistan

From the sixteenth to the nineteenth centuries the Kurds occupied the borderlands between the Ottoman Empire, ruled from Constantinople (now Istanbul), and the Persian Empire, ruled from Isfahan and, after 1800, from Teheran. In the early sixteenth century the Ottoman rulers concluded a pact with Kurdish chieftains that recognized sixteen autonomous Kurdish principalities and many smaller fiefdoms. Their hereditary rulers were confirmed in office and were granted privileges, but in exchange they were required to provide military support to the Ottoman rulers in time of war. Because of these conditions most Kurdish leaders willingly accepted Ottoman authority. The Persian rulers also had client Kurdish chiefs and tribes. By the nineteenth century there were nine major Kurdish principalities and many lesser ones, two within the Persian sphere of influence and the rest within the Ottoman Empire. The approximate domains of the largest historical principalities are shown in Map 3.2.

Beginning in the early nineteenth century the pattern of indirect rule was disrupted when the Ottoman Empire forcibly moved to establish direct control over the Kurdish principalities for reasons that now would be called state-building. The northern areas of Kurdistan needed to be strengthened against the threat of Russian expansion; rebellious leaders in southern Kurdistan had to be checked. Moreover, in 1826 the Ottomans had decided to establish a "new army" along European lines, which meant they needed to recruit more foot soldiers and secure new tax revenues. The Kurdish areas of the empire were seen as a major untapped source for both resources.

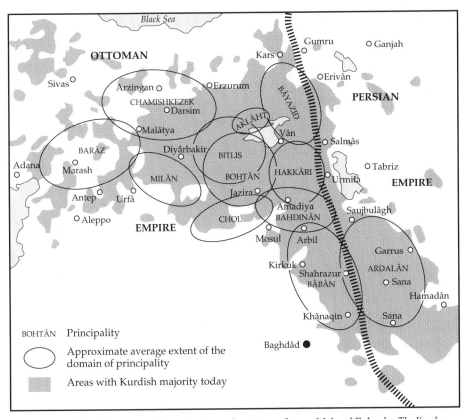

MAP 3.2   Kurdish principalities of early modern times. *Source:* Mehrad R. Izady, *The Kurds: A Concise Handbook* (Washington, D.C.: Taylor and Francis, 1992).

Resistance to the tightening Ottoman rule led to more than fifty rebellions. Among these were five major revolts that, had they occurred in the twentieth century, would have been called wars of national independence. The Kurdish princes who led these wars, from Abdurrahman Pasha in 1806 to Shaik Ubaydullah in 1880, mobilized up to one hundred thousand fighters, sustained their campaigns for as long as six years, and, in several instances, conquered and briefly held large sections of both Ottoman and Persian Kurdistan.

The Kurdish rebellions failed to stop the inexorable imposition of direct rule and the deconstruction of the autonomous principalities. Kurdish and Western scholars who have studied the Kurdish revolts attribute this failure to two factors. First, they were fought by traditional leaders of tribes and tribal federations who had no political organizations or programs that might attract and hold long-term support. And however widespread and enthusiastic immediate support for the leaders of the great revolts seemed to be, all leaders were envied and openly opposed by rival Kurdish leaders. Second, Ottoman and Persian rulers quickly took advantage of tribal divisions among the Kurds; despite their own rivalries, the two empires cooperated with one another to defeat Kurdish armies, and both encouraged defectors, some of whom ended up fighting fellow Kurds.

Twentieth-Century Changes in Kurdish Society

One important source of change in Kurdish life and society during the past century has been the increase within the Kurdish population of the number of people whose interests and politics have diverged from those of the traditional leaders referred to previously. First, a small urban elite, relatives of traditional leaders, began to emerge in the nineteenth-century imperial capitals of Constantinople and, to a lesser extent, Teheran. They and their descendants were the Kurds that were the most likely to become army officers, politicians, and officials in the governments of the ruling empires. These urban Kurds were also the first to articulate modern ideas of Kurdish nationalism. They were influenced especially by the nationalism of the Young Turks, who staged a constitutional revolution in Constantinople in 1908, and by the Western-inspired ideals of national self-determination that were in vogue at the end of World War I.

A second change involves the growth in the numbers of Kurds who live a settled existence in the valleys and plains. Some are farmers; others are concentrated in towns and growing cities like Diyarbakir in Turkey and Sulaymaniya and Kirkuk in Iraq. They include professionals and merchants as well as craftspersons and unskilled workers, and they provide much of the support for modern political movements.

A third source of change is seen in the dispersion of hundreds of thousands of Kurds away from their homeland through voluntary or involuntary migration. Hundreds of thousands of other Kurds were forcibly resettled in Turkey in the 1920s and 1930s and in Iraq during the 1970s and 1980s.[7] Similarly large numbers of Kurds have been displaced as refugees fleeing twentieth-century rebellions. Although some recently resettled Kurds and most refugees have eventually returned to their villages, many others have not. Some have swelled the populations of the Kurdish or mixed Kurdish towns and cities of Turkey, Iraq, and Iran; others live as an underclass minority among non-Kurds, especially in Anatolia.

Finally, since the 1950s many Kurds have migrated far from their homeland in search of employment. Istanbul now contains more Kurds than any city in Kurdistan, and more than half a million others are in Western Europe, 90 percent of whom live in Germany's Turkish community.

This dispersion of Kurdish people has important political implications. The typical Kurd is now as likely to live in a modern town or city as in the mountains. Contemporary Kurdish leaders have wide international networks of communication and support. Their political movements are more likely to emphasize modern political objectives, such as regional autonomy and access to resources, than the defense of traditional privileges and ways of life. The mountain villages still provide most of the fierce *peshmerga* fighters who fascinate outsiders, but they represent a dwindling share of the total Kurdish population. Clan and tribal loyalties remain important for the vast majority of Kurds, in cities and the countryside, and continue to provide the basis of support for contending political movements.

The Kurdish Quest for Autonomy in the Twentieth Century

The idea of national identity tied to a territorial state was a European import to the Middle East. The Ottoman religious-social-political system was centered on the idea of community, especially the religious community of Islam. Separate Christian and Jewish religious communities—*millets*—had a recognized place within the larger Ottoman society. Peoples like the Kurds, Armenians, Greeks, and Slavs who lived within the empire had no such place. Ethnic consciousness was supposed to be subordinated to identification with the imperial state, which was reinforced by the practice of coopting local leaders into the hierarchy of Ottoman rule—or, in the case of traditional Kurdish leaders, granting them autonomy on the condition that they remain loyal to the empire.[8] Viewed from this perspective, the rebellions in Kurdistan were not *Kurdish* rebellions but were efforts by traditional leaders to extend or defend their privileges.

Prior to World War I the idea of a separate Kurdish state was of interest only to a few urban intellectuals. During World War I the Ottoman Empire was defeated by the Allies, and the British occupied the lower Tigris-Euphrates valley and southern Kurdistan. At first the British planned to establish separate Kurdish and Armenian states, both to be carved out of the defeated empire. U.S. President Woodrow Wilson was also sympathetic to the idea: His Fourteen Point Program for World Peace included the statement that non-Turkish minorities of the Ottoman Empire should be "assured of an absolute unmolested opportunity of autonomous development." In 1920 the representatives of fifteen Allied powers convinced the defeated Ottoman state to accept the Treaty of Sèvres, one of whose provisions included the establishment of an independent Kurdistan, as shown in Map 3.3.[9]

The treaty was never implemented. Mustafa Kemal Ataturk, the reformer who founded the modern Turkish state, came to power committed to the creation of a unitary nation-state that included northern Kurdistan.

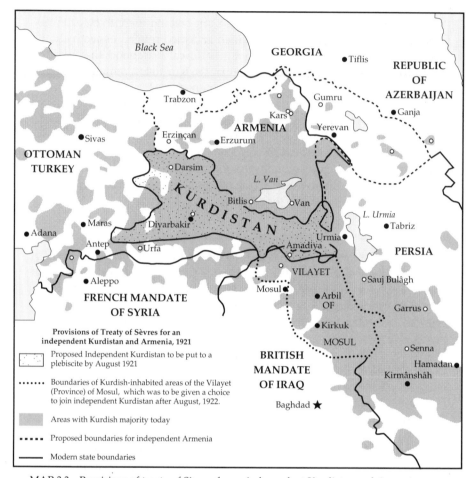

MAP 3.3   Provisions of treaty of Sèvres for an independent Kurdistan and Armenia, 1921. *Source:* Mehrad R. Izady, *The Kurds: A Concise Handbook* (Washington, D.C.: Taylor and Francis, 1992).

The British and French became preoccupied with establishing their spheres of influence in the former Ottoman territories of Mesopotamia and greater Syria. The British particularly wanted to ensure their control of the Mosul oil fields, over which Turkey was also making claims. They also found that the people of southern Kurdistan, which includes Mosul, were divided as to whether they wanted to be part of an autonomous Kurdish state or of the new Arab-Kurdish country of Iraq. So in 1923 the Allies abandoned the Treaty of Sèvres and replaced it with the Treaty of Lausanne, which recognized the state of Turkey within its modern boundaries. As a result, Kurdistan, already divided between the Ottoman and Persian Empires, was further divided among Turkey and the two new

Arab-dominated territories of Iraq and Syria, which were to be administered for an interim period by the British and the French, respectively. As a result, the Kurds never achieved the political statehood that was restored to the Turks and granted to the Arabs. Kurdistan remains the largest nation in the Middle East without its own state.[10]

After 1920 the history of Kurdish nationalism is mainly the history of three separate conflicts in which one or more Kurdish political movements have challenged the governments of Turkey, Iran, and Iraq.[11] These movements and their leaders have sometimes cooperated with and sheltered their kindred from adjoining regions; at other times they have been persuaded by outside powers to fight fellow Kurds. We review briefly the situation of Kurds in each of the three states.

Kurds in Turkey

About half of all Kurds live in Turkey. At the beginning of the 1920s some Kurds were attracted to the Turkish nationalist ideal of establishing a state in which Turks and Kurds had equal standing. But from the Turkish point of view equality was an individual concept: Kurds were encouraged to assimilate into Turkish society; their separate identity was rejected. When the last vestige of Ottoman rule, the Caliphate, was abolished in March 1924, "all public vestiges of separate Kurdish identity were crushed. Kurdish schools, associations, publications, religious fraternities and teaching foundations were all banned."[12]

From 1924 to 1990 the separate identity of Kurds was denied as part of the effort to establish a unitary Turkish nation and state. Kurds were referred to officially as Mountain Turks and were prohibited from teaching, writing, or publishing in Kurdish. Even public speech was forbidden. In the 1930s peasants marketing their produce were subject to a fine of five piasters for every word of Kurdish they spoke, even though few of them knew any Turkish.[13] From the mid-1920s to the late 1930s the most serious rebellions in Kurdistan occurred in Turkey. These were suppressed harshly and with great loss of life; many thousands of Kurds—Kurdish sources say over 1 million—were deported from areas that supported the rebels. Young Kurds today speak of continuing discrimination: "I have lived with Turks for as long as I can remember. ... When I was young, without even knowing what being Kurdish or Turkish was, we were looked down upon. They called us names I dare not repeat. ... When it came to schools there was segregation everywhere between Kurds and Turks. The teachers would just make it obvious ... we could never understand why they treated us in that way."[14]

As noted previously, official policy in Turkey was directed not toward segregation but toward assimilation of Kurds and all other minority peoples in the country. In practice, many individuals have subordinated their

Kurdish identity to that of the Turkish nation, and some have played an active role in political life. Following Turkey's first democratic elections in the 1950s, Kurds were able to take a more open political role: They joined political parties, entered parliament, and advocated policies of "Eastism," a euphemism for urging development of the backward eastern part of the country—Turkish Kurdistan. But the basic prohibitions against the public use of the Kurdish language and any reference to collective Kurdish interests continued to be enforced until early 1991.

In response to international pressures and growing concern in Turkey about the spillover of rebellions in Iraqi Kurdistan, Turkish President Turgut Ozal made important symbolic gestures to Kurds in 1990 and 1991. He spoke sympathetically about their plight, acknowledged meeting with Iraqi Kurdish leaders, tolerated public references to Kurds, and, in February 1991, introduced legislation that legalized public uses of Kurdish—although it did not allow publications in Kurdish. These accommodations, however, were strongly opposed by right-wing politicians and many Turkish military leaders.

An episode in Diyarbakir following the passage of the law illustrates the Kurdish dilemma in modern Turkey. On June 30, 1991, two young Kurdish teachers were sitting in a café listening to a concert. One asked a singer, who was also a Kurd, to sing a Kurdish song. When the singer did not respond, the two teachers began to sing aloud in Kurdish. Several policemen surrounded them and ordered them to leave. The two began to argue that the new law granted Kurds the right to speak and sing in Kurdish. The police shot both of them, and one of the killers reportedly said, "The Kurds should not be allowed to open their mouths and raise their heads." The day after the killings the president of the local People's Labor Party (a legal party), Vedat Aydin, filed a criminal lawsuit against the policemen. On July 5 Aydin was abducted and killed by armed police.[15] This incident reveals the depth of resentment still felt against the Kurds by some elements of Turkish society. The negative publicity the incident received from journalists and in parliamentary debate, however, shows that it is now possible, although risky, to defend Kurdish interests in public.

The gains for Turkish Kurds implied by the shift in policy were also undermined by the activities of the militant Kurdish Worker's Party (PKK). Since 1983 the PKK, with a training center in Lebanon's Bekka Valley and base areas in Iraqi Kurdistan, has used guerrilla and terrorist tactics in the pursuit of independence. In 1991 and 1992 it sharply escalated its attacks on government forces in Turkey's Kurdish provinces. This campaign provoked reprisal attacks by soldiers and police, many indiscriminately targeted against Kurds engaged in legal political activities. The 1991 events in Diyarbakir, described earlier in this section, are one example.

Meanwhile, many PKK fighters sought to escape Turkish reprisals by moving across the border to autonomous Iraqi Kurdistan. This move

Kurdish family in Sanandaj, Iran, 1991. Photo by Salah Aziz, Badlisy Center for Kurdish Studies, Tallahassee, Florida.

prompted intensive ground and air attacks by Turkish forces in early 1992—attacks that were sometimes indiscriminate, hitting Iraqi Kurdish villages as well as PKK camps. In October, under pressure from both the PKK and the Turkish government, the autonomous government of Iraqi Kurdistan fought a month-long war with the PKK that effectively neutralized its sanctuaries.[16] The PKK was hurt badly enough in these encounters that in March 1993 its leader declared a unilateral cease-fire and sought peace talks with the Turkish government.

Kurds in Iran

From the 1920s to 1979 the governments of the shahs of Iran, father and son, followed policies that encouraged Kurds to assimilate into the dominant society, although after 1960 limited publications and broadcasting in Kurdish were allowed. Pressures to assimilate do not seem to have been as consistent or as severe as they were in Turkey, in part because the shahs governed a multiethnic state that included the Turkic-speaking Azeris, the Arabs of Khuzistan, and the Baluchi, as well as the Kurds. Together these groups made up half of Iran's population. There were only two serious uprisings in Iranian Kurdistan during the 1920s and 1930s, both led by traditional Kurdish chiefs.

During World War II northern Iran was occupied by the Russians and southern Iran by the British to ensure that Iran did not join the Axis alliance. With Russian encouragement (but no military support) the Kurdish Republic of Mahabad was declared in January 1946. It was governed by a coalition of pro-Soviet Kurdish nationalists and a popular traditional leader from the town of Mahabad, Qazi Muhammad. It controlled less than half of Iranian Kurdistan; its government was opposed by many tribes in the region; and it was defendable only because of the presence of Mustafa Barzani, the leader of Iraqi Kurds, who had fled to Mahabad in 1945 and was soon joined by three thousand armed followers, as we discuss in the next section. The republic survived less than a year before it was conquered, without resistance, by the Iranian army. Its printing press was closed, the teaching of Kurdish was prohibited, and the leaders of the revolt were hanged in public in Mahabad's main square. Weak and short-lived though it was, the Mahabad Republic continues to be celebrated by Kurdish leaders as their closest approach to national independence prior to 1992.

In early 1979 some Kurds took advantage of the temporary weakness of the new Islamic government of the Ayatollah Khomeini and established control of Iranian Kurdistan. The same kind of leadership coalition emerged as that which had governed the Mahabad Republic: The left-linked Kurdish Democratic Party of Iran (KDPI) joined with a widely respected local religious leader, Shaik Izzeddin Hosseini. And like Mahabad's leaders, they sought autonomy rather than outright independence. During 1979 a number of serious proposals for local autonomy were exchanged between the Teheran government and the KDPI, but no agreement was reached. From 1979 to 1984 the Kurds and the Teheran government alternated between negotiation and warfare. The government ordinarily held the towns, and the Kurdish fighters held most of the countryside. By early 1984, however, the Kurdish-controlled areas were virtually eliminated, despite some continued assistance from Iraq; since that time Kurdish resistance in Iran has taken the form of sporadic guerrilla actions. In 1989 the leader of the KDPI, Dr. Abdul-Rahman Qassemlou, still searching for accommodation with the government, was invited to meet in Vienna with Iranian representatives, where he was assassinated.[17]

Kurds in Iraq

The British who occupied the Baghdad-Mosul area in 1918 were generally sympathetic to Kurdish aspirations, as noted previously. Their initial plan was to establish an Arab state with one or more autonomous Kurdish provinces loosely attached to it. In 1919, to forestall Turkish efforts to take control of central Kurdistan, British forces encouraged Shaikh Mahmud Barzanji, the Ottoman-appointed Kurdish governor of Sulaymaniya province, to run such a government. His authority was rejected by Kurds elsewhere in Iraq and by educated Kurds in Sulaymaniya. In 1923, after he proclaimed himself king of Kurdistan, the British suppressed his government.

Thereafter, the British sought to ensure that the Kurds would be incorporated into Arab Iraq with recognition of their separate cultural and political rights. Since the 1920s all Iraqi governments have accepted this principle. In 1954 Colonel Abdul Karim Qasim overthrew the monarchy and introduced a constitution that declared that Iraq was composed of two distinct nations, the Arabs and the Kurds. In the late 1950s Qasim's government offered concessions to the Kurds, as did the **Baathist** (Arab socialist) regime of Hasan Al-Bakr in the late 1960s. The Kurds' repeated rebellions since 1961 have arisen over questions of implementation. Each time accommodation seemed within reach, escalating Kurdish demands and political distrust and maneuvering on both sides led to the breakdown of negotiations and the outbreak of fighting.

A key cultural issue that has led to conflict has been that of whether the Kurdish language can be the language of instruction and government in Iraqi Kurdistan. During periods of accommodation Baghdad governments have permitted it; at other times they have sharply restricted its use and have attempted to replace Kurdish with Arabic.

There have been two major political issues: One involves the extent of autonomy in Kurdish regions; the second is whether the regions should include places like Kirkuk and Mosul that have mixed Kurdish and Arab populations. The minimalist position, taken by the most nationalistic Baghdad leaders, is that Kurds should have limited self-government only in narrowly drawn Kurdish areas. After 1974 the Baghdad government relocated Kurds and sponsored Arab settlement in mainly Kurdish areas, reducing still further the areas of Kurdish administration. The broadest demand, made by leaders of the Kurdish Democratic Party (the KDP, founded in 1946) and leaders of its principal rival, the Patriotic Union of Kurdistan (PUK, which split from the KDP in 1976), has been that a unitary government be established that has broad powers over all predominantly Kurdish areas. There are various subsidiary issues—for example, the number and role of Kurdish officials in the Baghdad government, the mix of Kurdish and Arab officials in autonomous regions, and the question of whether a Kurdish administration should share in revenues from the Kirkuk oil fields.

The first modern Kurdish rebellion occurred in 1943 under the leadership of Mustafa Barzani, the most influential twentieth-century Kurdish nationalist. Defeated in 1945, he retreated from his native district of

Barzan, near the Turkish border, to Iranian Kurdistan; his role in defending the Mahabad Republic was discussed in the previous section. After the short-lived republic fell, Barzani took refuge in the USSR for twelve years. In 1958 the Iraqi monarchy was overthrown in a military-led revolution, and Barzani returned to lead KDP participation in the democratic reforms promised by the Qasim government.

By 1960 the government had backed away from its cultural and political concessions to the KDP and had begun to crack down on KDP activists. This pushed the party into armed rebellion, which continued episodically until 1976. Qasim's government and its successors used all military means at their disposal in efforts to suppress these rebellions, beginning with heavy air attacks on Kurdish villages in September 1961. Barzani's KDP turned to outside support, which at various times was provided by the shah of Iran, the U.S. Central Intelligence Agency, and Israel.

Fighting was interrupted periodically by attempts to reach agreement on Kurdish demands. The leftist Baathist government that came to power in 1968 was willing at first to make significant concessions. In 1970 Barzani and the government negotiated a peace agreement that met many long-standing Kurdish demands. But in 1971 the agreement collapsed, in part because the KDP insisted that Kirkuk be included in a Kurdish autonomous region and in part because an attempt was made on Barzani's life. By September 1973 Barzani had secured promises of substantial support from the shah of Iran and had resumed fighting. The next year a new round of negotiations collapsed, and the government **unilaterally** implemented an abridged version of the 1970 agreement. It established an autonomous region with its capital in Arbil; the region encompassed three provinces that contained about half of Iraq's Kurdish population and Kurdish-inhabited areas. Little information is available about the region's policies or administration. It is worth noting that the autonomous Kurdish government established in northeastern Iraq in October 1992 under Allied protection, shown in Map 7.1 in Chapter 7, controls approximately the same area.

In 1975 the shah of Iran made a deal with the Iraqi government, which was represented by its vice president, Saddam Hussein. In return for Iraq giving up its claim to the Shatt-al-Arab waterway (the Tigris-Euphrates River outlet to the Gulf), the shah agreed to close the Iranian border to support for the Kurds. Barzani decided to stop the war, and again many of his followers fled as refugees to Iran. This was the worst defeat the Iraqi Kurds had suffered. Many of the refugees who returned to Iraq later that year were resettled away from the border zones.

In 1980, with Saddam Hussein now president, Iraq invaded Iran on Hussein's mistaken assessment that the revolutionary Iranian regime could be easily defeated and forced into concessions over the Shatt al Arab waterway and other boundary issues. The elder Barzani was now dead, and the KDP was led by his son Masoud. The PUK had split from the KDP in 1975, under the leadership of Jalal Talabani, who had rejected the elder Barzani's decision to stop fighting. During the next six years the PUK and the KDP fought both one another and the Iraqi government, accepted help from the Iranians, negotiated cease-fires with Baghdad and with one another, and fought again.

By early 1987 PUK forces held large areas of Iraqi Kurdistan, but they were soon devastated by an overwhelming government campaign. An area encompassing more than a thousand villages was declared a killing zone by the Iraqi defense minister, who issued orders on June 20, 1987, that concluded with these two points:

□ The corps commanders shall carry out sporadic bombardments using artillery, helicopters and aircraft, at all times of the day or night, in order to kill the largest number of persons present in those prohibited zones, keeping us informed of the results.

□ All persons captured in those villages shall be detained and interrogated by the security services and those between the ages of 15 and 70 shall be executed after any useful information has been obtained from them.[18]

Tens of thousands of Kurds died in this episode of **politicide.** By August 1988 the PUK and the KDP had suffered not only a military defeat but had caused the destruction of more than three thousand Kurdish villages and forced the deportation of Kurds from most of their homelands. In response the Kurdish leaders suspended armed resistance, but they did not trust Saddam Hussein sufficiently to begin new negotiations. Matters remained suspended until Saddam Hussein's invasion of Kuwait in 1990, the coalition's assault in February 1991, and the March 1991 Kurdish uprising described at the outset of this section.[19]

The 1991 uprising and the Allies' intervention, which established a protected zone in northern Iraq, led the Kurds to proclaim an autonomous "federated state," as noted previously. A parliament was elected, and an administrative system was established that continued to function in late 1993. But the region's economy is in crisis, and both its political and economic survival depend on international factors that are analyzed in Chapter 7.

THE MISKITOS: AN INDIGENOUS REVOLUTION CONFRONTS A SOCIALIST REVOLUTION

On September 18, 1989, former U.S. President Jimmy Carter spoke to two hundred Miskito Indians packed into a church in Puerto Cabezas, a ramshackle town on Nicaragua's Atlantic Coast. He announced that he had reached a compromise with Tomás Borge, the interior minister of the revolutionary Sandinista government, that would allow the return of rebel Miskito leaders from exile and decisively end eight years of armed struggle. The unofficial mediation of President Carter and representatives of the world indigenous rights movement was the final step in sporadic peace talks about autonomy between the government and Miskito leaders that had begun in January 1988. Brooklyn Rivera, one of the most important Miskito leaders, soon returned to Nicaragua and later joined the government of Violetta Chamorro as minister-director of the Nicaraguan Institute for the Development of Autonomous Regions.[20]

The Miskito People

To understand why the Miskitos were at war and why international actors were involved in ending that war we must begin with a brief look at Miskito society and history. About 150,000 Miskito Indians live in the humid tropical lowlands of eastern Nicaragua and Honduras, as shown in Map 3.4.[21] Their villages are the most heavily concentrated on the banks of the Coco River, the heart of their traditional homeland. Because of a decision of the International Court of Justice in the Hague, the Coco River has also been the international boundary between Nicaragua and Honduras since 1960. This decision resolved a long-standing dispute between the two countries but gave no consideration to the prior Miskito political claims to the entire area; thus, many Miskitos abandoned their villages on the northern, Honduran bank of the Coco River and moved to the southern bank.

The Miskitos share Nicaragua's Atlantic Coast region with much smaller numbers of Sumu and Rama Indians, thirty thousand to forty thousand Creoles of African origin, and Spanish-speaking **mestizos,** most of whom have migrated to the lowlands in recent decades from Nicaragua's densely settled Pacific and northcentral regions. The Miskitos and their Indian and Creole allies differ sharply from the dominant Spanish-speaking peoples of both countries. They speak indigenous languages and English, are mostly Moravian Protestants rather than Roman Catholics, and have closer cultural and economic ties to the English-speaking Caribbean and North America than to their nominal rulers, whom they refer to dismissively as "Spaniards."

The Miskitos have been more successful than most indigenous peoples in the Americas in defending their political and cultural domains against outsiders. The historical sketch that follows shows that the Miskitos' participation in the U.S.-sponsored "**contra**" war against Nicaragua's Sandinista government during the early and mid-1980s was merely the

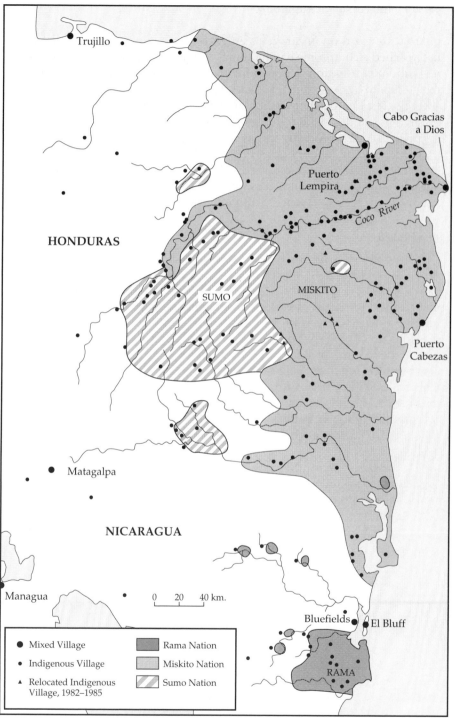

MAP 3.4 Miskito settlements in the 1980s. *Source:* Dunbar Ortiz, *The Miskito Indians of Nicaragua* (London: Minority Rights Group, 1988).

Miskito and Creole children in Puerto Cabezas, 1982. Photo by Cordelia Dilg. Reproduced by permission of the International Work Group for Indigenous Affairs.

latest and best publicized instance of Miskito resistance to attempts at political domination.

The Rise and Fall of the Miskito Kingdom

Before their first sustained contact with European pirates and traders in the 1630s, the Miskitos lived by subsistence farming, hunting, and fishing. Political organization evidently did not extend beyond the village level. Beginning in the 1640s Miskito chiefs joined with pirates in attacks on Spanish settlements along the coast and in the interior of the country to the west. The first Africans also began to arrive on the coast—some from Jamaica, some freed from shipwrecked slave ships. Africans intermarried with the Miskitos but retained a separate identity as Creoles, whose descendants continue to dominate Bluefields and other towns on the southern Nicaraguan coast.[22]

For more than two hundred years after the 1640s, the Miskitos were allies and agents of British political and commercial interests on the Atlantic Coast. Their access to firearms and British political support gave them superiority over other Indians in the region, some of whom they conquered, enslaved, or incorporated. The institution of kingship evolved from the belief among Miskito leaders that to be legitimated as chief, they had to be recognized as such by the British. In 1687 the governor of Jamaica established an English protectorate over the area and crowned a leading Miskito chief King Jeremy I. His successors governed the autonomous Mosquito Kingdom, later called Mosquitia and the Mosquito Reserve, until it was overthrown by Nicaraguan troops in 1894.

Miskito society and polity were buffeted by many external changes during the two centuries of autonomy. Spanish authorities carried out punitive expeditions in the region in the late eighteenth century but never established effective control. From 1848 to 1869 the southern part of the region was the eastern terminus of one of the major routes across Central America from New York to the California gold fields; North American cultural and commercial influence in the region was firmly established from that time onward.

In 1860, under U.S. pressure, the British government signed a treaty with the Nicaraguan government that ended its protectorate over the coast and acknowledged Nicaraguan sovereignty but that also provided for the establishment of a self-governing district in most of the area of the former kingdom. At this time the indigenous population of the coast numbered no more than fifteen thousand, almost equally divided between Miskito Indians and Creoles. The Creoles of the coastal towns became the dominant political and economic class in the newly established Mosquito Reserve, although Miskito kings still ruled; effective authority in Miskito villages continued to be exercised by village headmen called *whita*.

The most profound change in nineteenth-century Miskito society began with the arrival of German-American Moravian missionaries from the United States at the end of the 1840s. They worked hand in hand with Miskito and Creole authorities, first to convert and educate the coastal peoples and then to inculcate in them the Protestant ethic of individual morality, moderation, and hard work. The missionaries backed Mosquitia's autonomy for both secular and religious reasons: They wanted to maintain their close working relations with local authorities, and they opposed the extension of Catholic influence to the coast. The missionaries and their native assistants came to have great administrative and political influence as well as religious authority in the villages. The Miskito pastors who gradually replaced the missionaries in the twentieth century inherited this dual secular and religious authority and were among the strongest proponents of Miskito rights and autonomy in the 1980s.

In 1894 the Nicaraguan government decided to assert effective control over the coast in the interests of what would now be called state-building and modernization. The Nicaraguan government wanted to move troops to the region as a maneuver in its conflict with Honduras, and it sought customs duties from Mosquitia's port at Bluefields; leading merchants from the Pacific region, meanwhile, wanted to open up the coast for coffee production. Only a small contingent of troops was needed to occupy Bluefields and remove the authorities of the reserve. Creole resistance prompted intervention, at Nicaraguan request, by U.S. Marines and a few British troops. Resistance ended within a few months, and the Miskito king and 150 of his supporters were exiled to Jamaica. Miskito villagers remained mostly passive.

Nicaraguan governance of the coast, renamed the Province of Zelaya, was not repressive. Local affairs and tax revenues of Indian villages remained largely in the hands of village authorities, and after 1905, Indian villages were granted titles to their communal lands. In the late nineteenth century Mosquitia's economy changed more fundamentally than did its political status. From 1880 until the onset of the Great Depression in the 1930s, U.S. firms were heavily engaged in lumbering, running banana plantations, and mining, thus providing employment for much of the male coastal population. During World War II rubber plantations were a major source of employment; after the war, mining took on this role. The growth of a wage labor economy provided opportunities for small-scale commerce in which Miskitos and Creoles participated along with immigrant Chinese. During periodic slumps Miskito men returned to the subsistence farming that had continued to occupy their wives and children, or they worked abroad and sent their remittances home.

From the Somoza Dictatorship to the Sandinista Revolution

From 1936 to 1979 Nicaragua was ruled by the Somoza family, a dictatorship whose main interests in the Atlantic Coast region were economic rather than political. Especially during the 1950s and 1960s the Somozas promoted such projects as reforestation, commercialization of fishing, community-based cooperatives, and agrarian colonization by mestizos (people of mixed Spanish and Indian descent) from the Pacific side of the country. By 1981 the mestizos made up more than half of the population of the province, but most lived on the "agricultural frontier," near the foot of the highlands and well to the west of the areas of Miskito settlement. Some projects, like the creation of forest preserves on traditional lands, antagonized some villagers, but on balance the Miskitos benefited from government policies during this period because of employment and commercial opportunities. Many were said to admire English-speaking President Anastasio Somoza Debalye, and few Miskitos supported the Sandinista revolutionary movement that began in the Pacific region of the country in the mid-1970s.

In 1979 the Marxist-populist Sandinistas ousted the Somoza dictatorship from power in the Nicaraguan capital of Managua and instituted the policies that drew the Miskitos into protracted and internationalized conflict. Their war is best understood as a conflict between two political movements with contradictory ideologies. The Sandinista authorities had ambitious plans for revolutionary modernization of the Province of

Zelaya, which made up 60 percent of the country's area. Their program of state-directed economic growth in the interests of the country's predominantly mestizo peasantry and workers was fundamentally inconsistent with the emerging political program of the Miskitos. The Miskitos' mobilization had begun in 1974 when Moravian pastors and young Miskito professionals founded ALPROMISU (Alliance for the Progress of Miskitos and Sumus) to promote Indian economic interests vis-à-vis the Somoza government and merchants. ALRPOMISU was part of the international movement of indigenous peoples that emerged during the mid-1970s; one of its representatives became president of the Regional Council of Indigenous Peoples formed in January 1977 and served as an executive member of the World Council of Indigenous Peoples, founded two years earlier.

In November 1979, shortly after the Sandinistas came to power in Managua, a convention of five hundred Indians met in Puerto Cabeza and established a successor organization to ALPROMISU called MISURASATA (Miskitos, Sumus, Ramas, and Sandinistas United). The new organization appeared at first to embrace the revolutionary program and was granted a seat on the Sandinista government's National Council of State. Within a few months, however, MISURASATA leaders were making strong claims that indigenous people had a fundamental right to communal land and resources and the right to promote the language and culture that set them apart from others, including the Hispanic revolutionaries. The Sandinistas agreed to policies that met some MISURASATA demands, but the officials charged with implementing revolutionary programs on the coast were Spanish-speaking mestizos. Their actions, often heavy-handed, and attitudes, often racist, undermined efforts at compromise. MISURASATA demands and tactics simultaneously became more radical and threatening to the government.

Rebellion and Reconciliation

Violent conflict began in February 1981 when Miskitos resisted Sandinista attempts to arrest MISURASATA leaders at a Moravian church in Prinzapolka and four people on each side were killed. In August MISURASATA was banned; in December one of its leaders, Steadman Fagoth, operating from the Honduran side of the Coco River, began what the Miskitos called the Red Christmas campaign of attacks on Sandinista garrisons. The government responded in January 1982 by sending troops to forcibly remove 8,500 Miskito villagers from the south bank of the Coco River to resettlement camps fifty miles further south; about 10,000 others escaped across the river to Honduras.

Between 1982 and 1984 about four thousand armed soldiers from two Miskito groups waged guerrilla war on the Sandinistas. MISURASATA, now led by Brooklyn Rivera, operated from Costa Rica. Miskitos, Sumus,

Steadman Fagoth, July 1981. Photo by Leo Ga-
briel. Reproduced by permission of the International Work Group for Indigenous Affairs.

and Ramas (MISURA), led by Steadman Fagoth and armed and supplied by the U.S. Central Intelligence Agency as part of the "contra" war against the Sandinistas, operated from Honduras. Miskitos still living in Nicaragua were encouraged or coerced by contra forces to flee to Honduras.

In 1984 and 1985 the Sandinistas shifted their policies toward the coast. Zelaya Province was placed under the personal control of Interior Minister Tomás Borge, and "Spanish" officials in the region were gradually replaced with local people. A National Autonomy Commission was established, and talks were begun with local and exiled Miskito leaders. Some of the talks led to limited cease-fire agreements.

In September 1987 the National Assembly passed an Autonomy Statute—written with input from most coastal communities—which established two autonomous regions (north and south), each with its own representative council and administration. Substantial political, economic, and cultural rights were guaranteed. In January 1988 exiled Miskito leaders and the government began the autonomy and peace talks, referred to in the previous paragraph, that provided for the return of exiles and of thirty-five thousand refugees from Honduras, including fighters. The September 1989 agreement mediated by Jimmy Carter guaranteed the safe return of fifty rebel leaders, including Rivera and Fagoth, so they could participate in the national elections planned for spring 1990.[23]

The unexpected outcome of the elections was the defeat of the Sandinistas. In April 1990 Miskito leaders signed an agreement with the government of newly elected President Violetta Chamorro that affirmed truce accords and plans for demobilization. The autonomous region of Yapti Tasba was established, and elections were held for separate councils

Brooklyn Rivera speaks at a MISURASATA meeting in July 1981. Photo by Michael Rediske. Reproduced by permission of the International Work Group for Indigenous Affairs.

for its northern and southern parts; the Miskitos control the northern council and share control of the southern one with Creoles and others. Regional autonomy has not ended conflict between the Miskitos and the central government, but it has transformed it. The councils are currently enmeshed in a series of disputes with the Managua government over who will control development of the natural resources of the region and its offshore waters. The Miskitos have been able to check most of what they regard as abuses, but the regional government has been denied funding by a virtually bankrupt Nicaraguan state.[24]

CONCLUSION

Conceptual analysis and comparison of conflicts involving these two peoples are provided in Chapters 6 and 7. The history of the two groups and their fates offer striking contrasts. The Kurdish peoples' aspirations for autonomy, their cultural cohesion, and their common historical experience of subordination to other states have repeatedly motivated rebellions throughout Kurdistan. In Iraq and, to a lesser degree, Iran they have also led to frequent negotiations aimed at accommodating both government and Kurdish interests. All of these attempts have failed, often because of political divisions among the Kurds themselves, and they have usually been followed by escalation of conflict. Autonomous political entities have sometimes been established briefly in parts of Kurdistan, but political unity has never been achieved, not even within one region of Kurdistan.

The Miskitos are a much smaller group than the Kurds and have been involved in fewer instances of violent struggle against outsiders, yet they have been luckier in the outcome of their struggles. They have achieved a significant degree of regional autonomy without massive destruction and loss of life. One intriguing question is, Why the difference? What combination of domestic and international factors made it possible for the Miskitos to win a small victory, whereas the Kurds have suffered great and recurring losses in the largely futile pursuit of their own state?

The Miskitos provide evidence for another kind of conclusion. There is a tendency in Western societies to romanticize the lives of indigenous peoples, to think of them as surviving fragments of a lost world in which people lived without conflict in simple harmony with their natural environment. It should be clear, even from our brief account, that within the semiautonomous domain of the Miskitos, their culture and ways of life have evolved by incorporating Western elements. At various points in their history they have adapted to trade-based and wage labor economies and have converted to a strong and indigenously controlled Protestant faith. Miskito leaders did use the language and politics of the indigenous rights movement during the 1980s to justify and gain support for their opposition to the Sandinista government, and the broader war of the U.S. government against the Sandinistas did both coopt and empower them. But the society they were protecting is not a static fragment of pre-Colombian traditional society: The Miskitos are a dynamic and outward-looking society that has used Western political means and outside support to assert a distinctive local culture and interests that can be traced only in part to indigenous origins.

FOUR

□ □ □

Protecting Group Rights
in Plural Societies:
The Chinese in Malaysia
and Turks in Germany

The Chinese in Malaysia and the Turks in Germany are examples of two types of ethnopolitical groups identified in Chapter 2. The Chinese are communal contenders, cohesive and culturally distinct groups that are mainly concerned about using their limited political influence in a Malay-dominated society to protect their economic advantages and cultural interests. They provide an illustration of the ways in which the rights of a large communal group are both protected and restricted in a rapidly developing democracy. The Turks are an ethnoclass, a classlike immigrant minority that was originally expected to work temporarily in Germany and then return to Turkey. Most of its members are now permanent residents of Germany without full citizenship, their security threatened by right-wing attacks. Their uncertain status is the source of intense political debate in Germany. Their situation parallels that of the growing numbers of visible minorities in other advanced industrial democracies.

THE CHINESE IN MALAYSIA

During what became known as "the Emergency" in the British protectorate of Malaya (1948–1960), 6,710 Chinese insurgents and 2,473 civilians were killed (in addition, 510 civilians were missing), whereas 1,865 members of the government forces died. The government forces consisted mainly of British Europeans and Malays; all of their opponents were Chinese, who were concentrated on the country's west coast, as shown in Map 4.1. The Emergency was one of the numerous insurrections that swept Southeast Asia following World War II. Founded in 1930, the Chi-

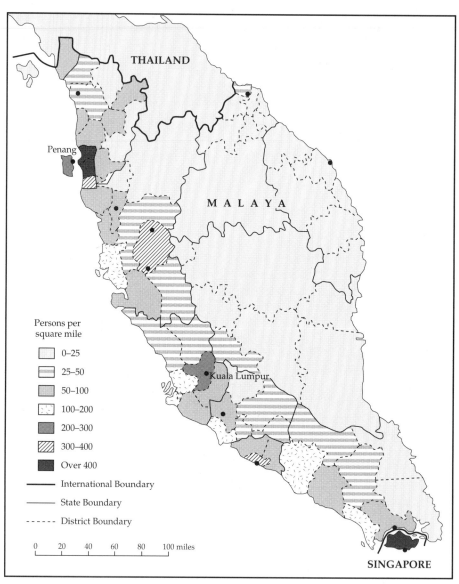

THAILAND

Penang

MALAYA

Persons per
square mile

	0–25
	25–50
	50–100
	100–200
	200–300
	300–400
	Over 400

——— International Boundary

——— State Boundary

- - - - - District Boundary

0   20   40   60   80   100 miles

Kuala Lumpur

SINGAPORE

MAP 4.1   Distribution of Chinese population in Malaya, 1957. *Source:* Ooi Jin-Bee, *Land, People, and Economy in Malaya* (New York: Longman, 1963).

nese Communist party became the principal resistance force during the Japanese occupation. Although it collaborated loosely with Allied forces during World War II, its main goal was to drive the British out of Malaya. Its youthful leader, Chin Peng, received his ideological direction from Moscow by way of the Comintern (International Communist Movement) and his revolutionary modus operandi from the Communists in China.

During the 1930s the Malay Communist party followed a rather unorthodox path by abandoning class struggle in favor of winning over labor unions and emphasizing the democratic and nationalistic character of the movement. This changed in 1948 when Peng's party was declared an illegal organization and, thus, was forced underground. Harsh British policies coupled with Malay reprisals led to the deaths described in the previous paragraph.[1]

The Status of the Chinese in Malaysian Society

Despite hardship, because of Japanese occupation and also as a result of the suppression of Chinese guerrilla activity, the Chinese have become prosperous in their adopted land. Although the Malay-dominated government has actively pursued Malay advancement through ethnic hiring quotas for the professions, commercial ventures, and the civil service, all citizens are guaranteed equal protection under the law. The government has justified preferential policies by arguing that if Malays continue to be less prosperous than their Chinese counterparts, ethnic tension will increase.

Since independence Malaysia has been committed to a multiparty parliamentary form of government, a working democracy in which Chinese and other minorities are represented. Nonetheless, the underlying competition and conflict between Chinese and Malays has dominated all political discourse.

In the eyes of many Malays, the Chinese are immigrants who have no particular loyalties to the overwhelmingly Malay political establishment. Distrust has also existed in Chinese circles, as has been evident in the platform of opposition parties challenging policies favoring Malays (one example is the Democratic Action Party, founded in 1965). With the increase in Islamic orthodoxy worldwide, some Malay Muslims now call for an Islamic polity that, if instituted, would circumscribe Chinese political participation.[2]

Despite ethnic rivalries, with the exception of communal riots in 1969 that led to a brief period in which democracy was suspended and a state of emergency declared, Malaysia's political elite has managed to maintain relative ethnic harmony. However, with the flare-up of ethnic violence worldwide and the increase in Islamic militancy, Malay-Chinese relations are vulnerable. The government has taken precautionary steps to counteract extremist propaganda by legally limiting civil liberties, especially in the area of freedom of communication. Thus, all opposition voices have been muted and public discussion of sensitive issues curtailed through the Internal Security Act of 1960 and later legislation. Unfortunately, by suppressing expressions of discontent, a sense of how deeply grievances are rooted is also lost. It is an open question whether Chinese-Malay relations will deteriorate in the present global climate of worldwide ethnic and religious assertiveness or whether both peoples will find the common ground needed to build a successful multiethnic polity.

Ethnic Divisions in Malaysia

Approximately 32 percent of Malaysia's multiethnic population of 18.2 million people (1990 estimate) is of Chinese background, 46 percent is Malay, and 8 percent is of Indian and Pakistani origin, as shown in Figure 4.1. Most others are tribal people of Sabah and Sarawak (see Map 4.2), such as the Dayaks and the Kayan, who are close cultural kindred of the Malays. The population also includes about one hundred thousand indigenous peoples, descendants of the aboriginal peoples of the Southeast Asian peninsula and Borneo. They are known collectively as Asal, a name assigned by the governing authorities.

Malays have populated the states of modern-day Malaysia for centuries, whereas most Chinese and Indians arrived during the late nineteenth century. Malay origin is uncertain: Myth and oral history claim they are descendants of a Caucasian tribe originating in China that migrated to the Malay peninsula seven thousand to four thousand years ago. The bulk of Chinese immigrants arrived from South China after 1860, lured by British promises of a better life. Some trace their ancestry back to the Straits Chinese migrants in earlier centuries, who settled in the islands of Penang and Singapore and in Malacca. Indians are largely Tamils from southern India brought by the British colonizers to work the rubber plantations.

Malays are Sunni Muslims, Indians are largely Hindus, and the Chinese are predominantly Buddhists, with some Confucianists and Taoists. The indigenous people are mainly Animists, and the few Eurasians and Europeans are Christians. Before World War II Malays were overwhelmingly agriculturalists; they were also heavily represented on the police force, and some were civil servants. The Chinese provided most of the labor for building roads and plantations and for working the tin mines; later they dominated the commercial sector. Most Indians worked in the mines and on the rubber plantations; some moved to the cities and opened small businesses. The tribal peoples are largely hunters and fishers, and they occasionally farm.

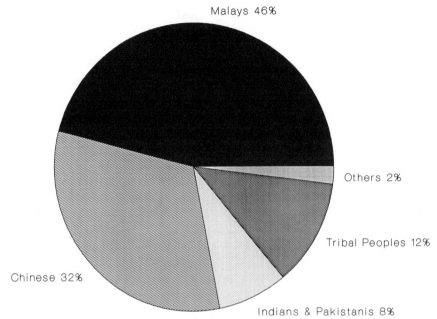

FIGURE 4.1   The population of Malaysia, 1990.

Before independence in 1957, Malaya's ethnic communities were separated not only by language, religion, custom, and geography, but they were divided among themselves. Ethnic consciousness and divisiveness were probably enhanced by the colonial experience. For example, Chinese elite consciousness was fostered and encouraged by the British, who from the early nineteenth century onward used the Straits Chinese as clerks in their firms. These Chinese often spoke English as their first language and had only a rudimentary understanding of Mandarin, Cantonese, or other Chinese dialects (Hokkien, Hakka, and Cantonese dialects are fairly different from one another and are not readily understood). Most of these people were descendants of longtime residents of Malaya, and they saw themselves as "Malay" citizens of the empire. Some of the more recent immigrants from China also came to see Malaya as their home, especially those who fled the civil war in China in the 1930s and 1940s. Others wavered in their sympathies between China and Malaya, and they envisioned Malaya as a temporary residence away from the Chinese motherland. Businesspeople, whose political sympathies were with the anti-Communist Kuomintang forces in China (before their defeat in 1949), were basically loyal as long as their business interests were protected by the local and colonial elites.

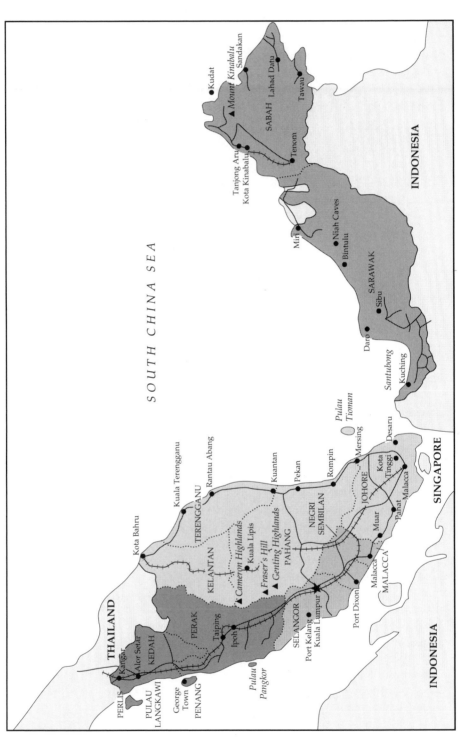

MAP 4.2   Modern Malaysia.

Malays were mostly rural people who lived in areas belonging to one of the nine sultanates that eventually became part of modern Malaysia. Malays seemed content to live under the patronage of their respective sultans, whose feudal systems remained largely intact until World War II. Dependence on the benevolence of individual autocratic rulers was firmly imbedded in Malay political culture prior to independence. Although sultans had an open-door policy under which citizens could ask for personal favors, voice their grievances, and utter complaints, once they reached a decision individuals had few avenues for redress.

Most Malays were illiterate, partly because the sultans discouraged Western-style education. In most instances people had to rely on their local qadis (Muslim judges) and religious leaders for education and dispute settlement. Literacy was further impeded because some of the classical texts of Malay literature were written in Arabic, reflecting the Islamic impact on the civic culture. Cultural exchanges with Europeans, Chinese, and Indians were discouraged by local leaders for fear of having their authority undermined.

Wealthier Chinese established their own elementary and secondary schools prior to independence, but most attended the secular institutions established by the British. Secret societies and special bureaus (established by the British) that dealt specifically with Chinese civil affairs served as the equivalent of a modern-day patronage system in preindependence Malaya. Under the colonial system the Chinese were restricted in their access to ownership of land, to which they responded by becoming traders; from there they moved on to become bankers and manufacturers.

Indians who worked on rubber plantations had their own security system and social services; the plantations were largely self-contained units. Indians typically divided their loyalties among the Crown, their home provinces in India, and Malaya. Most were either subjects of the Crown or Indian citizens; thus, they were doubly dependent on the British.[3]

The Emergence of Democratic Malaysia

Britain's role in Malaya was largely that of a protector rather than a colonizer, with the notable exception of the Crown colonies of Singapore, Malacca, and Penang. Penang effectively became a dominion of the British East India Company (the commercial predecessor of Imperial Britain) in 1785, when the sultan of Kedah ceded the island in return for military support and an annual salary. Singapore was similarly taken over by 1824, and Sarawak and Sabah on the island of Borneo became Crown colonies in the late nineteenth century. Malacca was first held by the Dutch, who gave it to the British in 1796. The interior of Malaya was never effectively colonized. By playing one sultan against the other and offering military assistance, the British were able to establish dominion over the sultanates of Negri Sembilan, Selangor, Perak, and Pahang by 1875. These states merged into a federation known as the Federated States of Malaya. The sultanates of Kedah, Perlis, Kelantan, and Trengganu, all either previously allied with Thailand or vassals of the same, were freed of Thai domination by 1909 but at first declined to join the British-sponsored Malay federation. Johore, the last independent sultanate, formally accepted British supervision in 1923.

Britain's rule was relatively benign. Colonial officials interfered in dynastic conflicts among the pretenders to the sultan's throne and similarly intervened when hostilities broke out among the Chinese secret societies.

At the beginning of the twentieth century, political power was divided among the British governor and high commissioner, the Conference of Rulers, the prime minister of each state, and members of the Legislative Council. The council included representatives of the trade unions and chambers of commerce (including Chinese), who were chosen by their respective organizations and appointed by the high commissioner.

World War II and the Japanese invasion of the peninsula exposed the tenuousness of British rule in Malaya. The Chinese especially were the targets of ruthless treatment by the invading Japanese. When the Japanese invaded China in 1937, all Chinese in Asia were treated as enemies. Deprived of work, they became impoverished squatters on the fringes of the Malayan jungle.

After World War II the British were slow to reestablish colonial rule in interior Malaya. Visible only in Penang and Singapore, their tentative plans to extend central rule triggered widespread Malay protests. Compromises between the British and communal leaders in the late 1940s and early 1950s led to a formal alliance of three important communally based parties. What emerged in 1957 as the independent country of Malaya consisted of eleven states; in 1963 Sabah and Sarawak (on the island of Borneo) and Singapore (for a period of two years) joined the federation and formed the country of Malaysia.

During decolonization and the early stages of independence, executive and legislative powers were somewhat decentralized, as each state retained the power to run its own internal affairs. This situation changed when Malaysia entered a new era that included what became known as "the Emergency."[4]

The Emergency

Subsidized by the British during World War II as a local resistance force against the Japanese occupiers, the Malayan Communists gained a degree of respectability among ethnically divided Malayans. The Chinese and the

Chinese resettlement camp in Sarawak, 1965. Although not directly affected by the Emergency in peninsular Malaya, 8,000 Chinese in Malaysian North Borneo were moved into camps as protection against Communist influence. Photo courtesy of UPI/Bettmann.

Communists were the prime targets of ruthless Japanese elimination campaigns. Communist sympathizers were often killed on mere suspicion. Upon the Japanese surrender, the British sought to disarm the guerrillas, of which there were about six thousand in 1945. Alarmed by what the Chinese perceived as the British catering to Malay dominance, the guerrillas refused to disarm. The sultans' refusal to join a more centrally organized federation that would give representation and full citizenship to minorities added to the mistrust. Chinese Communists were convinced that only full independence, preferably under their leadership, would lead to full emancipation of all ethnic groups in Malaya.

Authorities' treatment of the Chinese was often harsh and discriminatory. Until 1948, for example, Chinese accused of the tiniest infractions were regularly sent back to China. In 1948, emboldened and inspired by the impending Communist victory in China, the Malayan Communists embraced armed struggle. The British responded with a scheme whereby thousands of squatters were resettled into camps hermetically closed off from their surroundings. The Chinese were given land and were allowed to farm but were simultaneously deprived of free movement. Villagers became pawns of the Communists and the British. Totally dependent at first on British support and often forced to collaborate with Communist infiltrators, they were targeted by both sides. Informants were typically killed by the Communists; upon suspicion of Communist support, government forces responded with food rationing, deportations, prison sentences, and other forms of collective punishment. Eventually, the hamlet policy, as it was known, of closing off the villages from the outside world robbed the guerrillas of the much-needed political and physical support of the Chinese squatters and, thus, gradually led to the dissipation of the movement.

The Emergency disclosed the weakness of a decentralized political system and forced a reevaluation of existing arrangements. With the realization that the insurgents were a force to be reckoned with, state-level executive committees cooperated with federal authorities, local police chiefs, and army commanders to fight the insurgents. At first, lacking military and police forces to fight the rebels, the British passed emergency regulations that gave the police extraordinary powers. They created special forces trained in jungle warfare, gave arms to community guards, and, later, encouraged non-Malays to join the struggle against the Communists. By the early 1950s the **insurgency** had faded, and Malays and Chinese, under the able leadership of Tunku Abdul Rahman, joined to form an alliance that became the basis for cooperation among the three ethnic groups.

The son of the sultan of Kedah and a Thai princess, Tunku Abdul Rahman was one of the bright nationalists who organized the Alliance Party in 1952, which convinced the British that Malaya was ready for independence. The party consisted of the Malay Nationalist Organization, the Malayan Chinese Association, and the Malayan Indian Congress. Until 1969 it provided the type of political formula that led to relative ethnic stability. The formula consisted of a series of compromises that favored the Malays: The Malays were to dominate politics, the official religion was to be Islam, the official language would be Malay, and the head of state was to be a sultan elected from among the nine hereditary rulers.

Malaysia Since 1969

The preindependence social contract that favored Malay status and protected non-Malay cultures, which allowed for relative ethnic harmony, collapsed in the riots that followed the elections of 1969. The urban-based, largely Chinese Democratic Action Party had wrested votes from the Malaysian Chinese Association by promoting equal rights for all citizens regardless of race. This position directly opposed the aims of the alliance, which promoted racial harmony by acquiescing to Malay political hegemony. The electoral gain of the Democratic Action Party was interpreted by impoverished Malays as a direct threat to the continuance of political dominance. In the ensuing riots 143 Chinese, 25 Malays, 13 Indians, and 15 others were killed.

These riots led to the emergence of a new generation of leaders committed to protecting communal rights for all. New policies were enacted to eliminate poverty among all ethnic groups. The long-term objectives were to narrow the gap between rural poverty and urban wealth and to eliminate economic inequalities between the Chinese and the Malays. Estimates showed that in 1969, nearly 65 percent of all Malays lived below the official poverty line, compared with 26 percent of the Chinese and 39 percent of the Indian households.

Broader initiatives included funding for research and development, especially in technical fields, providing additional funds for regional development schemes, stressing the value of education, and encouraging peasants to take wage-earning jobs. Furthermore, the government hoped to reduce foreign investment by replacing foreign corporations with Malaysian owned and managed ones. In 1969, an estimated 62 percent of all corporate assets were foreign-owned, whereas Chinese Malays owned more than 30 percent and Malays less than 2 percent. Government policy aimed to change this within twenty years to 30 percent foreign, 40 percent non-Malay, and 30 percent Malay. Although the Malay-owned percentage had increased significantly by the early 1990s, it still fell short of these targets.

In reality, the New Economic Policy (NEP), as it was called, favored the Malays through special subsidies. Newly established government-financed agencies served as clearinghouses in commercial ventures, job quotas were introduced, Chinese quotas were introduced at universities, and various other programs were instituted that were designed to help Malays gain economic parity with the Chinese.

To many Chinese these policies amounted to a Malay takeover and an attempt to convert potential Chinese economic losses into Malay gains. For the Malays the change of direction was long overdue. Although many earlier policies had favored Malays by requiring quotas in occupations, they had done little to alleviate rural Malay poverty. Thus, the new policies were directed primarily toward trying to narrow the gap between rural poverty and urban wealth and eliminating economic inequalities between the Chinese and the Malays. The official goal was to "eliminate the identification of race with economic function."[5]

Since the implementation of the New Economic Policy, Malays have enrolled in universities in unprecedented numbers, whereas because of quotas, many Malaysian Chinese study abroad. Malays are still underrepresented in the professions and in technical jobs. All ethnic groups have gained in relative income, but the distribution within ethnic groups has changed only slightly in favor of Malays, and income disparities remain.

Malaysia's export-oriented economy is not easily manipulated through government-sponsored programs. Economic growth may promote more overall wealth but may do little to alter existing income inequalities, despite governmental intervention, because of the independent nature of a globally oriented market economy. The very real Malay gains in education may eventually challenge Chinese domination in the professional and technical fields and, thus, in the long run improve overall Malay economic standing.

Malaysia in the 1990s

Despite regular elections, an orderly leadership succession, a federal bicameral legislature, and a sharing of legislative powers with thirteen states, democracy in Malaysia is still somewhat limited. After the 1969 riots the democratic system was suspended for eighteen months and replaced with a National Operations Council with full emergency powers. Also, emergency legislation was enacted that has yet to be repealed. Under the provisions of the Internal Security Act, party activists, Christian evangelists, and other activists from various community organizations have been arrested. The act is supposed to allow people to criticize the government as long as the criticism has no racial or ethnic connotations. The curtailment of freedom of expression to such a degree, coupled with the occasional use of preventive detention, is incompatible with democratic values; on the other hand, there is continuity in the democratic process, and few question politicians' commitment to parliamentary democracy. On the positive side, despite economic and political inequalities and internal threats posed by a long-lasting insurgency, Malaysians prospered and enjoy relative freedoms in a quasidemocracy, a rare accomplishment among multiethnic Third World countries.

It is important to reiterate that obstacles to complete ethnic harmony in Malaysia still remain, obstacles that would present a tremendous challenge to any polity. Malays have yet to achieve economic parity in their native land. **Islamic fundamentalists** who are found in universities and in politics stress the Islamic character of the polity. Kinship ties remain a strong force in Malay life—Chinese can only enter the circle if they convert to Islam, as few have done. Some Chinese have converted to Christianity, which is an affront to pious Muslims, who see proselytization as an attempt to diminish their faith (the government actively opposes Muslim proselytization). Quotas preventing Chinese from entering universities have led to emigration and to a brain drain of needed professionals. State legislatures have frequently challenged the central government, especially when it is controlled by opposition parties. In response, the federal government has sometimes invoked emergency powers to remove opposition leaders. Divisions exist not only between Chinese and Malays but also between the educated elite and their rural counterparts. Communal tensions are exacerbated by the various demands of the indigenous groups in Sarawak and Sabah, who, although they are ethnically related to Malays, have interests similar to those of indigenous peoples elsewhere. Aborigines in peninsular Malaysia form yet another group within the communal pie. Indians, the third-largest ethnic group in Malaysia, are largely ignored in the ongoing struggle involving Malay political dominance and Chinese economic preponderance. Malaysia enjoyed healthy economic growth during the 1980s, until the retrenchment of the global economy in the early 1990s, and it was considered one of the fastest growing economies in Asia. Because of declining demands for natural rubber and tin, Malaysia has undergone a recession. Thus, the future stability of Malaysia depends in part on international economic factors beyond the control of its multiethnic government.[6]

TURKISH IMMIGRANTS IN GERMANY

On November 23, 1992, a fifty-one-year-old Turkish woman and two girls, ages fourteen and ten, were killed and eight other Turks injured by the firebombings of two apartment buildings in the western German town of Moelln, near Hamburg. Ten days later two neo-Nazis, ages nineteen and twenty-five, confessed to having thrown the gasoline bombs. This was one of the most deadly episodes in a yearlong wave of more than 4,500 attacks on foreigners and citizens who were thought to be foreign in recently reunited Germany. The arrested killers were typical of the young skinheads who were responsible for virtually all of the attacks. The victims, however, were atypical, because most targets of antiforeign attacks in 1992 were recent refugees such as Vietnamese, Angolans, and Romanian gypsies, who were protected by German law, which guarantees temporary asylum—including shelter and support—to people fleeing from repression. In 1993, attacks on Turks escalated; the worst episode occurred in Solingen on May 29, when three Turkish women and two girls were killed in another firebombing.

The immediate political questions raised by these incidents are why there is a Turkish minority in Germany, and why they and other foreigners should be targets of often-deadly hostility. The larger questions are whether an analysis of the German situation helps explain the rise in antiforeign sentiment in other European democracies, and what kinds of public policies are being devised to cope with such problems.

Origins and Status of Turks in Germany

In 1990 Germany had more than 5 million resident foreigners, as shown in Figure 4.2, the largest proportion of whom were Turks, who numbered

Turks and others pray in front of a burned-out house in
Solingen, Germany, on May 30, 1993. Five Turks died and
three were injured when the house was destroyed by neo-
Nazis in an arson attack. Photo courtesy of Reuters/
Bettmann.

nearly 1.7 million. Most are long-time residents who make a major contri-
bution to the German economy. Many, like the two girls who died in
Moelln, were born in Germany, went to local elementary and secondary
schools, and are bilingual and bicultural. Their situation within German
society is deeply ambiguous, however. The great majority want and ex-
pect to stay in Germany, but official policy has been that Germany is not a
"society of immigration," a policy that justified raising almost insur-
mountable barriers for Turks and other foreign residents who sought citi-

Total: 5242

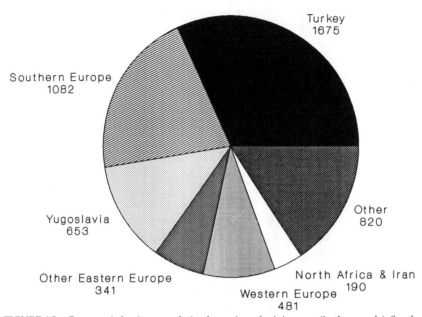

FIGURE 4.2   Germany's foreign population by region of origin, 1990 (in thousands). South-ern Europe includes Spain, Portugal, Italy, and Greece. *Source: Continuous Reporting System on Migration, Trends in International Migration* (Paris: Organization for Economic Coopera-tion and Development, 1992), p. 136.

zenship in the past. Turks are entitled to full social benefits, but those who are not citizens cannot vote or run for political office. Their lack of citizen-ship symbolizes foreigners' exclusion from the community of Germans and provides a kind of implicit license allowing subtle, yet persistent and widespread, discrimination.

The presence of Turks in Germany is a consequence of policies of the former West German and the Turkish governments. Germany's rapid eco-nomic growth in the 1950s and 1960s created a demand for labor that could only be satisfied by encouraging immigration of workers from poorer countries. At first they were recruited mainly from Italy, Greece, and Yugoslavia, but in 1961 the governments of West Germany and Tur-key signed a bilateral agreement that regulated the recruitment, employ-ment, and wages of Turkish workers. During the next fifteen years 650,000 Turks migrated to Germany—two-thirds of them recruited by the Turkish Employment Service, one-third nominated by German employers. Con-trary to the popular German image of migrants as unskilled Anatolian villagers, more than half came from urban areas, one-third were skilled workers, and one-fifth were women. Many were members of Turkey's Kurdish minority, some of whom were recruited into Kurdish nationalist organizations that soon established branches in Germany.

Both governments expected that the workers' stay was temporary and that they would return to their homeland. One-third of Turkey's skilled workers emigrated during the 1960s and early 1970s, mainly to West Germany, and the Turkish government was eager for their return.[7] Opinion polls from the mid-1960s to the 1980s showed that the majority of Germans wanted the foreign workers to leave. A 1966 survey found that 81 percent of respondents agreed that "even though there is a shortage of labor in Germany, nonetheless, too many foreign workers have entered the country." Other surveys in 1966 and 1967 showed that about two-thirds of Germans wanted foreign employees to leave the country. Negative stereotypes were also common: Two-thirds of the German workers who were included in these surveys—the people most likely to interact regularly with foreign workers—thought the foreigners chased German women, nearly half blamed them for starting fights, and others said they used too many social services.[8]

In the early 1970s all West European economies were hit by recession and rising unemployment, and the federal German government promptly moved to halt emigration, beginning with the *Anwerbestop* (recruitment stoppage) legislation of 1973. The influx of new workers slowed to a trickle, but most Turks already had long-term residence permits and were reluctant to leave. During the next decade new restrictions were imposed, and new incentives to return to Turkey were established. To discourage family reunions, for example, work permits were denied to dependents who emigrated after December 1, 1974, until authorities realized that the policy was creating a subclass of unemployed, potentially delinquent youths. In the early 1980s tougher restrictions were placed on family reunions, Turks were offered substantial premiums and early payouts of social security benefits if they left the country, and additional grounds for deportation were specified. Although some Turks left voluntarily, the restrictions increased the determination of most Turks to bring in their spouses and children from Turkey and to maintain permanent residence.[9]

A 1982 survey, one of many taken during this decade, showed a hardening of attitudes. Sixty-eight percent of Germans polled rejected the proposition that "guestworkers wishing to remain in Germany should be given the possibility [to do so]," and 66 percent thought they should "return to their native soil."[10] Incidents reported in West German newspapers during this period show how such attitudes were manifested in racist acts. In June 1982, in a Frankfurt housing complex occupied by foreigners and poor Germans, a middle-aged German was disturbed by the noisy games of Turkish children. He grabbed a three-year-old and pushed him into a concrete box filled with garbage bins, slamming the door after him. In response to a German woman who criticized his action, he said, "They're just filth, they must get out of here."[11]

By the early 1990s almost all of the 1.7 million Turks in Germany were permanent residents, most of whom lived with their families in urban neighborhoods like Berlin's Kreuzberg district, where 150,000 Turks were concentrated. Males slightly outnumbered females by a ratio of five to four; one-third were children under sixteen. In the late 1980s more than 400,000 Turkish youths were enrolled in primary, secondary, and technical schools—nearly 20,000 of them in Gymnasiums, the academic secondary schools that are the gateway to universities and professional training. Polls show that more than 80 percent of Turks want to remain in Germany, including virtually all of those born in the country. The Turkish community is relatively prosperous, even though most Turks live in old inner-city districts. There are 33,000 Turkish-owned businesses, Turkish unemployment rates are lower than those of German workers, and Turks are enthusiastic consumers—for example, only one German in thirteen drives a Mercedes, but one Turk in five does so. As one authority remarked, German-born Turks are "not foreigners with German residence permits, but Germans with foreign passports."[12]

The Changing Political Situation of Turks

In contrast to this picture of immigrant economic success are political threats and restrictions. The political threats come from right-wing political parties that have campaigned against the foreign presence in Germany. From the 1960s to the 1980s the National Democratic Party advocated compulsory repatriation and other restrictive measures, although it never won seats in the federal German legislature, the *Bundestag*. In 1989 a new right-wing party, the Republicans (founded in 1983), capitalized on antiforeign sentiment and won seats in Berlin and later in several other German localities. In the industrial city of Essen, for example, the Republicans increased their share of the votes from less than 1 percent in 1989 to 8.3 percent in 1993. Polls suggest their popularity continues to rise.[13] Also increasing are skinhead and neo-Nazi attacks on foreigners, which more than doubled between 1991 and 1992, then declined slightly in 1993. Between January 1992 and August 1993, these attacks were responsible for at least twenty-five deaths.

Although political threats to the Turkish community come from a small right-wing minority, of greater import is government policy, the effect of which has been to restrict the citizenship rights of Turks. The basic assumption of (West) German public policy, until very recently, was that the

Turks were temporary residents, which justified raising barriers to their citizenship and, hence, to their political participation. The citizenship law in effect at the beginning of 1993 allowed foreigners who had lived in Germany for fifteen years—or for eight years if they were under age twenty-three—to apply for citizenship. This meant giving up foreign citizenship, which some Turks have been reluctant to do. Further, fees of up to $3,000 were required. Most applicants reportedly were rejected by police investigators—sometimes for minor tax or traffic offenses, sometimes for reasons authorities would not reveal to unsuccessful applicants. The citizenship process has been so difficult that only thirteen thousand Turks were able to achieve citizenship between 1977 and 1990.[14] The stringent citizenship law has been widely criticized in Germany by experts like Klaus Bade (see Chapter 4, note 9), by the opposition Social Democratic Party, and by many Turks.

In response to the crisis of rising numbers of antiforeign attacks, in 1993 the major German parties began to debate proposals to make the citizenship process more open and routine. Administratively, application fees were reduced to $60, and promises were made to speed up the process. Alternative proposals under consideration by the *Bundestag* would reduce the fifteen-year residency requirement to ten or even five years and give automatic citizenship to children of foreigners born in Germany. Serious consideration was also being given to allowing dual citizenship, which had been legal in Germany prior to 1934.

Given our concern with the analysis of ethnic conflict, a major question is why Turks have not organized any kind of sustained political action to improve their status. In fact, some of them have done so. In the 1970s, encouraged by grassroots political organizations, some Turks participated in major strikes, demonstrations, and building takeovers to protest poor housing conditions. A Federation of Turkish Workers was established in 1977. Many Turkish workers joined trade unions, and some have joined political parties—despite the fact that they cannot vote—and have participated in special advisory councils set up in some localities to represent foreign workers. A number of ad hoc groups composed of German citizens and immigrants have been formed locally and regionally to pursue common interests.

The attacks on Turks and other foreigners in 1992 and 1993 led to a marked increase in Turkish political activism. After the Moelln and Solingen killings described previously, Turks participated in large nationwide demonstrations that were organized by Germans opposed to racism and neo-Nazism. In June 1993, there were clashes between stone-throwing, club-wielding Turkish demonstrators and police in Solingen and other cities, and four teenage Turks were arrested for trying to set fire to the office of a conservative political party in Bavaria. These events and the

Turkish women and children march in Berlin to protest persecution of Turks in Bulgaria, March 1985. Photo by Ahmet Ersöz, Berliner Institut für Vergleichende Sozialforschung.

public statements of militant Turks have raised concerns that future ethnic violence will no longer be one-sided. Nonetheless, as we suggest in Chapter 6, a number of factors combine to inhibit large-scale political action.

Events since the dissolution of the Soviet bloc in 1990 and 1991 and the unification of Germany in mid-1991 have added greatly to antiforeign sentiment. First, other flows of immigration to Germany have increased greatly. Germany's liberal political asylum law attracted nearly 800,000 refugees between 1990 and 1992, more than half of whom arrived in 1992. They are given housing and support while their cases are being reviewed, which is a source of German resentment. Until late 1993 there were long delays in reviewing applications for asylum. Most of the right-wing attacks mentioned previously have been directed against these immigrants and the temporary quarters in which they live.

Second, 173,000 ethnic Germans migrated to Germany in 1992, principally from Eastern Europe and Russia. German law, in effect since 1913, grants citizenship to any immigrant who can demonstrate that he or she is of German descent. Public policy guarantees these immigrants housing and support as well as citizenship. Third, economic crisis in the former East Germany has pushed many people, an estimated 200,000 in 1991 alone, to emigrate to the former West Germany.

Thus, German society is under great and growing pressures from outsiders, some of whom have a right to residence and citizenship—ethnic

Germans from the former East Germany and abroad—and others of whom have a right to temporary asylum. The costs of accommodating these people are high, and they are especially resented because of the economic problems, including rising unemployment, caused by unification. It is not surprising, then, that foreigners are attacked mainly by unskilled and semiskilled youths, many of whom are unemployed.[15]

There is much evidence that mainstream German society deplores the recent upsurge in antiforeign violence and discrimination. Attacks against foreigners have prompted public reactions throughout Germany: Thousands of people have acted as human barricades between neo-Nazis and immigrant hostels, and hundreds of thousands have marched in protests against right-wing violence. The federal government, led by Chancellor Helmut Kohl, in 1993 belatedly cracked down on the right-wing organizations most directly responsible for the attacks. Domestic pressures on German politicians to take further action has led to two kinds of responses. One, discussed previously, involved moving toward granting citizenship to most long-term foreign residents, especially the Turks. The other was to restrict the rights of asylum seekers to cross the German border; this was the aim of a new law that went into effect on July 1, 1993. Moreover, Germans are keenly aware of international concern and criticism, which provides added incentives to put their house in order.

MINORITIES IN OTHER WESTERN EUROPEAN SOCIETIES

The problems posed by immigrant minorities in Germany are greater in magnitude but otherwise similar to those in other Western European democracies. In 1990 the foreign population of the thirteen most prosperous European countries totaled more than 15 million, as shown in Figure 4.3. France, with 3.6 million foreigners, and the United Kingdom, with almost 1.9 million, have both experienced an upsurge in antiforeign violence and increasingly strident demands from right-wing political organizations to stop future immigration and to force those already there to return to their countries of origin.

The main targets of these anti-immigrant pressures in France are the Maghrebins, Muslims from North African countries. The openly racist National Front Party advocates their repatriation; the party's leader, Jean-Marie Le Pen, received 14 percent of the votes in the first round of the last presidential elections, held in 1988. In the United Kingdom the targets include Afro-Caribbeans from Jamaica, Trinidad, and other West Indian islands, and Asian immigrants from India, Pakistan, and Bangladesh. British officials report that there were 7,700 racial attacks against members of

Total: 15533

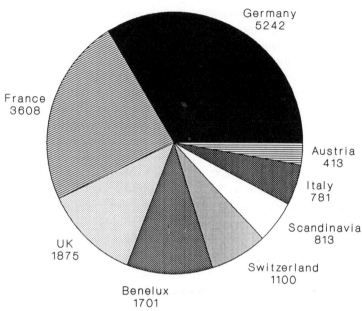

France
3608

Germany
5242

Austria
413

Italy
781

Scandinavia
813

Switzerland
1100

UK
1875

Benelux
1701

FIGURE 4.3   Foreign population of thirteen European countries, 1990 (in thousands). Legal residents only. Benelux includes Belgium, the Netherlands, and Luxembourg. Scandinavia includes Denmark, Norway, Sweden, and Finland. *Source: Continuous Reporting System on Migration, Trends in International Migration* (Paris: Organization for Economic Cooperation and Development, 1992), p. 131.

these groups in 1992 and that about a dozen people died from such attacks in 1992 and 1993.[16]

The attacks on visible minorities in these societies raise serious questions about the ability and the will of Western democracies to protect the basic rights of all of their residents. Citizenship is the key symbolic issue for German Turks. The underlying issue is that of popular resentment against visible minorities, whatever their legal status. Many French Muslims and most Afro-Caribbeans and Asians in Britain have citizenship, but it does not protect them from individual attacks or demands to send them back to their countries of origin. Resentment of visible minorities has increased virtually everywhere in Europe for a combination of reasons. One is prolonged economic recession and high unemployment throughout Western Europe, which increases hostility against "outsiders" who are thought to take jobs away from "real" citizens. Second is the rising tide of refugees and asylum seekers: Germany hosts the largest numbers, but the trends in other countries are also sharply upward. Third is the susceptibility of democratically elected politicians to public pressures, which means it can be very risky for a governing party's leaders to ignore demands for restrictions on foreigners.

In response to this near-crisis situation, a two-track policy is being charted by virtually all West European governments. One is to devise increasingly tighter restrictions on new immigrants and refugees. In Britain such policies date back to the 1960s; in Germany they are more recent, but they share a common objective: to restrict the influx. The parallel policy is to speed up the incorporation of people of foreign origin who have already established residence. This has also been a long-standing policy in some countries, but it is being accelerated, especially in Germany and France. There are and will be significant differences among European governments in the details, timing, and emphasis of these two policies. Their larger objectives are clear: to close the gates to outsiders, even if this violates some individual rights and ignores humanitarian needs, and to incorporate or assimilate immigrants already inside the gates into the dominant culture.

CONCLUSION

The internal dynamics of the conflicts in which the Malaysian Chinese and the German Turks have been involved are analyzed in Chapter 6; their international dimensions are assessed in Chapter 7. Here we can point out that both cases provide correctives to some simplistic assumptions about the nature and outcomes of communal conflict in the last decade of the twentieth century.

First, at a time when serious ethnopolitical conflicts are escalating throughout much of Africa and Asia, Malaysia offers a modest success story. It shows that restraint and accommodation can be more effective than policies of cooptation and repression. Despite often mutually exclusive communal demands, Malaysian authorities have not succumbed to temptations to replace democratic rule with autocracy, although present policies favor Malays and restrict the expression of potentially divisive communal demands. Malaysia's remarkable economic growth results in no small part from a political system that balances contending communal interests, and the country's sustained growth in turn reinforces all groups' acceptance of its political arrangements.

Second, the German case highlights some of the dilemmas facing prosperous Western democracies. Many people in Western societies are smugly confident that their systems have an almost infinite capacity to respond to internal crises. Germany in the 1990s is up against the limits: It is simultaneously trying to incorporate the crippled economy of former East Germany, rebuild that region's civil administration and infrastructure, *and* accommodate a flood of immigrants and refugees that, in proportional terms, is probably unparalleled in the history of Western societies. Few observers doubt that German democracy will survive the process, and most think long-term immigrants will eventually be incorporated. But Germany also illustrates a dilemma common to all democracies that face the challenge of incorporating visible minorities. Germans who oppose further immigration or citizenship for people of Third World origin have the right to work for those objectives within the political system. And if their views are widely shared, they will almost inevitably shape future public policy in ways that will restrict the influx and rights of noncitizens. Political leaders in all democracies, including the United States, are obliged by the basic rules of their political systems to create compromises among the rights, interests, and demands of both majorities and minorities.

FIVE

□ □ □

A Framework for Analysis of Ethnopolitical Mobilization and Conflict

I n Chapters 3 and 4 we recounted the distinctive historical, political, economic, and social experiences that shaped the identities, status, and grievances of four different ethnopolitical groups. We also showed when and how each group became involved in political conflict with the state in which it lives and pointed out the ways in which members of each group have been restricted and sometimes victimized by governments.

Most social scientists are committed to going beyond describing single cases to provide more general explanations. How do we explain the reasons for, and the causes of, ethnic conflicts in general? In this chapter we begin with a brief review of some social science approaches (or theories) for explaining why ethnic groups mobilize and become involved in conflict. We then introduce a variety of concepts and **propositions** that together form a preliminary theory of ethnopolitical conflict. By identifying general determinants of ethnic groups' behavior, our aim is to provide the common ground that will enable any citizen to critically analyze accepted wisdom about what causes ethnic conflict. In subsequent chapters we use information from the four cases in the previous chapters to illustrate our propositions and try to strike a balance between providing a sophisticated theory to explain all cases of ethnopolitical conflict and offering historical interpretations of single cases.

APPROACHES TO EXPLAINING ETHNOPOLITICAL CONFLICT

Many theories have been proposed to explain political conflict and violence, either in general or in specific forms such as revolution.[1] But there is no comprehensive and widely accepted theory of the causes and consequences of ethnopolitical conflict. Rather, there are approaches and **hypotheses** that seek to explain particular aspects of ethnic conflict. Some of these are concerned with how ethnic identities form and change over time.[2] Others examine the sources of competition and conflict between ethnic groups.[3] We are most interested in explanations of why and how ethnic groups **mobilize** (organize for political action) and enter into open conflict—often violent conflict—with the governments that claim to rule them.

New theories usually begin as efforts to explain puzzles—that is, new political phenomena that are not explained by older theories. This is clearly the case with ethnopolitical conflict. In the 1950s and 1960s many social scientists thought economic development, the migration of rural peoples to cities, and growing literacy would lead to the creation of complex and integrated societies throughout the world. **Modernization** theory, as this argument was called, made a specific prediction about ethnic identities: that greater political and economic interaction among people and widespread communication networks would break down people's "parochial" identities with ethnic groups and replace them with loyalties to larger communities such as Canada, the European Community, or an emerging pan-Africa. The political facts of the 1970s and 1980s contradicted this prediction: Rather than declining, conflicts based on the assertion of ethnic identities and interests increased sharply. Moreover, ethnopolitical conflicts increased not only in modernizing societies but also in developed Western societies, which experienced an upsurge in regional **separatist** movements and ethnoclass protests in the 1960s.[4]

Several alternative approaches have been used to explain the persistence of ethnic conflict in a modernizing world. One approach argues that people's ethnic and religious identities have deep social, historical, and genetic foundations. From this perspective, sometimes called **primordialism,** modernization is a threat to ethnic solidarities that prompts minorities to mobilize in defense of their culture and way of life.[5] A second alternative emphasizes the **instrumental** nature of ethnic mobilization. The main goals of a group are assumed to be material and political gains; cultural identity is invoked only as a means to attain those goals. In this perspective the most important effect of modernization is to increase economic differences, or awareness and resentment of differences, between dominant groups and minorities. "Political entrepreneurs" capitalize on these differences to establish ethnically based political movements aimed at increasing the economic and political well-being of their group or region. A version of this argument, called *internal colonialism,* was proposed to explain one source of growing ethnic conflict in developed European societies—the regional separatist movements like those of the Welsh and

Scots in Britain, the Bretons and Corsicans in France, and the Basques in Spain.[6]

The primordial and instrumental approaches to explaining ethnic mobilization and conflict emphasize different factors; the first emphasizes defense of ethnic identity, and the second stresses the pursuit of group material and political interests. But they are not fundamentally inconsistent. We think ethnic groups are most likely to mobilize when both conditions—a strong sense of ethnic group identity in combination with imposed disadvantages—are present. Recent theories of specific kinds of ethnic conflict incorporate both conditions. Scholars have proposed, for example, that secessionist movements like those of the Kurds and the Miskitos result from three general conditions: (1) the existence of a separate ethnonational community or society, (2) actual or perceived disadvantages in comparison with the central government, and (3) territorial contiguity. If we borrow from international legal arguments, a group's territorial base shapes its decision to pursue its interests by fighting wars of secession.[7] We also find primordial and instrumental elements in theories designed to explain how conflict arises in multiethnic societies like Malaysia and modern Germany, where peoples of different ethnic origins compete with one another in the pursuit of jobs, political influence, and status. A common argument is that when peoples of different ethnic groups compete *directly* for the same scarce resources and positions, their ethnic identities become more important to them. And if some groups are more successful than others, inequalities increase, which provides the second general condition for ethnic mobilization and conflict.[8]

The mobilization of ethnic groups is the immediate precursor of the political actions used to make demands on governments. The extent and intensity of the resulting conflict depend upon the strategies followed by ethnic groups' leaders *and* those followed by governments. Few theorists have tried to explain what strategies governments have used in response to challenging groups in general or to ethnic groups in particular. One important exception, however, is directly relevant to our subject: theories about the causes of genocides and politicides (mass political murder). These theories are important for our subject because they show how competition between subordinate ethnic groups and dominant groups can lead to discrimination and repression of subordinate groups. In response to privation and repression, some ethnic groups mobilize for political action, which is then used to justify their destruction. Others, like the victims of the Holocaust and the Muslim Chams in Cambodia under the Khmer Rouge, are targeted because they are defined in the dominant group's ideology as a threatening group.[9]

We have identified five internal factors that, in combination, make genocides and politicides likely: (1) Persisting cleavages exist among ethnic groups; (2) elites have a history of relying on repression to maintain power; (3) elites use their power to reward groups differentially for their loyalty; (4) the society has recently experienced a political upheaval, for example, a revolution or a defeat in war; and (5) exclusionary ideologies arise that define target groups as expendable.[10] When all of these five factors are present, ethnopolitical conflict is likely to have genocidal consequences.

Many of the foregoing arguments about the causes of ethnic mobilization, conflict, and genocide are incorporated in the theoretical model developed in the next section.

USING SOCIAL SCIENCE THEORIES
TO EXPLAIN ETHNOPOLITICAL CONFLICT

Some people think the terms *theory* and *model* are too removed from harsh political realities. Theories use abstract concepts, which some regard as irrelevant to their perceptions of events in the real world. We recognize that there are different ways of looking at the world of ethnopolitical groups, one of which is to become so deeply immersed in information about a group—by direct observation, for example—that one gains an almost intuitive understanding of its members' perceptions and intentions.

Our view is that systematic comparison of different cases is needed to reach more general conclusions about how and why ethnic groups become involved in conflict. Therefore, we provide here a rationale and guidelines for students who seek more general, empirically grounded knowledge about ethnic conflict. Use of the theories and language of social science can generate the kind of satisfaction that comes with an increased understanding and appreciation of the complexity of political life. The reasons are not just "scientific"; we think general knowledge is essential if scholars and policymakers are to understand, anticipate, and respond to ethnic conflicts in ways that can reduce human suffering and improve the chances for accommodation.

Scientific analysis requires precise communication, a key to which is the development of a common vocabulary. The technical language of the social sciences is supposed to convey the same meanings to anyone who reads or reanalyzes a researcher's findings. Scientific analysis also requires the use of standardized concepts, categories, and indicators so as to eliminate as much as possible the observer's own subjective interpretations. Objectivity and logic, after all, are the tools of the scientist.

Assume one wants to argue that the UN-sponsored **sanctions** against Iraq preceding the 1991 Gulf War increased the conflict potential of the region. The concepts—here, sanctions and conflict—ought to have the same meaning to all and should be measured by commonly accepted indicators. In order to describe something, we need to be able to observe or experience it. In order to be persuasive, we need to demonstrate that the conflict potential increases when sanctions are applied.

Now let us assume the following hypothetical scenario. The United States unilaterally cuts off trade relations with all Middle Eastern states that are either neutral in their policy toward Iraq or that subvert UN-sponsored sanctions against Iraq. The U.S. action is designed to enforce compliance with the sanctions. The targeted states respond by accommodating the United States: They abandon their hostile rhetoric and stop letting Iraq use their territory to smuggle in its food. Saddam Hussein reacts with open defiance by attacking Kurdish villagers and imprisoning some foreign nationals. The Kurds in turn attack Iraqi positions. Turkey, fearing unrest among its own Kurds, attacks Kurdish villages inside Iraq. It seems that the U.S. trade embargo has had the desired impact by forcing a change in the behavior of the target states. Yet it led simultaneously to the Iraqi attack against Kurdish villagers and to Turkey's intervention. At this stage of analysis we cannot assume that the changes in political behavior resulted from U.S. pressure, however likely this may seem. Perhaps Saddam Hussein had long planned an attack to reestablish government control over Kurdish rebels, and Turkey had used the circumstances to resurrect a long-standing policy of intimidating Kurds by force. We need to further test our argument.

An untested argument or idea about a specific kind of relationship is called a proposition. How do we test our proposition that sanctions against Iraq increased the conflict potential within the region? The standard procedure used by social scientists is to put the proposition into testable form: A testable proposition is a hypothesis. If we expand our ideas to include more than one hypothesis about the conflict potential within the region, we can call this a theory. In other words, logically related testable ideas (hypotheses) that specify relationships between concepts are commonly called a theory.

We argued that sanctions against Iraq increased the conflict potential in the region, but this is simply an untested idea (proposition). How do we change propositions into testable hypotheses? Let us briefly conclude our theoretical excursion by transforming our proposition into a hypothesis and **operationalizing** its concepts.

The hypothesis states that the degree of compliance in countries' political behavior increases relative to the strength of sanctions imposed by external actors. Sanctions imposed on states engaged in open conflict increase their degree of hostility toward internal and external opponents.

By specifying the type of pressure applied by the United States and relating it to a specific type of performance (stop supporting Iraq), we can determine with much greater confidence whether and under what conditions the United States is able to influence a specific type of political behavior. Of course, we cannot assume that all of the countries in question would act similarly if the United States were to ask them to disarm, for example. In the second part of the hypothesis we argue that once a country is involved in open conflict, sanctions may have the opposite effect—namely, they may increase conflict behavior. Thus, we have qualified our statement because we recognize that political behavior and conflict are multifaceted phenomena, that they occur in different domains (domestic policies versus foreign policy behavior), and that they are applied with different degrees of strength (sanctions that force total versus partial compliance).

Another important step in social science analysis is to introduce criteria that enable us to disprove a hypothesis. If we were to identify only those instances in which the targeted countries complied with U.S. demands and ignored instances in which they did not, our task would be easy and our conclusions wrong. By selecting information to suit our particular argument, we overlook other information and may reach false conclusions.

What have we learned about states' behavior in our example? If we have observed the region's relations with the United States for some time, we probably recognize that many states were already in the process of changing their behavior vis-à-vis Iraq and only reacted more quickly than they would otherwise have done because the United States exerted pressure. This implies that the United States truly influenced some states' behavior, but possibly not to the extent we had thought. And we do not know with any certainty whether either Turkey or Iraq responded with increased hostility toward Kurds because of the U.S. sanctions or because they had long-standing designs to do so anyway. How much influence did the United States truly exert compared with states' own desire for change? Answering this question is far more complicated. Only if we were able to observe the same sequence of events at another time or in another area and find similar outcomes could we say with increased certainty that in some instances U.S. policy leads to changes in political behavior and under particular circumstances increases the conflict potential of a particular area.

Because of these difficulties we more often propose *likely* explanations rather than definitive ones, our statements are more often tentative than conclusive, and our tested statements (hypotheses) are **probability statements** rather than truths. Students should consider these obstacles as challenges, not barriers. The best we can do in most instances is to be as specific as possible, to be modest in our goals and objectives, to scrutinize as much information as we can obtain, and to follow procedures that can easily be duplicated by others.

Is the scientific approach we have just described worth using? Consider the alternatives. In the early stages of social science, scholars offered little more than learned opinions, similar to journalistic interpretations. The social sciences had little or no basis for claiming that their explanations had any general validity. Political science was little more than a combination of descriptive historical interpretation and philosophical discourse on human destiny. We have advanced at least to the stage of weather forecasting; that is, we can assert with some plausibility that certain actions lead to likely outcomes.

What, then, is our goal in this chapter? Our propositions about ethnic mobilization and conflict are essentially tentative statements describing likely relationships. We invite students to develop hypotheses based on the propositions and to test them against the reality of ethnic groups in various situations. Our model introduces a set of testable hypotheses (theory) and operationalizes some of the concepts (the building blocks of propositions and hypotheses). Operationalization involves the process of defining the concepts so they can be measured in real quantities. Thus, for example, if conflict is the concept, its **variable** properties can include the amount of conflict—such as numbers of armed attacks involving two countries—the extent of participation in street protests, or a number of other properties. In other words, variable properties differ depending on the context in which they are observed.

EXPLAINING ETHNOPOLITICAL MOBILIZATION AND CONFLICT

What contributes to ethnic mobilization? Here we use two concepts: discrimination and ethnic group identity. By discrimination we mean the extent of socially derived inequalities in group members' material well-being or political access in comparison with other social groups. An ethnic group consists of people whose identity is based on shared traits such as religion, culture, common history, place of residence, and race.

On the most basic level, people resent and react against discriminatory treatment. They may use their anger constructively or destructively, or they may be apathetic. In the former case they may opt for peaceful activism, channel anger into greater personal efforts to succeed, or emigrate to escape discrimination. Others are willing to openly challenge their opponents and attack the principal sources of their discontent. The extent of their grievances usually varies with the extent of their actions, and vice versa. Let us examine these arguments more closely.

We propose that when people with a shared ethnic identity are discriminated against, they are likely to be resentful and angry. Anger is expressed in a number of ways: Some people opt for accommodation; others vent their frustrations openly (proposition 1). For people who are motivated to action, the greater the discrimination they experience, the more likely they are to organize for action against the sources of discrimination (hypothesis 1).

Rare is the individual who single-handedly challenges institutions or society at large. Finding like-minded individuals with similar grievances intensifies discontent and increases willingness to take action (proposition 2). The more strongly a person identifies with an ethnic group that is subject to discrimination, the more likely he or she is to be motivated into action (hypothesis 2a). Factors other than shared grievances, including a shared religion, language, history and culture, and place of residence, strengthen group identity. The greater the number of traits common to a group, the stronger the group identity (hypothesis 2b).

What triggers political action and turns action into open conflict with the government and other groups? And what kinds of action or types of violence are most likely to occur? Collective actions are shaped by the political context in which an ethnic group is situated. The type and extent of political conflict are determined by such factors as the cohesion of the group, the strategies and tactics of its leaders, the nature of the political system that governs it, and outside encouragement. Here we examine group cohesion and ethnopolitical leadership, the political environment, the severity of force used by governments, and outside encouragement. We examine each of these in turn.

A major determinant of the occurrence of ethnopolitical conflict is the cohesion of the challenging ethnic group and the strength and unity of its leadership (proposition 3). Cohesive groups are those that have dense networks of communication and interaction that link leaders with followers. Strong ethnopolitical leaders generate the type of climate in which peoples willingly subordinate personal preferences to group preferences. Cohesive groups with autocratic leaders are not likely to face internal constraints on decisions to use violent forms of political action, whereas democratically organized challengers are typically less cohesive and have more diverse views about the preferred form of action.

Group cohesion increases to the extent that groups are regionally concentrated, share many common traits and grievances over long periods of time, and have widely accepted autocratic leadership (hypothesis 3). Thus, if and when leaders decide to use violent forms of political action to protest grievances, they are more likely to do so in cohesive groups that share a history of discrimination and that accept strong, autocratic leadership.

The concept of political environment refers to the type of regime governing a state. We distinguish four types: institutionalized democracies and **autocracies,** and **socialist** and **populist states.** Democracies typically tolerate a wide range of political participation that at various times includes protests, riots, and open rebellion (proposition 4). However, we must keep in mind that fully functional democracies protect core values, such as equality before the law and full political and civil rights; therefore, discrimination is less likely, and violent protest and rebellion are less common. Thus, the more democratic the political environment, the more likely ethnopolitical groups will be to voice opposition nonviolently (hypothesis 4).

In political environments other than democracies, violence is more likely to be used to quell protest and riots (proposition 5a). The more violence is used by political authorities, the greater the likelihood that challengers will respond with increased violence (hypothesis 5a). However, state authorities that have used *extreme* force, such as massacres, torture, and genocide, to subdue challengers are also less likely to be openly challenged (proposition 5b), either because groups cannot organize open resistance or they fear the consequences of doing so. Thus, the more *extreme* force is used, the less likely the chances for open rebellion (hypothesis 5b). A curvilinear relationship thus exists between state violence and the extent and level of violence of political action taken by the challengers. Clandestine movements that use terrorism and guerrilla warfare are typically responses to situations in which government authorities have used deadly force in dealing with challengers.

What external factors contribute to ethnic conflict? Here we develop two concepts that relate to the international environment in which ethnopolitical groups act: external support and economic status.

As shown previously, the domestic political environment substantially determines the kinds of actions chosen by ethnopolitical groups. In addition, many groups depend on external support (proposition 6), which includes verbal encouragement, financial support, weaponry, military personnel, and other forms of active or passive support the ethnic group receives from outside the state. The greater their external support, the greater the chances groups will use violent means to challenge authorities (hypothesis 6). Of course, we need to point out that minor grievances do not provoke violent political action. Thus, the kind of action taken depends on the combination or interaction of the political environment (type of regime, external support) with the severity of discrimination.

A second external factor is the status attributed by the international community to the government that is facing ethnopolitical challenges. International status is awarded to groups and states according to the number and value of economic resources they command. States blessed with an abundance of resources are more likely to enjoy the support of the international community, which is dependent on such resources (proposition 7). They are also more likely to be free from unwanted interference

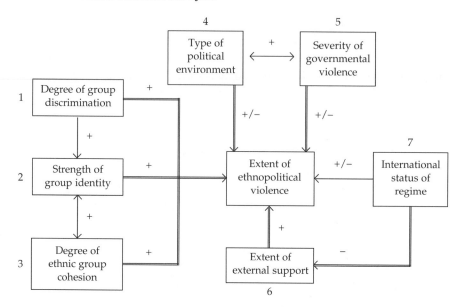

Numbers refer to the propositions and hypotheses that develop these concepts.

━━━━━━━━ relations for which hypotheses are developed in the text

──────── relations for which hypotheses are not developed in the text

FIGURE 5.1   Framework for explaining ethnopolitical violence.

than are those with fewer resources. Domestic stability, by whatever means it is achieved, guarantees the free flow of goods, currency, and primary resources. Therefore, the greater international status accorded to a state, the less it is likely that its challengers are externally supported (hypothesis 7).

During the Cold War two factors combined to favor ethnic and other challengers to Communist rule. First, the centrally planned, or "command," economies of Communist states rarely interacted in the global economy to the same degree as their capitalist counterparts. Second, internal challengers opposed to Communist rule were more likely to find outside support from states that opposed communism than they were to find challengers among states closely tied to the global economy.

The propositions and hypotheses spelled out in this section describe interactive relationships among concepts. Together they constitute a model that is shown schematically in Figure 5.1. The relationships are represented in the figure by bold arrows that connect the variables. No attempt is made to express the model in more formal ways, such as by using mathematical expressions. Positive relations (an increase in x leads to an increase in y) are represented by plus signs. Combined plus and minus signs represent complex relationships—for example, the argument, in hypotheses 4, 5a, and 5b, that ethnic mobilization and conflict are likely to be greater in authoritarian political environments than in democratic ones. In Figure 5.1 we use thin arrows to depict potentially important connections among the variables that are not discussed in the text. For example, the double-headed arrow between strength of group identity and degree of group cohesion summarizes two kinds of probable relationships: First, groups with strong identity are likely to be more readily organized into cohesive groups, and second, once cohesive leader-follower networks are established, group identity tends to become even stronger. This kind of mutually reinforcing connection is sometimes called a feedback relationship. Students are encouraged to identify and analyze other significant relations that are not developed in this chapter.

We next briefly review the concepts and variables introduced in this section and then suggest indicators for the variables. However crude some indicators may appear, they should guide students' efforts to collect and evaluate information more systematically.

CONCEPTS, VARIABLES, AND INDICATORS

In general, social scientists seek to minimize error in the interpretation of theoretical ideas by describing concepts like group identity and external support in clear and unambiguous ways. Concepts derive their meaning from careful observation of real-life situations. The challenge for researchers is to define variables and construct standardized indicators of those variables that can be used to make reliable observations of a number of groups and situations. Observations, or measurements, are said to be reliable if similar measurements are obtained by anyone who collects information.

A simple example involves the concept of the size of ethnic groups. The variable property is the number of people who belong to each group. But alternative indicators might be used for "belonging." One such alternative is to estimate the number of people who share the group's culture (which is difficult to observe in most cases). Another is to count the number who live in the group's homeland (but some will have emigrated, and outsiders may have moved in). A third is to rely on censuses that use standardized procedures for determining people's ethnic identification. Census data are usually the most reliable indicators for measuring and comparing the sizes of different groups, but not all governments conduct censuses or ask people's ethnic identity. If census data are not available, less precise indicators of group size must be found.

Now we turn to concepts identified in the hypotheses of the theoretical model.

Concept 1: Discrimination. *Variable property: degree of discrimination.* The concept of discrimination was defined in the previous section as the extent of socially derived inequalities in ethnic group members' material well-being or political access in comparison with other social groups. The greater the differences in status by comparison to other groups, the greater the degree of discrimination.

Indicators of discrimination. Government policies that treat ethnic groups unequally are the least ambiguous indicators of discrimination. Inequalities between ethnic groups may also result from historical discrimination or from economic and cultural differences that give some groups persistent advantages over others.

Indicators of economic discrimination

☐ Public policies that restrict the economic activities or roles of group members

☐ Low income, poor housing, and high infant mortality rates compared with other groups in the society

☐ Limited group access to education, especially higher education

☐ Proportionally few group members in commercial, managerial, or professional positions

Indicators of political discrimination

☐ Public policies that limit the group's participation in politics and access to political office

☐ Low participation in politics compared with other groups in the society

☐ Proportionally few group members in elective offices, civil service, or higher-ranking police and military positions

Concept 2: Group identity. *Variable property: strength of group identity.* We proposed in the previous section that the strength of ethnic group identity depends upon the number of traits shared by group members. The greater the number of shared traits, such as religion, culture, common history, place of residence, and race, the greater the strength of identity.

Indicators of strength of group identity. The more of the following traits members of an ethnic group have in common, the greater the strength of group identity.

- The extent to which they share and use a common language
- The proportion of people who share a common religious belief
- Visible racial characteristics
- A shared history over at least a one-hundred-year period
- A common culture—identifiable social and legal customs developed and practiced within close proximity

Concept 3: Ethnopolitical leadership and group cohesion. *Variable property: degree of cohesion among leaders and followers.* Cohesive groups are those that have dense networks of communication and interaction linking leaders with followers. The more factions that exist within the group, the less cohesive it is. We proposed in the previous section that the type of leadership also influences cohesion within the group. Strong leaders generate a climate in which people willingly subordinate personal preferences to group preferences. Autocratic leaders are more likely to be able to mobilize people than their democratic counterparts, because democratic practices emphasize individual rights rather than the rights of the collective body over and above the individual.

Indicators of ethnopolitical leadership and group cohesion. Cohesion within ethnic groups increases with increased communication and interaction. In contrast, the greater the number of factions or self-proclaimed leaders, the less cohesive the group. Factors indicative of cohesion include

- Degree of acceptance of traditional roles of leaders
- Degree of acceptance of established social order within the group
- Number of factions within the ethnic group
- Number of identifiable leaders within the group
- Extent of open conflict within the group
- Number of newspapers and radio stations used by the group

Concept 4: Political environment. *Variable property: type of political environment.* The political environment sets the stage for political action. Here we propose guidelines for identifying the four types of regimes with which ethnopolitical groups may come in conflict: institutionalized democracies, autocracies, and socialist and populist states. Note that most contemporary states have one of these four types of political regimes; a few combine elements of several.

Indicators of institutionalized democracies

- Guarantee political and civil rights for all citizens
- Effective constitutional limitations on the power of the executive
- Multiple political parties that compete for office and transfer power by constitutionally prescribed means

Indicators of institutionalized autocracies

□ Concentrate most or all political power in the executive
□ Limit or ban political parties and sharply restrict civil rights and political participation
□ Political power usually transferred and distributed among members of a tiny political elite

Indicators of socialist states

□ Concentrate power in a single party used by the elite to mobilize mass support for the regime
□ Encourage participation only within the party and restrict other political and civil rights
□ Transfer political power through competition within the party

Indicators of populist states

□ Weakly institutionalized political systems in a transitional state to either democracy or increased autocracy
□ Transfer political power through military coups or popular uprisings, short of revolution
□ Frequent leadership changes, with no predictive sequence
□ Wide, often disruptive political participation through functional groups, and many transient political parties and movements

Concept 5: Use of violence by governments. *Variable property: the severity of force used by governments against ethnic groups.* The systematic annihilation of an ethnic people is the rarest and most severe form of violence used by governments and is called genocide. Less severe kinds of force include massacre, torture, execution, detention without due process, forcible relocation of a people, and many others.

Indicators for use of force by governments against ethnic groups. Governmental violence directed against ethnic groups varies with the type of government. Autocracies and socialist states use violence against political challengers more often than do their democratic counterparts. Populist states often alternate erratically between severe repression and accommodation. Means used to oppress ethnic challengers, in ascending order of severity, include

□ Number of arrests
□ Forcible relocation of group members
□ Widespread torture and executions

□ Massacres
□ Political mass murder and genocide

Concept 6: External support. *Variable property: extent of external support.* As described in the previous section, the concept of external support refers to the entire range of active and passive support an ethnic group can receive from outside the country. Military support is, of course, more valuable than verbal support. The more numerous the sources, the larger the volume, and the longer it is provided, the greater the extent of support.

Indicators of external support. Ethnic groups may receive support from other states, from kindred groups in neighboring states, from international movements like the indigenous people's movement and the Islamic movement, and from international organizations. Major types of support include

□ Verbal encouragement and advice
□ Financial support
□ Provision of intelligence information
□ Provision of safe havens for exiles and refugees
□ Mercenaries and military advisers
□ Weaponry and supplies

Concept 7: International economic status. *Variable property: degree of international economic status.* We proposed previously that the international community awards economic status to states according to the number and value of resources they command. Resource-rich states are likely to enjoy higher status than resource-poor states and are more likely to deal with ethnic challengers as they wish.

The status accorded to challenging groups depends upon the position accorded to their state by the international community. Thus, movements fighting regimes with low status that are autocratic and have command economies are likely to enjoy higher international status than ethnic challengers fighting capitalist states.

Indicators for degree of international economic status. High economic status is accorded to states that

□ Control large reserves of scarce resources (such as gold, uranium, titanium)
□ Control a high percentage of the global trade of valuable commodities
□ Have a high level of per capita income
□ Rank high in gross domestic product and gross national product

☐ Have a global network of trading partners
☐ Have a large surplus in balance of payments

OVERVIEW OF THE MODEL

Remember that we want to explain *why* ethnic mobilization and conflict occur. The logical consequence of accurate explanation is to be able to *predict* under what circumstances ethnic conflict will occur. The model illustrated in Figure 5.1 represents our effort to tie our hypotheses together in a systematic fashion. The hypotheses are testable propositions about real-life events. By using a diagram we are able to demonstrate visually the underlying structures of complex relationships.

Scholars have produced many data-based **empirical generalizations** that are the premises upon which we have built our propositions. In other words, we know much about ethnic conflict thanks to the work of many historians and area specialists who are concerned with describing and interpreting particular ethnic conflicts in specific countries. A viable model is one that re-creates the process leading to ethnic conflict, not in one country but in all countries that have experienced ethnic unrest. Of course, there are idiosyncratic factors that are important in one or two particular situations but not others. It is impossible to incorporate literally all factors that lead to ethnic conflict, and, typically, the use of large numbers of specific factors yields no better predictive results. Instead, one should concentrate on key factors. The best models are those that explain the largest number of phenomena based on a small number of hypotheses.

Our model identifies seven key factors we consider important predictors of ethnic mobilization and conflict. Most of these factors are interrelated or interdependent—that is, they influence one another. The factors also differ in importance. Thus, research on a number of cases may show that external support has a greater impact on the extent of ethnic conflict than does group cohesion. This does not mean our model is incorrect; instead, it gives us additional information that may enable us to improve its accuracy.

Our seven key factors are also likely to vary over time. Thus, information about them needs to be updated periodically, especially in ongoing cases of ethnic conflict. When a rapid increase is observed in one or more of the variables in the model, we can infer that conflict is likely to intensify.

This brief review of the key factors emphasizes the way in which they are interrelated: We propose that a people who strongly identify with their ethnic brethren and who live in an autocratic political system with low international economic status, one that has used discrimination and intermittent violence to repress its ethnic peoples, are the most likely to challenge their oppressors. The conflict potential is greatest if the group has traditional (autocratic) leaders who enjoy the widespread support of international organizations and actors.

PROBLEMS AND ISSUES IN MODELING ETHNIC CONFLICT

Most of our indicators are straightforward and should provide reliable measurements of the variable properties of the concepts. But available information is sometimes difficult to assess. Take, for example, our indicator *the extent to which people share and practice the same religion.* One can usually estimate the number of Catholics or Protestants in a group, but how does one determine whether they truly practice their religion? This is possible only if we have access to surveys that report details about people's beliefs and practices. The same is true for all indicators that deal with attitudes—in essence, they are not readily observable and must usually be inferred from other information.

With regard to group identity, innate characteristics such as race are readily observable, but other factors may require judgment calls. Even more difficult are situations in which group identity is superimposed by outside groups on the basis of one or two traits whose significance is not self-evident or even visible to outside observers. The group identity of *Indios* (Indians) in Latin American countries is an example: The label reflects a social judgment by the dominant group about the culture of a number of rural peoples who to the observer may appear indistinguishable from mestizo villagers. In these and other situations, self-identification is the optimum measure of people's sense of belonging to an ethnic group.

Our indicators of discrimination are readily observable, with the possible exception of *public policies that restrict economic activities or roles of group members and that limit the group's participation in politics and access to political office.* Here we should look for widespread official and political practices, such as quotas that limit various groups' access to jobs and institutions of higher learning or that restrict them to token political roles and activities.

More difficult is our scheme that divides polities into four different categories. It is hard to make a neat separation between populist and autocratic states because of the transitional nature of the former. One may end up treating populist states as those that do not fit any of the three other categories. As a rule, democratic states should be classified as such if they possess most of the defining traits listed for institutionalized democracies.

Our indicators for external support include verbal support and intelligence information. We can focus our search for evidence on verbal support by analyzing the content of speeches made by major policy figures, such as officials of international organizations and presidents and foreign ministers of neighboring states and major powers. The sharing of intelligence information can sometimes be observed in the actions that occur during or after episodes of significant conflict. For example, Israel's nonintervention in the Gulf War was evidently partly a result of its lack of tactical information. Israeli fighters were reportedly discouraged from engaging Iraqi fighters over Iraq because the Allies withheld critical information; thus, Israeli aircraft would have been subject to attack by the coalition forces. Kurdish nationalists fighting Saddam Hussein in Iraq likely had access to intelligence information from the Allies. Unfortunately, we rarely have decisive information on such intelligence issues.

Our indicators for a country's degree of economic status include its relative independence of international trade and control of world trade through industrial capacity, two seemingly contradictory indicators. The United States, an economic superpower, provides an example. The United States dominates trade of a number of items and has large reserves of scarce resources but is not self-sufficient in some other scarce resources; it has a surplus in balance of payments but has a negative trade balance; and it trades extensively but receives a small proportion of its national income from trade compared with other industrial nations such as Germany. In times of international instability or civil conflict, the United States is less vulnerable than Germany to economic blackmail or sanctions because of its lower degree of trade dependence, although the U.S. standard of living would undoubtedly suffer if sanctions were imposed over the long run. Therefore, if the United States committed gross human rights violations against some segment of its population, its high status would likely deflect international responses. Significant support for the victims, therefore, would not likely to be forthcoming. High status, however, carries international visibility, and the internal behavior of high-status states is carefully scrutinized. All U.S. internal affairs attract world attention. If a situation of gross human rights violations were to develop in Mali, a country with low economic status, other states would be more likely to provide substantial aid to victims of government abuse.

CONCLUSION

The U.S. example in the previous paragraph is hypothetical: Oppression of ethnic people is much less likely to occur in a democracy than in other political systems. Two concluding observations follow. First, only the combination of indicators of economic status, with their relative weights assessed against each other, provides the necessary information to allow us to generalize about a country's international status. The same principle applies to discrimination against ethnopolitical groups, to group cohesion, and to all of the variables in the model that is summarized in

Figure 5.1: Reliable measurement requires us to obtain information on a number of indicators of a variable, not just one or two. Second, the assessment of the conflict potential of an ethnic group and of a country must take into account the combination and interactions of all of the variables included in the model, both domestic and international.

SIX

□ □ □

The Internal Processes of Ethnic Mobilization and Conflict: Four Cases

I n this chapter we use the theoretical framework developed in Chapter 5 to interpret and compare the domestic processes of ethnopolitical conflict in the four cases described in Chapters 3 and 4. First we analyze and compare the Kurds in Iraq and the Miskitos in Nicaragua. As is the case with national and indigenous peoples elsewhere, the most fundamental issue of conflict is that both groups have sought greater autonomy from state control. We then examine the Chinese in Malaysia and the Turks in Germany. Like other communal contenders and ethnoclasses, they are in conflict with dominant groups over protecting and improving their status within existing social and political institutions. In each pair of cases we begin with variables that refer to characteristics of the group, then move to the state level of analysis. The concept of **levels of analysis** is explained more fully in Chapter 7, where we examine the international context of these four conflicts. Most of the information used for the analysis is taken from Chapters 3 and 4; some additional information on specific variables is also used.

We make one other preliminary observation: The framework developed in Chapter 5 is designed to help us understand the extent of ethnic mobilization and conflict. It also calls our attention to an important related issue, which is how the policies and responses of governments and international actors affect the extent and the outcomes of ethnopolitical conflict. In this chapter we give special attention to the ways in which changes in government policies shape the internal processes of ethnic mobilization and conflict; we examine international responses in Chapters 7 and 8.

CONFLICT PROCESSES: THE KURDS IN IRAQ AND MISKITOS IN NICARAGUA

Group Sources of Mobilization

The framework identifies three variables at the group level of analysis: the degree of political and economic discrimination that affects an ethnic group (hypothesis 1), the strength of group identity (hypothesis 2), and the degree of cohesion among leaders and followers (hypothesis 3). We assess each in turn and then suggest how their interactions have contributed to mobilization for political action. Our assessments are summarized in Table 6.1 at the end of the chapter.

Political Discrimination. None of the Iraqi or Nicaraguan governments during the 1970s and 1980s deliberately restricted the political participation of *individual* members of communal groups. This is not to say Kurds or Miskitos enjoyed Western-style civil and political rights: No one enjoyed such rights in Saddam Hussein's Iraq or the Somozas' Nicaragua.

Kurds had more opportunities than Miskitos for political advancement. The Iraqi government recruited many assimilated Kurds into the lower and middle ranks of the army, the **Baath Party,** and the bureaucracy. Some advanced to high levels, but not to the highest levels; those were reserved for the Sunni Arab clique from the town of Tikrit, who formed Hussein's inner circle.

The Somozas made no effort to encourage or discourage the participation of people from the Atlantic Coast in public life, although, except in local affairs, virtually none of them did participate. The Sandinistas, however, actively sought to recruit Miskitos into the governing party and decisionmaking bodies. The price was the same as it was for Kurds in Iraq: The Miskitos had to accept the dominant group's means and ends. The Miskitos who initially joined the Sandinista organizations used their positions to advocate Miskito communal interests; therefore, most were expelled, were arrested, or fled into exile.

The most serious political grievance of Kurds and Miskitos is not discrimination in the usual sense but, rather, involves restrictions on their efforts to express and pursue their group interests. Three such interests are common to both groups and to most other national and indigenous peoples: the right to exercise political control over the internal affairs of their own region and communities, the ability to control and benefit from the development of the region's resources, and the freedom to protect and promote their own culture and language. The immediate precondition of the mobilization of both the Kurds and the Miskitos has been their resentment of failures to reach satisfactory agreements on these issues.

It is important to recognize that the governments of the two countries did not reject outright the validity of group claims. On several occasions from 1961 to the 1980s the Baathist regimes in Iraq offered significant concessions to Kurds, as pointed out in Chapter 3. In each instance the offers were rejected as inadequate by some Kurdish leaders, who then began a new round of mobilization, which quickly led to armed conflict and repression. In the case of the Miskitos, at first the Sandinistas brought indigenous leaders into state organizations, but they rejected those leaders' insistent pursuit of communal interests and instituted new policies that created the conditions for mobilization. By arresting Miskito leaders and taking direct control of economic and political life in the Atlantic Coast region, they created resentments and stimulated organized opposition where little had existed previously.

Economic Discrimination. All Kurdish and Miskito villagers live in relative poverty compared with dominant groups, but their poverty is mainly the result of ecological circumstances rather than of deliberate economic discrimination by dominant groups. Kurds living in Iraqi towns and cities have long participated in the economic life of modern Iraq. There have been no formal barriers to Miskitos' economic participation, but few are fluent in Spanish, and most have not had access to technical or higher education; thus, in practical terms, they can only pursue the limited economic opportunities available in the coastal region.

The economic development policies of the Iraqi and Nicaraguan governments have adversely affected the economic interests of local peoples. The Mosul oil fields are located in a predominantly Kurdish region, but Iraqi governments have consistently refused to consider demands that a share of oil revenues be devoted to Kurdish regional governments and development. The Somoza regime promoted economic development along Nicaragua's Atlantic Coast by giving outsiders—companies from "Spanish" Nicaragua and North America—concessions to exploit the agricultural, timber, and mineral resources on land to which Miskitos had traditional claims. Development did provide employment opportunities for some Kurds and Miskitos; however, the process was controlled by and designed mainly for the economic benefit of dominant groups rather than the people whose traditional lands and resources were being exploited.

During the 1980s the regimes of both Saddam Hussein and the Sandinistas initiated policies that harmed the economic interests of both communal groups. The Iraqi government devastated the rural Kurdish economy by destroying thousands of villages and forcibly relocating their residents. The policy was a response to Kurdish rebellions and support of the Iranians during the Iran-Iraq War. The Sandinista government, motivated by socialist ideology, evicted foreign concessionaires from the Atlantic Coast region and sought to induce Miskitos to join fishing and farming collectives. The end of the concessions meant loss of employment, and the collectives were regarded as an infringement on Miskitos' freedom of economic action. The net impact of these policies on the Miskitos was modest compared with the hardship inflicted on the Iraqi Kurds, but it sharpened their sense of grievance against the new government.

Strength of Group Identity. The Miskitos should have a somewhat stronger sense of group identity than do the Iraqi Kurds, based on the five indicators identified in Chapter 3. Each group has at least four centuries of common history, but the unity of Kurdish culture has begun to be eroded by urbanization and modernization; as observed in Chapter 3, a substantial minority of Kurds have assimilated into modern Iraqi society. Most Miskitos, however, continue to live in their traditional villages and a few coastal towns and to share a common, gradually evolving culture that incorporates both traditional and modern elements.

With regard to religion, the third indicator of group identity, most Kurds in Iraq are Sunni Muslims, as are the dominant Sunni Arabs. Some are Shi'is; others are Alevis or Yazidis, sects whose members have been persecuted in the past. These religious differences may contain the seeds of future divisions within an autonomous Kurdish society. Almost all Miskitos, by contrast, are Moravians and are acutely aware of the differences between their faith and that of the Roman Catholic "Spaniards."

Language, the fourth indicator, points in the same direction. There are different dialects of Kurdish, and many Iraqi Kurds—our sources do not specify proportions—speak the Arabic language of the dominant group as well as Kurdish. Most Miskitos, by contrast, speak two languages—Miskito dialects and English—which differentiates them sharply from the "Spaniards," who speak neither.

The final indicator of strength of group identity is the presence of visible racial or ethnic traits. Outsiders would probably find it impossible to distinguish Kurds from Arabs or Miskitos from "Spaniards" solely on the basis of physiological characteristics. The visible markers people use to determine ethnic identity in these and many other cases are culturally prescribed—manner of dress, speech, and social behavior. Men in rural Kurdistan, for example, wear distinctive headgear that makes them instantly recognizable even to outsiders. Our sources do not give us enough information to allow us to judge whether urban Iraqis or Nicaraguans can make reliable distinctions between "us" and "them" based on other markers of this sort.

Consideration of the two groups' geopolitical situations suggests a background factor that affects strength of group identity. Both groups live in terrain that is inhospitable to outsiders—humid and swampy lowlands for the Miskitos, rugged mountain valleys for the Kurds—yet that permits

its residents to move freely. The separate identities of both groups have been nurtured and protected by these conditions. Of course, the mountains that separate areas of Kurdish settlement surely have played a major role in the emergence and persistence of tribal divisions within rural Kurdish society. Modern national identity seems strongest in cities, even among Kurdish migrants in Europe, where Kurds of different origins interact on a regular basis.

Group Cohesion and Leadership. This variable refers to the degree of cohesion among members of an ethnopolitical group. Cohesion is likely to be higher in groups that share a number of common traits, as discussed previously, but cohesion per se depends on whether group members accept a common authority structure, whether they have close communication with one another, and how fragmented or unified their political organizations are.

The political histories of the Kurds and the Miskitos provide strong clues about their potential for cohesion in the modern political era. Throughout their history, Kurds have been divided among a number of contending principalities, tribes, and clans. Past and present, each Kurdish political movement and rebellion has been supported by some of these segments and opposed by others. This generalization applies equally to all of Kurdistan and to the Kurds in Iraq. The Miskitos, by contrast, have recognized the local authority of village chiefs and for three centuries also recognized a line of kings who nominally ruled them all. Our sources do not mention serious rivalries or warfare among different segments of the Miskitos, although we cannot rule out the possibility that they occurred.

We have little information on communication networks within the two groups. Interesting research could be done on the use of newspapers and legal and clandestine radio stations to build solidarity among ethnic peoples and on the use of radiotelephone facilities for organizational work by bodies like the Moravian church.

The Kurds of Iraq had one widely respected traditional leader, Mustafa Barzani, and a dominant political movement, the Kurdish Democratic Party (KDP), from the 1940s to 1975. Barzani returned from his long residence in the USSR in 1958 and for seventeen years was the Kurds' preeminent leader in negotiations and conflict with the government. From the 1950s onward there were two competing tendencies within the movement, however. Barzani represented more traditional and rural interests; Jalal Talabani, a member of the KDP politburo (governing council), led a more modern, socialist, and pro-Arab faction. Barzani's 1975 unilateral decision to end the rebellion after the Iranians cut off support provoked a political split. Talabani's faction broke away and established the Patriotic

Union of Kurdistan (PUK). The elder Barzani died soon thereafter, and the KDP has since been led by his son, Masoud Barzani. Since 1975 the two major organizations have sometimes cooperated but more often have followed opposing strategies; on some occasions they have had armed clashes.

The Miskito political movement, MISURASATA, which was founded in 1979, divided in May 1981 over disputes about whether to continue to cooperate with the Sandinistas. Steadman Fagoth led the breakaway MISURA into exile in Honduras, where his followers formed an army the U.S. Central Intelligence Agency (CIA) funded as part of its support for the Contras. Within a year Brooklyn Rivera, disillusioned with Sandinista policies, led the rest of MISURASATA into exile in Costa Rica. The Sandinistas' 1985 policy shift toward offering regional autonomy to the Miskitos prompted further splits and realignments. For example, one MISURA leader, Eduardo Pantin, broke with Fagoth, participated in peace talks with the Sandinistas, then was assassinated. In 1987 Fagoth, Rivera, and other leaders joined in a new organization called YATAMA, but it was not cohesive enough to overcome persisting splits between CIA-supported Miskito groups, which continued to fight the Contras, and the growing numbers of leaders and field commanders who participated in the peace process. The conclusion of the peace agreement in 1989 and steps toward implementing regional autonomy were accompanied by a decline in factionalism. The rivalries that continue among Miskito leaders are similar to those of competing politicians in democratic societies rather than being deep-rooted sources of violent factionalism.

Getting It Together, or the Mobilization of Ethnic Groups

Cohesive groups, as described previously, have dense networks of communication and interactions between leaders and followers. The concept is analytically separate from the extent of mobilization, which refers specifically to how much of a group's resources are being committed to political action against other groups and the government. Mobilization depends on decisions of leaders combined with the willingness of their followers to make the commitments and take the risks necessary for protest and rebellion.

The general proposition is that mobilization is likely to be highest and most sustained among groups whose members share a strong sense of grievance about discrimination, have a strong common identity, and are highly cohesive. Comparison of the Iraqi Kurds with the Nicaraguan Miskitos suggests that both had strong grievances against their governments. Both sought greater cultural autonomy and had economic grievances, but their political grievances were far more important. For the Miskitos, the political grievances were the result of new government policies; in Iraq, repressive government policies made existing political grievances worse. Group identity was relatively strong in both groups and was undoubtedly strengthened by heavy-handed government policies. At the beginning of open conflict each group was represented by one political movement. The cohesion of the Iraqi Kurds in the 1960s resulted from the charismatic leadership of Mustafa Barzani; the evidence reviewed earlier points to many underlying cleavages. There were no obvious cleavages among the Miskitos in 1979 and 1980. In both cases, however, rivalries within the political leadership came to a head over differences about strategies of rebellion; as a result, both the KDP and MISURASATA split into two major factions (in 1975 and 1981, respectively). This reduced effective mobilization and made it easier for governments to contain rebellion. The Iraqi government played the two Kurdish groups against one another, which made it easier to defeat subsequent uprisings. The Nicaraguan government was able to draw less-militant factions into negotiations, which eventually paved the way for a settlement.

Political Context and Responses

Ethnic groups' political environment affects the ways in which they formulate and pursue their objectives. Democratic principles and practices encourage ethnically based political movements to use conventional politics and protest in the pursuit of limited demands (hypothesis 4 in Chapter 5). Most leaders of democratic states respect the civil and political rights of opposition groups and accept the principle that democracy requires that competing interests be accommodated. Politically, demands that are expressed persistently by a numerically significant group need some kind of positive response, because to ignore them is to risk loss of electoral support.

The leaders of authoritarian and populist states have different principles and political concerns. They usually feel no moral or political obligation to reach accommodation with challengers and generally rely on force to deal with threats to their positions and policies. If they do decide to accommodate demands from ethnic or other groups outside the power structure, it is usually because they have calculated that the costs of compromise are lower than the costs of protracted conflict. Ethnopolitical leaders in this type of political environment are likely to mobilize their followers for rebellion with far-reaching objectives—seeking independence rather than limited autonomy, revolution rather than reform (see hypothesis 5 in Chapter 5). First, their chances of achieving any success depend on their mobilizing strongly committed followers for high-risk conflict with high potential gain. Second, by thus raising the costs of conflict for regimes, they may convince autocratic leaders that compromise is cheaper than fighting.

The responses of governments to the beginnings of ethnopolitical activism decisively influence later stages of conflict. They may do nothing in the hope that activism will simply go away. If activism is based on serious grievances and a strong sense of identity, however, it is likely to continue until regimes are provoked into some kind of response. The mix of policies of forceful suppression and of accommodation used at this stage is critical. The use of force, we argue, is a two-edged sword: It may dissuade some ethnic activists but is likely to encourage others to greater resistance, to the point at which the costs and risks become prohibitively high. Accommodation poses a lesser set of risks: The regime that responds to ethnic demands with prompt reforms may inadvertently encourage some activists to escalate their demands, but it usually satisfies moderates and minimizes the chances of rebellion. The optimum response from the perspective of a government that wants to limit escalation of ethnopolitical conflict is usually a mix of concessions that meet some grievances and the show or threat of force to discourage militants from escalating their demands and tactics.

Ethnopolitical conflicts escalate for many reasons, despite the best intentions of people on both sides. The accumulated grievances may be so great that activists cannot be satisfied with limited concessions; outside supporters may encourage leaders to fight rather than compromise; governments may decide not to implement promised reforms and, thus, frustrate ethnic expectations that were raised by earlier promises. Many observers of ethnopolitical conflicts have noted that the more protracted and deadly they are, the more difficult it is for governments and rebels to reach negotiated and enduring settlements.

The Iraqi Kurds and the Nicaraguan Miskitos operated in contrasting political environments and were met with different sequences of responses. All Iraqi regimes since the 1950s have had authoritarian leaders who gained their positions through popularly supported coups or internal power struggles and who relied on force to control opposition. The Baathist regime, which first came to power in 1968, was motivated by ideals of Arab socialism and nationalism and was prepared to accommodate Kurds who accepted those principles. But the concessions it offered at various times never satisfied the most militant Kurdish leaders, especially the Barzanis. As a result, proposals for limited autonomy were never fully implemented, and each phase of negotiation and concession was followed by renewed fighting in which the Kurds suffered increasingly costly defeats.

The revolutionary Sandinista regime was not a purely Marxist authoritarian regime, despite its portrayal as such by the Reagan administration. Its leaders were motivated by a mixture of socialist and democratic ideals, and they pursued them by populist means—by attempting to mobilize mass support for the new government among all social groups. When the Sandinistas tried to incorporate the Miskito leaders into the regime, however, the Miskitos pursued their own objectives rather than those of the revolutionaries. The consequences were summarized previously: The Sandinistas abandoned policies of incorporation in 1981 and decided to rely on their own (and Cuban) personnel to implement revolutionary policies on the Atlantic Coast. When the Miskitos protested and began to arm for rebellion, the revolutionary government responded with force. The Sandinista decision to shift from incorporation to the use of force was paralleled by shifts in Miskito tactics from conventional politics to protest and then rebellion.

In 1984 and 1985 the Sandinistas again shifted their policies, this time toward accommodation based on recognition of the Miskitos' demands for autonomy (for reasons analyzed in Chapter 7). Cease-fires, regional self-government, and the return of refugees and guerrilla fighters were negotiated, but it took five years for accommodation to bring peace to the region.

The outcomes of the two conflicts contrast sharply. From 1960 to the 1990s Iraqi governments responded to a series of Kurdish rebellions with escalating force. The 1988 Al-Anfal campaign was genocidal in intent and effect. As the model in Chapter 5 postulates, this extreme level of force led the Kurds to suspend hostilities. But when the regime was weakened by its defeat in the Gulf War, the Kurds who remained immediately rose again in rebellion. Thus, each military defeat succeeded only in contributing to the conditions—intensified grievances, stronger sense of common identity—that prepared the way for future rebellions whenever the strategic balance shifted. Such a pattern is characteristic of most protracted communal conflicts.

Conflict between the Sandinistas and the Miskitos, by contrast, never escalated to the highest levels. Once it became clear that forcible relocation intensified rather than reduced rebellion, the Sandinistas drew back from armed confrontation and shifted decisively toward negotiation. The Sandinista leader, Tomás Borge, was personally committed to ending the rebellion by dealing with its root causes. Even in this case, though, the negotiations were long and difficult.

This case illustrates another general principle: It is always difficult and sometimes impossible to bring ethnic conflicts to a peaceful conclusion once they have escalated to rebellion. First, as a result of the fighting, the opponents are intensely hostile toward one another and are suspicious of each other's motives, usually for good reason. Second, some factions on both sides usually think they have more to gain from continued fighting than from accepting compromises. Participation of outside parties—foreign governments, international organizations, private mediators—and promises of outside assistance may help to overcome these problems.[1]

CONFLICT PROCESSES: MALAYSIAN CHINESE AND TURKS IN GERMANY

These two minorities have similar origins and face similar problems: Both are descended from economic immigrants to long-established societies, and both live with political restrictions imposed by governments acting in the interest of dominant groups. And both groups have responded in similar ways: Rather than mobilizing for collective action, almost all of their members are pursuing their interests through conventional political and economic means—community associations, labor unions, and political parties. One important reason for considering these groups is to explain why they have *not* been politically more assertive.

Analysis of the contemporary situation of these two groups should also help us to understand the situation of many similar groups. Other Southeast Asian societies—Indonesia, the Philippines, Thailand, Vietnam, and Cambodia—contain Chinese minorities who are or have been subjected to discriminatory treatment. The Turks in Germany are one of many recently arrived groups that have migrated from less-developed societies to Western industrial societies, minorities that are often the targets of public hostility and the objects of both positive and restrictive government policies. Peaceful relations among groups in all such multiethnic societies depend upon delicate, government-managed balancing of the interests of minorities and majorities. Our two cases offer examples of how the potential for violent ethnic conflict has been contained in two democratic societies; a summary of our assessments is found in Table 6.1 at the end of the chapter.

Group Sources of Mobilization: Discrimination

Most Chinese in Malaysia are economically advantaged compared with the politically dominant Malays, and economic discrimination takes the form of "reverse discrimination" that gives preferences to Malays. Many Chinese fear their languages and culture are also threatened by pro-Malay policies in the area of education. One specific policy that vexes the Chinese is the use of quotas in university admissions that exclude many otherwise qualified Chinese youth, a policy that has both cultural and economic implications. As an alternative, many prosperous Chinese send their children to foreign universities.

In the 1960s the Turkish immigrants to Germany began at or near the bottom of the economic ladder, as did the first generations of Chinese immigrants in Malaya. At first the Turks encountered informal discrimination in access to better-paying jobs and good housing. By the 1990s, however, they had substantially improved their economic position, in ways similar to the Chinese, by establishing many small businesses. Moreover, by law their individual economic and social rights are guaranteed to the same degree as those of German citizens.

The most salient grievances of the Turkish community at present concern threats to their personal safety, which is a form of political discrimination. They are perceived by some Germans as constituting an economic threat, because they hold jobs when many citizens are unemployed. They are also seen as an affront to German society, because some still speak Turkish rather than German and some Turkish women still wear traditional clothing. These beliefs are used to rationalize anti-Turkish attacks and rhetoric.

A persisting source of political grievance for both groups has been restrictions on their citizenship rights. This was not an issue for the first wave of Turkish immigrants, because most expected to return to Turkey; it was also not an issue for those Chinese who came to Malaya in the 1930s and 1940s with plans to return to mainland China when the fighting ended. For immigrants and their descendants who have come to think of themselves as permanent residents, however, the citizenship issue becomes more important: It is both a passport to participation in democratic politics and a protection against deportation. In Malaya this issue was largely resolved through liberalization of the citizenship laws during the 1950s: By 1957 more than two-thirds of Chinese residents of Malaya were citizens, and, because of the rules in effect since that time, virtually all are now citizens.

By contrast, German law has made it very difficult for Turkish residents to obtain citizenship. Reforms debated in 1993 will ease the process, but it will likely be decades before all Turks who want to remain in Germany are granted citizenship. Germany has been slow to respond because it has long followed the principle that German citizenship is restricted to people of German descent; therefore, descendants of Germans who immigrated to Eastern Europe and Russia two centuries or more ago can and do return to Germany as citizens. In this respect Germany is out of phase with most other European countries, in which citizenship is determined by birth and residence, not by descent. Some countries, including the Netherlands and Sweden, routinely grant citizenship to immigrants after a few years' residence.

In summary, the Malaysian Chinese experience political restrictions on some economic activities that are justified by the goal of reducing inequalities between Chinese and Malays. The Chinese are also very sensitive to local and national policies that are seen as a threat to the teaching and use of Chinese languages. At the same time, they and all other communal groups are barred from making ethnic claims or criticisms that threaten the Malay-dominated balance among communal groups.

The Turks face political discrimination with respect to citizenship plus some day-to-day social and economic discrimination. Their greatest concern in 1992 and 1993 was the right-wing threat to their personal security. The Chinese grievances in the early 1990s, thus, are different in both degree and kind than those of the Turks, but we judge that both are much less intense and widespread than were the grievances of the Kurds and Miskitos in the 1980s.

Sources of Group Mobilization: Group Identity

The bases of group identity were weak during the early stages of both groups' immigration, especially for the Chinese. They came to Malaya over a long period of time from different regions of China speaking different languages or dialects. The Turkish immigrants arrived in Germany within a shorter period of time but included a mix of Turkish-speaking and Kurdish-speaking people from urban and rural areas. In each instance the group's identity was, in effect, defined and reinforced by dominant groups who labeled them as a distinct category of people and practiced discriminatory treatment toward all members of the category. Interactions with dominant groups also made minorities more self-consciously aware of defining differences: They were Buddhists or Confucianists in an Islamic society or Muslims in a Christian society; they dressed and acted differently in social situations than did Malays or British or Germans; and they were physically distinct, which meant Malays and British and Germans could recognize them and treat them according to their assigned status.

We also concluded previously that the degree of discrimination against Chinese and Turks is relatively low. Members of both groups continue to be reminded that they are "different," but not at great personal cost. For such immigrant groups, we think discrimination is the main negative source of group identity. In the absence of deliberate discrimination, their sense of cultural identity is likely to be benign and is not a source of social conflict; it may eventually weaken or disappear entirely as successive generations are absorbed into growing economies and an evolving social order. The greatest threats to ethnic harmony in such situations are economic decline and the resultant intensified competition among groups for shares of the shrinking pie. As we point out in Chapter 7, the economies of Malaysia and Germany are both vulnerable to international economic changes.

Group Cohesion and Mobilization

An attempt to explain the Chinese-based insurgency of the period 1948–1960 raises an important theoretical question, because the conditions for mobilization specified in our theoretical model seem to be missing. Group identity was weak and fragmented, as we suggested previously. Discrimination against the Chinese was widespread but minor, and it was no greater than that experienced by other communal groups under colonial rule. The Malayan Chinese also lacked the cohesion that would have been provided by a common authority structure, by leaders, or by a large-scale political organization. Secret societies were important forms of social organization for Chinese immigrant communities, but they were local rather than countrywide. Trade unions were concerned mainly with economic issues, not ethnic issues. The Communist Party of Malaya (CPM), founded in 1930, was not established as an ethnic political movement, nor did it pursue exclusively Chinese interests. It attracted little external support from either the USSR or the Chinese Communists.

These conditions help to explain why few Chinese in Malaya openly supported the CPM's rebellion; they do not explain why the CPM's leaders initiated it. The most plausible answer to the theoretical question begins with the fact that the CPM was already mobilized and had credibility because it had led armed resistance to the discriminatory and repressive policies of the Japanese occupiers during World War II. Its leaders feared the postwar British policy of decolonization would lead to a decline in their political status in an independent, Malay-dominated society, so they made a strategic decision to direct the energies of an already armed and mobilized organization into a nationalist, anticolonial uprising.

The CPM example leads us to an important general conclusion: Once militant communal organizations have mobilized for rebellion, they may decide to continue or resume fighting for strategic or tactical reasons, even in the absence of some of the conditions that prompted their initial mobilization. This may help to explain why the leaders of the KDP, for example, so quickly rejected government concessions and resumed fighting in 1970 and at other times.

In Malaysia in the 1990s, the principal organizations that promote Chinese interests are legal political parties. The Malaysian Chinese Association (MCA) has been part of the Malay-dominated government coalition since the early 1950s. It is a politically acceptable channel through which Chinese can pursue their interests and ambitions, albeit within Malay-dictated limits. The principal alternative for Chinese who are dissatisfied with the probusiness, procoalition stance of the MCA is the Democratic Action Party, which has taken more assertive pro-Chinese positions and, for most of the past three decades, has been the principal opposition party at the national level, although it usually holds only a handful of seats in the Malaysian parliament.

In summary, the Malaysian political system gives the Chinese (and other communal minorities) a limited but guaranteed role in the political process and restricts the divisive pursuit of communal interest. Thus, it encourages participation in conventional politics and discourages any efforts to mobilize Chinese for ethnic protest or rebellion. In the absence of serious grievances or threats to their status, the Chinese have little reason to attempt more militant actions.

The Turkish community in Germany has fewer of the conditions for political mobilization. Group identity has been diluted by the partial assimilation of second-generation Turks into German society. Citizenship restrictions alone are not sufficient to create serious grievances. And, like the Chinese in Malaysia, the Turks have established an economic niche. These factors help to explain why the Turks have not developed political associations that command widespread support or promote political action. However, the wave of right-wing attacks in 1992 and 1993 prompted more Turks, especially younger second-generation people, to consider becoming politically more proactive. If the attacks subside and citizenship restrictions are eased, as seems likely, the most probable scenario is that Turks' political energies will be channeled through existing political parties and grassroots community organizations in the cities in which most live.

Political Context and Responses

The Chinese in postindependence Malaysia and the Turks in Germany both illustrate the argument, made previously, that minorities in democracies are likely to pursue their collective interests through conventional means. There are two important reasons for this—one specific to immigrant groups like these, the other a general trait of democracies. The group-specific explanation is that both minorities are descendants of economic migrants who have prospered—the Chinese more than the Turks— in their adoptive countries. In other words, they have been preoccupied mainly with material concerns and have been more accepting—or realistic—about the political restrictions placed on them by the dominant society. The second reason is that the governments of both host societies have sought to accommodate the immigrants, within limits. The Chinese have maintained their leading economic role in rapidly developing Malaysia and have more than token political participation. The Turks are eligible for the full, substantial range of social and economic benefits provided to German citizens; they mainly lack citizenship and, at present, physical security. The Malaysian limits on communal politics are sometimes criticized as being undemocratic. The Malaysian response is likely that in a divided society, a perfectly egalitarian democracy is at risk of destructive communal conflict that would have to be controlled by instituting authoritarian rule.

Both governments have also used coercive means to counter minority political militancy. The British and Malays' successful **counterinsurgency** tactics against the Communist Party in the 1950s are discussed in Chapter 4 in "The Chinese in Malaysia." The resurgence of guerrilla activity in the far north of Malaysia in the 1970s was also met with force, which was sweetened by offers of amnesty for fighters who were willing to come in from the jungle. Furthermore, Malaysian authorities have invoked national security considerations to justify the arrest and detention of political opponents; in October 1987, for example, 119 political members of legal political and religious movements were detained.

During the 1970s and 1980s a widely feared policy of both governments was deportation, which was used by Malay and German authorities to deport political activists as well as immigrants who violated various regulations. For example, Turkish Kurds who organized support for the Kurdish Worker's Party (PKK; see Chapter 3) and other radical causes were regularly deported. In a well-publicized 1975 case, a Malaysian Chinese citizen was deported for temporarily residing and pursuing university studies in the People's Republic of China. The threat of deportation is one of the reasons citizenship, or the lack of it, has been an important concern of immigrants. Without the protection of citizenship they have little or no recourse against administrative decisions to deport them.[2] And there is little doubt that some specific deportation cases have been decided arbitrarily. The effect of deportation policies did not increase opposition; since it was a policy aimed at a few individuals rather than entire groups, it seems to have encouraged political caution and conformity.

CONCLUSION

Ethnopolitical conflicts usually center on one of three general issues: the desire for "exit" or independence from the state (the Iraqi Kurds), the demand for greater autonomy within the state (the Miskitos), or the recognition and protection of minority interests within a plural society (the Malaysian Chinese and Turks in Germany). Observers often argue that such conflicts are likely to be protracted and deadly and are difficult or impossible to resolve. Resolution is difficult but not impossible, as our cases illustrate. We conclude this chapter with a brief analysis of the ways in which each of these three issues of ethnopolitical conflict can be accommodated.[3]

Ethnonationalist demands for independence imply the breakup of existing states. States usually counter secessionist movements with all of the political and military means at their disposal, as exemplified by the responses of Turkish, Iranian, and Iraqi governments to the episodic nationalist rebellions by Kurds. Autonomy of the kind negotiated with the Miskitos in Nicaragua is potentially a less costly alternative to protracted civil wars for all parties concerned. State officials who are prepared to consider this approach can usually find some leaders in virtually all ethnonationalist and indigenous movements who are open to compromises that guarantee regional autonomy within a federal framework. The Miskitos are one of seven peoples whose civil wars during the 1945–1990 period led to autonomy agreements; the others are the Basques of Spain, the Nagas and Tripura in India, the Afars in Ethiopia, the people of Bangladesh's Chittagong Hill region, and some of the Moros of the Philippines. This approach was also attempted by Iraq's Baathist government in 1970 to defuse Kurdish resistance. At least six other such conflicts, including those of the Palestinians and the Iraqi Kurds, are currently the subject of protracted and intermittent negotiations that have led to a preliminary agreement for the Palestinians. The autonomy gained through negotiations is generally more limited than that sought by ethnonationalist leaders and less limited than that desired by officials. Nonetheless, both sides may conclude that agreements regarding autonomy are preferable to starting or continuing destructive wars that cannot be won.

The interests of communal contenders like the Chinese Malaysians and the Turkish ethnoclass in Germany are not likely to be pursued or satisfied by open rebellion. The strategy of rebellion failed badly for the Chinese who supported the Malay Communist Party in the period 1948–1960. We can distinguish four patterns of accommodation that have been attempted in multiethnic societies in the last half of the twentieth century.

Containment is a strategy of keeping minorities "separate and unequal," as was done to African Americans until the 1950s and to Black South Africans under apartheid. Such policies are usually forced on minorities by dominant groups and are accepted only for as long as the groups have no opportunity to pursue alternatives. The German government's policies toward the Turks from the 1960s through the 1980s were a relatively benign form of containment.

Assimilation was long the preferred liberal alternative to containment. Assimilation is an individualistic strategy that gives minorities incentives and opportunities to forsake their old communal identities and adopt the language, values, and behaviors of the dominant society. Until the 1960s assimilation was the preferred strategy for dealing with ethnoclasses and indigenous peoples in most Western societies. In practice, the Turks in Germany have moved toward assimilation, even though it is contrary to the government's long-standing position that Germany is not a society of immigration—that is, one that incorporates people of non-German origin. Assimilation is also widely used by states in developing countries to complement strategies of containment. We pointed out that the Iraqi government has actively recruited Kurds and members of the Shi'i religious majority into the Baath Party, the officer corps, and the bureaucracy. The Turkish government has sought to assimilate Kurds by similar means. The strategy of encouraging national minorities to assimilate is attractive to dominant groups, because it diverts the talents of potential opponents into the service of the state. In the long run a stream of individual choices to identify with the dominant society causes a politically assertive ethnic group to lose much of its cohesion and human resources.

Pluralism is an approach to regulating intergroup relations that gives greater weight to the collective rights and interests of minorities. If containment means "separate and unequal," then pluralism means "equal but separate": equal individual and collective rights, including the right to separate identities and cultural institutions. In the United States and Canada the advocates of **multiculturalism,** which is another name for pluralism, seek recognition and promotion of the history, culture, language or dialect, and religions that define their separate identities.

The growing emphasis on pluralism in Western societies is a reaction to the limitations of assimilation. For Turks in Germany, assimilation is a potential solution to the discrimination most have encountered. But they are also aware that complete assimilation implies the loss of their distinctive identity as Turks, which most want to preserve. Furthermore, policies of assimilation in other Western societies have not meant an end to inequalities or informal discrimination, as the experiences of visible minorities in the United States and France show. So why, ask ethnic activists, give up our identity for incomplete integration? Pluralism has growing appeal for many minorities in this situation and can be expected to be favored by the next generation of Turkish activists in Germany.

Communal **power-sharing** is an alternative way of regulating group relations in multiethnic societies. It assumes that communal identities and organizations are the basic building blocks of society. State power is exercised through collaboration among the ethnic communities, each of which is proportionally represented in government and all of which have mutual veto power over policies that affect their communal interests. This kind of institutionalized power-sharing evolved historically between the Protestant and Roman Catholic communities in the Netherlands and has been extended in modified form to new visible minorities who have emigrated to the Netherlands from Indonesia, the Caribbean, and elsewhere. Power-sharing has intrinsic appeal to some ethnic activists because it seems to guarantee that a communal group can possess both status and access to power without compromising its social or cultural integrity.

One problem is that power-sharing arrangements are not easily constructed, especially when the groups begin from an unequal footing. Attempts to improve the status of disadvantaged minorities often trigger a backlash from advantaged groups that fear the loss of some of their own privileges. Ethnophobic political movements motivated by this kind of concern became increasingly common in multiethnic Western societies during the 1980s and early 1990s.

Malaysia illustrates the liabilities of power-sharing arrangements in Asian, African, and Middle Eastern countries. The main flaw has been the fact that Malays have used their advantaged position to selectively benefit the Malays. The Malaysian version of power-sharing has helped to maintain stability and the observance of most democratic principles, but it has worked mainly because the Chinese and Indian communities have been willing to accept their subordinate roles. If the Malay-dominated government were to impose more restrictions on the communal minorities—which is possible but unlikely in present circumstances—a situation like that described here as containment would result. The general point is that power-sharing among unequal partners can lead to exploitation and repression of the weaker parties. The less advantaged groups may be tempted to defect, even to rebel. Lebanon's power-sharing political system degenerated into civil war in this kind of circumstance.

In conclusion, the policies of regional autonomy, assimilation, pluralism, and power-sharing can be used in creative combination to accommodate the essential interests of most disadvantaged and politically active communal groups. To make such policies work, however, compromises among groups and an enduring commitment by leaders of all groups to adhere to agreements reached are necessary. If policies of accommodation are to be effective in any type of political system, they must be pursued cautiously but persistently over the long run—slowly enough that they do not stimulate a political backlash from other groups, persistently enough so disadvantaged minorities do not become disillusioned and mobilize for rebellion.

TABLE 6.1 Summary of Internal Factors in Ethnic Mobilization for Four Groups Since the 1970s

Variables	Kurds in Iraq	Miskitos	Chinese in Malaysia	Turks in Germany
Discrimination				
Economic	Deliberate destruction of rural economy	Some loss of opportunities	Restrictions on corporate ownership, education	Minor discrimination because of social practices
Political	Denial of autonomy demands, forcible relocation	Denial of autonomy demands, forcible relocation	Minor restrictions on civil service recruitment	Limited citizenship, right-wing attacks
Group identity	Medium to strong, strengthened by conflict with regime	Strong, strengthened by conflict with regime	Low to medium, reinforced by perceived discrimination	Weakened by assimilation, strengthened by attacks
Group cohesion	Weakened by clan and political divisions	High, but weakened by political divisions during war	Low to medium, weakened by partisan political divisions	Weak to none
Type of political environment	Authoritarian	Socialist	Democratic with restrictions	Democratic
Severity of governmental force	Escalating from severe to genocidal	Escalating from arrests to forcible relocation	Occasional arrests	None except to restrain protesters
Effects on ethnic mobilization and conflict	Recurring rebellions	Protest escalating to rebellion	Conventional political participation since 1960s, limited protest	Limited participation, limited protest

SEVEN

□ □ □

The International Dimensions of Ethnopolitical Conflict: Four Cases

The international system affects the process and outcome of ethnic conflicts in several ways. Its member states may extend support to the warring factions, discourage continuation of the conflict through sanctions, or actively intervene in the conflict. Protracted ethnic conflict often spills over boundaries, devastates economies, and contributes to environmental catastrophes; therefore, it has important international consequences. Ethnic conflicts sometimes coincide with massive human rights abuses that typically result in large refugee flows. Refugees usually flee to neighboring states, which reluctantly provide only temporary sanctuary with the expectation that international organizations will support and resettle the refugees.

We have focused thus far on the reasons ethnic groups challenge state authorities. In Chapters 5 and 6 we analyzed the internal sources of challenges; here we examine their international linkages. Thus, what follows builds upon and extends recent commentaries on the international dimensions of ethnic conflict.[1] More specifically, we look at international factors as they affect the mobilization of ethnic groups and at the aspects of ethnic mobilization that lead to international responses. We focus on three questions: How did the international environment affect the regime and challenging minorities in each of the four cases? Which regimes and challengers had high status, why, and with what consequences? And how does regime status affect external support for minorities?

THE EMERGING ETHNIC DIMENSION IN GLOBAL POLITICS

Students of international relations are taught that the international system consists primarily of nation-states, regional organizations like the European Community (whose members are also states), and supranational organizations such as the United Nations. The modern state system that emerged after the Peace of Westphalia in 1648 replaced one central authority—namely, the church in Rome—with a system of absolute rulers competing for space, power, and influence. Although the democratic state is apparently slowly replacing autocratic or absolute rule, other forms of political organization may yet be the answer to current ethnic unrest.

In the last half century other kinds of groups have been recognized as important independent actors. They include functional organizations such as the International Committee of the Red Cross; national groups such as the Palestinians, a dispersed group of national peoples who do not control their own territory; and multinational corporations—organizations that are not tightly connected to specific state interests. Typically, in municipal and international law individuals and groups are treated as an extension or an integral part of the state rather than as independent actors, as we show in Chapter 8.

The emerging ethnic dimension of global politics challenges our perception that the primary identity of people coincides with the territorial state, or, conversely, that people see themselves as members of larger regional units like the European Community. Arguably, the reassertion of communal identity may be the result of the alienation and frustration that accompany the decline of artificial states. The increasing fluidity of international borders is evident not only in the increase in ethnic strife and separatist movements but also in the ever-increasing pool of expatriate labor. Foreign capital penetration and global environmental concerns further diminish the importance of national borders. As borders become less significant, functional interest groups and **communal groups** may become the main focus of the study of international relations.

COMMUNAL IDENTITIES AND THE FORMATION OF NEW STATES

The assertion of communal identities by national and indigenous peoples often leads to demands for internal autonomy or for secession and the establishment of new states. Rarely has ethnic self-determination been achieved through negotiations or ratified by **plebiscites.** More typical are attempts to secede through rebellion, as is seen in the ongoing struggle of the Kurds and in the historical example of the Biafrans, who fought a deadly and unsuccessful war to secede from Nigeria in 1967 and 1968.

Regimes that are unwilling to accommodate or negotiate in such situations often respond violently to ethnic protests. Ethnic challengers may then organize, seek arms, and respond in kind, which in the worst cases leads to a spiral of violence that may include political massacres and genocide. The more intense these secessionist conflicts become, the greater the likelihood of strong international responses.

In reality, ethnic challengers are seldom able to compete with the well-equipped armies of states that are accustomed to relying upon force to settle internal and external conflicts. To do so they usually have to seek external support. To the outside observer the cohesion of ethnic groups may appear largely symbolic, derived from the cultural, social, and psychological symbols that tie the group together. However, once highly cohesive ethnic groups have organized politically and obtained external support, they have a good chance of attaining some of their objectives. The type and level of external support they receive depend, in turn, on the sympathies of international actors and on the **legitimacy** accorded to the group's demands. A group's legitimacy, in turn, increases when a national government accommodates its demands. States are usually less dependent on external support in the face of ethnic challenges, but their leaders may also find it necessary or useful to seek foreign recognition and support for their efforts to deal with secessionist challenges.

THE THEORETICAL MODEL REVISITED

Our analysis of each of the four cases traces the linkages between international and internal factors as they affect ethnic conflict. We move from the highest level of analysis—namely, the international system—to the group level of analysis. States and regimes form an intermediate level of analysis. We assume that the nature of the international system and the internal policymaking processes affect each other. The behavior of ethnic challengers is influenced by the relationship between states and the international environment, and vice versa. Ethnic mobilization is group-level analysis. Individual preferences do affect group behavior, and vice versa. If we were to shift our attention to the highest level of analysis, the international system, individual preferences would have few global implications; however, global characteristics are very likely to affect individual preferences. For example, global warming, pollution, and overpopulation have all affected personal preferences and behaviors.

Extent of External Support

We asserted in Chapter 5 that the types of actions ethnic groups take are determined in part by the resources of the group and by outside support and encouragement (hypothesis 6). Outside support may take the form of provision of supplies, training of combatants, and, in rare cases, aggressive intervention on behalf of the ethnic group. These material kinds of external support translate into group resources for protest and especially for rebellion.

Outside encouragement may come in intangible forms. Successful ethnic contenders may inspire their brethren, in adjacent territories or elsewhere, to mobilize for action. This may occur in two different forms: *contagion*—that is, the intentional transmittal of models of communal activism from abroad, or *imitation*, in which group leaders find inspiration and guidance in the successes of similar groups elsewhere.

International Status of Regime

We argued (hypothesis 7 in Chapter 5) that high international status is awarded to states that control large numbers of scarce resources, control a high percentage of the market trade of valuable commodities, have a high level of per capita income, rank high in gross domestic product and gross national product, have a global network of trading partners, and have a large surplus in balance of payments. We assume that high status allows states to deal with internal challengers as they wish. International responses also vary with the status of the challenging group, its demands, and the legitimacy of the dominant authority.

The model presented in Chapter 5 does not explicitly explore the linkages between the status and support of regimes and those of the challengers. We suggest that the status of the challengers is not independently determined but, rather, depends on their status in comparison with that of the regime with which they are in conflict. For example, the international status of, and support for, the Kurds increased relative to the declining international stature of Iraq in the aftermath of the Gulf War. Previously, the Kurds had little international clout and more typically were pawns of Turkey, Iraq, and Iran. The statuses of both regimes and ethnic challengers are examined in the sections that follow.

THE INTERNATIONAL CONTEXT OF THE KURDISH CONFLICT

Here we assess the international dimensions of the conflict between the Kurds and Saddam Hussein's regime. Since we assume that shifting international and regional alliances affect the status of regimes and challengers, we begin with an analysis of international alignments within the region. The analysis is summarized in Table 7.1 near the end of the chapter.

International and Regional Players in the Mideast During Baathist Rule in Iraq

The traditional Arab governments in the Gulf—such as the United Arab Emirates, Bahrain, Qatar, Saudi Arabia, and especially Kuwait—

viewed Saddam Hussein's regime with great suspicion even before the 1990 invasion of Kuwait. From one perspective, he was thought to give the Gulf nations a sense of security against Iranian adventurism in the Persian Gulf, especially in the Strait of Hormuz, where Iran had territorial claims to some islands. In contrast, Saddam Hussein's socialist Baath Party ideology was an anathema to the autocratic leadership of the Gulf states. Moreover, his secular tendencies were threatening to both Shi'i and Sunni fundamentalist aspirations in the Arab world, especially in Iran.

Through Israeli eyes Iraq was potentially a major threat. Iraqi anti-Israel rhetoric, combined with the largest and best-equipped army in the Arab world, and Iraq's program to acquire nuclear weapons were seen as ever-increasing threats to Israel's survival.

The United States, although it had condemned Iraq for using chemical weapons as early as 1984, had not imposed sanctions on Iraq nor seriously interrupted heavy trading prior to the beginning of the Kuwait crisis. After the Iranian revolution Iraq's status increased relative to the declining status of the Iranian regime. The United States officially changed its anti-Iraq position by reestablishing formal relations with Baghdad in 1984 and assisted Iraq's war effort by buying more oil. After the Iran Contra affair in 1986, the United States actively sought to stem weapons sales to Iran.

Despite Britain's role in drafting UN Resolution 620 (1988) "condemning the use of chemical weapons and calling for 'appropriate and effective measures' if they were used again," Britain only "reprimanded Iraq verbally" and simultaneously doubled "the amount of its export credit facility to Iraq."[2] The other European states, especially West Germany and France, continued trade as usual. Later inquiries revealed that German and Soviet manufacturers and exporters were heavily involved in developing Iraq's nuclear program.

Soviet relations with Iran were cool during the regime of the shah, who was seen by the United States as the bulwark against Soviet expansionism. After the fall of the shah, the Soviets tried to exploit the volatile situation by improving economic relations, but the Khomeini regime had little interest in pursuing closer relations. The Soviet invasion of Afghanistan in 1979 had convinced him that Soviet objectives were expansionist, anti-Islam, and hegemonic.

Regime Status

Iraq is potentially fairly prosperous given its crude oil reserves, but it has devoted most of its resources to military purposes. Iraq in the years 1987–1989 had the highest military to social spending imbalance in the Third World; its policy priorities clearly favored a massive military build-up.[3] Iraq has also had severe economic problems since its war with Iran. Although Iraq has been partially financed by friendly oil-rich Arab governments, Hussein's gamble to make Iraq the dominant regional power in the wake of the Iranian revolution failed. The war instead left Iraq with a large debt burden, with few gains from Iran, with fewer sympathizers within the Arab world, and with greater Kurdish and Shi'i unrest.

Despite its potential economic strength, its staunch anti-Khomeini posturing, and its large armies, Iraq's international stature was lower than its leader had envisioned. Iraq, after all, had attacked Iran in September 1980 to secure a preeminent position in the Mideast, to resettle the boundaries of the Shatt-al-Arab waterway in its favor, and to cut off any potential Iranian support for the Kurds. Saddam Hussein's abominable human rights record made him a less than ideal candidate for Western support. In 1988, when Baghdad attacked Kurdish villages with chemical weapons, the international community formally condemned Iraq and launched a UN-sponsored investigation. Although Iraq was eventually found guilty of repeatedly using chemical weapons against Kurdish fighters and civilians, no sanctions were imposed against the Iraqi regime.

The Status of the Challengers: The Kurds

Kurdish internal divisions along clan, religious, urban-rural, and political lines have not helped them to secure external support nor enhanced their international status. The division among Kurds is also evident at the leadership level. Mustafa Barzani, the traditional leader who commanded the largest amount of support from tribal leaders, at times was actively opposed by Jalal Talabani, whose ideological position was much closer to the Baathist ideas of socialism and Arab unity. Moreover, over the years Baathist regimes have tried to meet Kurdish demands by offering limited autonomy and equality in treatment of Arabs and Kurds; thus, the Kurds' demands were largely ignored by outside powers.

Gamal Abdel Nasser emerged as the undisputed leader of the Arab world in the mid-1950s by emphasizing pan-Arabism. This strategy also worked against Kurdish demands for recognition as a distinct ethnic group and their quest for special rights in predominantly Arab lands. Pan-Arabism stresses the unity of Arabs and favors social reforms but does not recognize special ethnic group rights. The union of Syria and Egypt in 1958 led to Kurdish repression in Syria. Thousands of Kurds were stripped of their citizenship, and some Kurds were expelled.

The Talabani faction always dealt more easily with Iraq and other regimes that were favorably inclined toward Arab unity. His ideological left leanings and his willingness to accept Arab Kurdish brotherhood put him at odds with the majority of Kurds but ingratiated him to the Baathist regime.

Some Kurdish groups have been adversely affected by the revival of Islamic fundamentalism. Although most are Sunnis, who adhere to the Shafi'i school of jurisprudence, some are mainstream Shi'is. About one hundred thousand, most of whom live in Iraq, are adherents of Yazidism, which is not recognized by Islamic religious authorities as part of the umma (community of believers). Others are Alevis (living largely in Turkey), an offshoot of Shi'ism that is also rejected by many pious Muslims. Although among themselves Kurds consider their Kurdishness to be the cornerstone of their identity, Arab regimes have sometimes persecuted Yazidis because of their unorthodox practices and beliefs. With the emergence of more radical factions among Sunni and Shi'i fundamentalists, religious identity may prove to be a greater issue for Kurds and Arabs than has previously been the case and may lead to continued persecution. Regional realignments have worked largely to the detriment of Kurdish aspirations. Syria, the other Baathist-governed state in the region, sponsored its own Kurdish fighters, who conducted raids into Turkish territory during the Iran-Iraq War.

External Support for Iraq

The Soviet Union was the main weapons supplier for Iraq prior to the Iran-Iraq War; France was a secondary source. The Soviets disapproved of Iraq's invasion of Iran and briefly interrupted arms deliveries but soon once again became Iraq's main supplier of weapons.

Iraq had seen itself as part of the Arab rejection front, which consists of the Arab countries determined to settle Arab claims against Israel through military means. In the past this hostility had added to Iraq's status in the eyes of many Arab states, and this had often translated into tangible support in the form of hard currency and increased trade.

After the collapse of the Soviet Union and the Iraqi invasion of Kuwait, Iraq became the pariah state of the Mideast. Russia and the United States have since collaborated on bringing limited stability to the region.

External Support for the Kurds

The shah of Iran, the United States, and Israel began to give tangible support to Barzani's Kurdish Democratic Party (KDP) during the 1960s as a way of maintaining pressure on the Iraqi regime. In the wake of the nationalization of the British-owned Iraq Petroleum Company in 1972, the U.S. government promised greater support to the Barzani forces that would be channeled through Iran.

Despite a formal agreement in 1970 that gave the Kurds some control over their own affairs in Iraq's northern Kurdish-dominated provinces, Barzani thought he could gain more by fighting. He was undoubtedly encouraged by what he perceived as continuing strong foreign interest in, and support for, his goals of internal autonomy and eventual indepen-dence, and he greatly overestimated these states' willingness to supply him with sophisticated weapons to fight the Baath regime in Baghdad. Al-though Barzani had secured some heavy guns and missiles, he was unable to secure victory. Reports that Barzani accepted help from Israel seem well-founded but were never acknowledged because any support that could be traced to Israel would have discredited the Kurds in the eyes of Arab and Muslim states.[4]

Soviet prompting and Arab mediation led to a meeting between the shah and Saddam Hussein (then vice president of Iraq) in Algiers in 1975 to settle officially Iraq's claim to the Shatt-al-Arab waterway. Iraq eventu-ally accepted the Thalweg line (that is, the middle of the river) partition.[5] The more important consequence of the conference was a tacit under-standing that Iran would immediately cease supporting Barzani forces and would ask its allies, especially the United States, to follow suit. The immediate termination of support led to the collapse of the Kurdish rebel-lion.

During the Iran-Iraq War, the Kurds intermittently launched their own revolts in border areas. In the later stages of the war, the Kurds, supplied by Iran with heavy guns and missiles, held their own against the Iraqi forces but were unable to secure victory. At times KDP forces supported Iranian efforts in Iraqi provinces, whereas Talabani's forces actively cooperated with regular Iraqi forces to supply Kurdish fighters inside Iran. The infighting between Kurdish pro-Talabani and pro-Barzani forces, combined with the raids by members of the Kurdish Worker's Party (PKK) who were fighting for independence from Turkey, did little to promote the cause of an autonomous Kurdish region. KDP support for Iran was especially costly for the Kurds. Internally, the Baghdad regime responded by razing thousands of villages, forcefully relocating tens of thousands of Kurds to the south of Iraq, and eventually using chemical weapons. Internationally, the Kurds' pro-Iranian stance probably reduced sympathy for their plight.

Only after Iraq invaded and then was forced out of Kuwait in 1990 and 1991 did the fortunes of the Kurds change. Encouraged by what they per-ceived as signs of imminent support, Kurds of all factions openly rebelled in March 1991. Early successes turned into defeat when the coalition forces failed to support Kurdish fighters. Thousands of Kurds fled into the border areas of Turkey and Iran; thousands died along the way. In re-sponse to this immense human suffering the United Nations eventually passed Resolution 688, which provided a safe haven for Kurdish refugees north of the 36th parallel (see Map 7.1). The Iraqi government very reluc-tantly agreed to the positioning of UN personnel in this zone. Accommo-

Kurds in Sulaymania demonstrate against the Iraqi government in March 1991. Photo by Salah Aziz, Badlisy Center for Kurdish Studies, Tallahassee, Florida.

dation between Saddam Hussein's regime and the Kurds remains highly unlikely.

THE INTERNATIONAL CONTEXT OF THE MISKITO CONFLICT

The International Environment

The conflict between the Miskitos and the Sandinistas was, at the highest level of abstraction, one between two global movements: a new movement that advocated indigenous rights to land and respect for the environment and an older one that sought rapid modernization within a classless society. Miskitos were among the charter members of the new indigenous rights movement; the Sandinistas were perhaps the last political movement anywhere in the world to win a revolution inspired by nineteenth-century Marxist ideals. From the Miskitos' point of view, the Sandinista program implied that revolutionaries would determine how their land and resources were developed and for whose benefit; it also foreshadowed pressures for assimilation into a homogeneous national so-

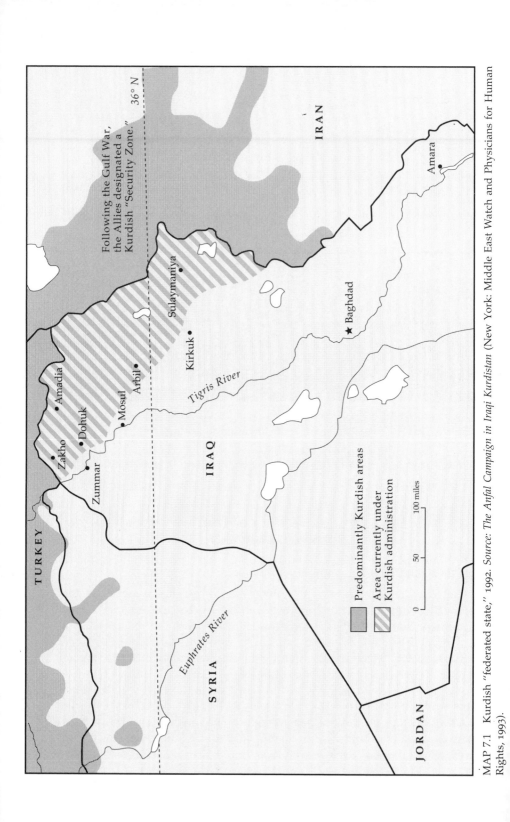

MAP 7.1 Kurdish "federated state," 1992. *Source: The Anfal Campaign in Iraqi Kurdistan* (New York: Middle East Watch and Physicians for Human Rights, 1993).

ciety. From the Sandinistas' perspective, Miskito claims were an obstacle to their economic plans and their vision of a classless society. There were grounds for political compromise between the two: The Sandinistas were sympathetic to people who claimed a history of exploitation by outsiders; the Miskitos wanted the benefits of some revolutionary social and economic programs. But the fundamental values of the two groups were antithetical. Recognition of the underlying conflict of values by leaders on both sides contributed to the breakdown of initial efforts at cooperation.

At the political level, the Miskitos were unintentionally caught up in the last stages of superpower competition between the United States and the Soviet bloc. Two general principles shaped U.S. policy in the Caribbean during the Cold War. The first was the 1823 Monroe Doctrine, a presidential message to Congress, which included the principle that U.S. foreign policy was directed toward minimizing European intervention in the Western Hemisphere. The second principle was the 1947 Truman Doctrine, another presidential message, which stated that it was U.S. policy to contain the expansion of Communist influence anywhere in the world. The existence of a Russian-supported Communist regime in Cuba after 1959 was a widely feared threat to U.S. security interests during the 1960s and 1970s. The Cubans fueled U.S. concerns by providing political support, military training, arms, and advisers to Marxist revolutionary movements throughout Latin America and the Caribbean. The Cuban threat was used to justify extensive U.S. military and economic assistance to regimes throughout Latin America and the Caribbean that were thought to be susceptible to Communist insurgencies.

The Nicaraguan Regime's Status and Support. Between 1960 and 1979 no Marxist- or Cuban-supported insurgency came close to toppling a non-Communist government in the Western Hemisphere. Then came the Sandinista revolution in Nicaragua, which overthrew one of the most blatantly corrupt regimes in the region. The Sandinista revolution was homegrown and was supported by a broad spectrum of Nicaraguan society, including much of the middle class and the business community, but many Sandinista leaders were sympathetic to Marxist ideals. During their first year in power the Sandinistas had the cautious support of the Carter administration, which, along with Mexico, Canada, and a number of Western European states, began to supply aid. They also received medical, educational, and technical advisers from Cuba plus increasing amounts of economic and military assistance from the USSR.

The international attention given to Nicaragua was a consequence of its revolution, not of its economic status. Nicaragua was one of the poorest and most heavily indebted countries in Central America. Agricultural goods such as coffee, cotton, sugar, bananas, seafood, and meats accounted for over 80 percent of Nicaragua's export earnings. At the outset the regime attracted the support of both Western and Marxist governments, which sympathized with its populist policies. But Western and especially U.S. support declined in proportion to increased support from the Soviet bloc.

When the Reagan administration took office in January 1981, its senior officials were convinced that the Sandinistas had become the instrument of Communist expansion in the Western Hemisphere. Sandinista support from Cuba and the USSR, expropriation of large land holdings, and cancellation of foreign concessions—many held by North American firms—were seen as steps toward turning Nicaragua into another Cuba. The new administration almost immediately began to use the Central Intelligence Agency (CIA) to channel support to the contras, opponents of the Sandinistas who included members of the defeated Somoza National Guard plus disillusioned former supporters of the Sandinistas. The Reagan administration also imposed a trade embargo against Nicaragua and used U.S. influence to block international development aid. In 1983 and 1984 the United States clandestinely mined Nicaraguan ports to discourage ships that ignored the embargo. In 1984 the Sandinista government brought a suit against the United States because of the mining to the International Court of Justice, which first ordered the United States to stop the mining and later ruled that Nicaragua could sue for damages. However, the Reagan administration rejected the decisions on grounds that the court had no jurisdiction in this case and that the U.S. Congress had determined that the Nicaraguan government was supplying military support to groups attempting to overthrow other governments in the region.[6]

The Miskitos' International Status and Support. By early 1982 it was widely known that the United States was organizing and supporting a substantial and expanding guerrilla war against the Sandinistas from bases in Honduras. The cooperation of the Honduran government and military in this effort were secured by substantial U.S. aid. Some of the twenty-five thousand Miskitos who fled to Honduras were resettled there with assistance from the UN High Commission for Refugees; others were recruited into CIA-supported Indian armies that soon were fighting a widespread guerrilla campaign in eastern Nicaragua.

From the perspective of the Reagan administration, support for the Miskitos was justified by the larger objective of crippling the Sandinista regime rather than by any sympathy for the indigenous rights movement. Brooklyn Rivera, leader of the Costa Rican–based MISURASATA faction, sought out individuals and organizations sympathetic to the movement in Ottawa, Geneva, and Washington, where he gained the attention of Senator Edward Kennedy and other members of Congress and the support of advocacy organizations like the Indian Law Resource Center. Later, when Rivera began MISURASATA's 1984–1985 round of negotiations with Sandinista officials, he was accompanied by interested observers from indigenous peoples' organizations.

Effects of International Linkages

International pressures contributed directly and materially to the negotiated settlement of the Miskitos' war with the Sandinistas. By 1984 the Nicaraguan economy was beginning to be badly hurt by the effects of U.S. economic pressure and the costs of fighting the contras and their Indian allies. It was estimated that the total economic cost of U.S. actions against Nicaragua during this period was $3.7 billion, an enormous burden for a poor country. From 1983 on the Sandinistas were also under diplomatic and political pressures from other Central American states, known as the Contadora group, who sought to initiate a regional peace process that would bridge the gap between the U.S. and Nicaraguan governments. The Sandinistas and the Reagan administration both rejected these regional efforts at first, but they were revived in 1987 by Costa Rica's President Oscar Arias. This time the efforts led to negotiations in 1988 between the Sandinistas and contra representatives and to a peace agreement, grudgingly accepted by the Bush administration, that culminated in the 1990 elections, which the Sandinistas unexpectedly lost.[7]

By the time of the Arias initiative, the Miskito-Sandinista conflict was well on its way to settlement, because the Miskitos wanted to return to their villages and the Sandinistas wanted to reduce U.S.-supported military pressures. When negotiations reached a stalemate, both sides accepted the mediation of a respected outsider, Jimmy Carter, to overcome the final obstacles to agreement. It is also important to call attention to what did *not* happen. Despite U.S. encouragement of the faction led by Steadman Fagoth to continue fighting, all Miskito leaders eventually accepted the terms of the agreement.

THE INTERNATIONAL CONTEXT
OF THE CHINESE COMMUNIST INSURGENCY
IN MALAYA

In Chapter 4 we observed that the Chinese uprising that became known as the Emergency was one of many insurrections that swept Southeast Asia after World War II. One can argue that the movement, although Communist-inspired, was part of the worldwide struggle of colonial peoples to drive out colonial powers.

Characteristics of the International System
During the Malay Emergency: The Players

Under President Harry Truman's leadership the United States eagerly supported British efforts to contain civil war in Greece in 1946 and 1947 and later backed the French in the first Vietnam war on the perception that the Communist states were actively pursuing hegemonic interests in the Far East and in Europe. The Truman Doctrine, which was prompted by the civil war in Greece, provided the rationale for future Western interventions. It was now U.S. policy "to support free people who are resisting attempted subjugation by armed minorities or outside pressures." Unfortunately, the "freedom fighters" in Greece, who were actively supported by Britain, with U.S. encouragement, consisted largely of reactionary forces—including former supporters of the Nazis—that were fighting an indigenous Communist movement that received no encouragement from Stalin.

The Soviet Union under Stalin's leadership had its own hegemonic agenda. Stalin's aspirations clearly went far beyond the Soviet Union's borders, as is shown by the Soviet involvement in the Berlin crises, the use of Soviet forces to suppress a popular uprising in East Germany (1953), and indirect Soviet involvement in the Communist coup in Czechoslovakia (1948). The USSR already had a presence in mainland China (Port Arthur), had bases on former Japanese islands (the Kurile Islands and South Sakhalin), and effectively controlled Outer Mongolia. This presence eventually came to be seen in the same light as U.S. imperialism.

Tangible Soviet involvement in Third World politics was limited to Korea, where during the Korean War the Soviets supplied North Korea with aircraft and weapons, and to China, where support was provided to the Communists in the last phases of civil war. The effect of Soviet support during Israel's war of independence was diminished by its simultaneous support of Syria. Ho Chi Minh received little support during Vietnam's war for independence. Tangible support was seldom given, partly because the Soviets were unable to provide it but also because they were ambivalent about the nationalist-Communist struggles of colonial peoples in the Far East. Thus, support was usually limited to advice and encouragement.

At the onset of the insurgency in Malaya, the Chinese Communists were in the midst of a civil war that was not won until 1949. Moreover, they had few hegemonic interests. Traditionally, China has taken its preeminent role in Asia for granted, and it did not forcefully colonize adjacent territories. It only took or attempted to take what it considered to be the ancestral lands of the Chinese people, broadly understood, including Tibet in 1959. It also claimed territory acquired by czarist Russia through a series of unequal treaties from the mid-eighteenth century onward. The

Chinese did provide material support to the Vietnamese nationalists against the French but not to the Malay Communist Party.

Regime Status: Britain After World War II

When the Cold War began, Britain tried to maintain its prominent status within the emerging Western alliance. Becoming embroiled in colonial wars was not popular with its U.S. supporters; Britain also lacked the ability and the interest to engage in protracted struggles in the hinterlands of the British Empire.

As we have argued previously, mainland Malaya was never fully colonized as India or Singapore had been, and Britain was committed to granting Malaya its independence. For the British, the Communists were just one more obstacle in their plan to introduce democracy, power-sharing, and a parliamentary form of government into Malaya. Progressive British policies, such as opening European clubs for Asians, encouraging non-Malays to join the civil service, and creating federation regiments that included all races, increased public sympathy for the British. In the early 1950s communal tensions were further mitigated through the able leadership of Tunku Abdul Rahman, who, with Indian and Chinese cooperation and British prompting, worked out a formula that provided the base for political stability. Under the agreement Chinese economic leadership and Malay political predominance were implicitly recognized.

The Status of the Challengers: Chinese Communists

The Chinese community in post–World War II Malaya was far from cohesive. A large number of Chinese in Malaya were relatively recent arrivals, and many did not envision Malaya becoming their permanent home. During the civil war in China in the 1940s, many had fled to await a Kuomintang victory or at least an end to the struggle. With the impending Communist victory in the late 1940s, however, most chose to stay in Malaya or, if they were prosperous enough, to emigrate to the West.

In contrast, Malaya was home for the Straits Chinese and for most second-generation and third-generation Chinese, who were descendants of laborers recruited to Malaya with the promise of a better life. Fighting colonial authorities made little sense to Chinese who were recuperating from an oppressive Japanese occupation. In their eyes the returning British authorities brought order, a limited sense of security, and a commitment to democratic principles. In 1946 talks were under way to establish a parliamentary form of government, which soon became independent.

The Communists, ironically, had been the backbone of the anti-Japanese resistance and, thus, were respected by the larger Chinese community and returning British authorities. Because of their British training and guerrilla activities during the war, they were the only fighting force capable of resisting the Japanese occupier and, later, the British colonizers. Emboldened by the emerging Communist victory in China and facing an uncertain future as an ethnic minority among Malay Muslims and their autocratic leaders, the Malayan Communists refused to surrender their arms when the British returned. Instead they chose to follow the Chinese Communist model by fighting for national liberation and an end to feudal rule. The party followed shifting political strategies. In the eyes of the rebels the emerging federation of Malayan states gave the sultans unequal shares of power, granted few citizen rights to the Chinese, and ignored Chinese sacrifices during the war. In 1947, after the British authorities had outlawed them, they embraced armed struggle, but their struggles were far from displaying the militancy of Communist movements elsewhere.

The Communists were part of a larger nationalist-socialist-Communist movement that made anticolonial slogans part of its ideological arsenal without necessarily advocating the violent overthrow of colonial regimes. Most Chinese viewed anticolonial struggles with anxiety, despite their sometimes discriminatory treatment by the British authorities. Thus, the Communist insurgents had little support among the Chinese community in Malaya, but they nonetheless chose to fight the British and Malayan authorities for both ideological and political reasons.

External Support for the Regime

Britain's status as one of the World War II victors was secure. Although the United States tacitly disapproved of the preservation of colonial empires, it nevertheless actively supported colonial powers fighting insurgents, such as the French during the first phase of the Vietnam War. In Malaya, however, Britain did not need, nor did it ask, for outside support. Instead it relied on the cooperation of Malays and of some Chinese to design and carry out an effective counterinsurgency campaign, some of the elements of which—like the hamlet resettlement policy—influenced U.S. policy during its phase of the Vietnam War.

External Support for Chinese Communists

The Malayan Communists evidently received little support from China, despite Chinese Communist meetings with their Chinese Malayan counterparts. As is typical, Chinese Communists rarely offered more than verbal support, in part because of their inability to do so at a stage when they were busy building their own base. Moscow's role is even more uncertain. The Soviet Union, taken by surprise by the revolutionary activities in colonial dependencies, verbally supported the so-called national liberation struggles against imperialism but did little else immediately following World War II. The Emergency simply died out.

In the late 1950s the remnants of the Malayan Communists, lacking external support and internal credibility, retreated into the border areas of Thailand. Because of British policy, lack of support among fellow Chinese, and lack of external support, the Communists had to rely exclusively on their own resources to support their campaign. The high status they initially held with Chinese Malay peasants quickly dissipated because of their harsh treatment of Chinese suspected of collaborating with the British. Lacking clear ideological commitments and fighting ability, they were probably of little consequence to either the emerging People's Republic of China or the Soviet Union.

THE INTERNATIONAL CONTEXT OF MINORITY ISSUES IN GERMANY

The influx of refugees is not just a German problem, but it has had a greater impact on Germany than on other countries in the European Community (EC). The number of refugees and asylum seekers entering the ten principal host countries in Europe more than tripled between 1987 and 1991, as shown in Figure 7.1. By 1991 Germany was receiving more than double the numbers going to France and the United Kingdom combined.

As a result of its economic interdependence and residual concerns about its pariah status at the end of World War II, Germany is highly vulnerable to international pressures and criticisms concerning domestic political issues, especially regarding the status of immigrants and refugees. In fact, much of the crisis in Germany in the early 1990s over refugees and immigrants is a consequence of laws and policy that guaranteed temporary asylum to anyone claiming to be a political refugee. This policy, which was among the most liberal in the world, was a legacy of Germany's attempt to atone for its past.

German sensitivity concerning the status of immigrants and refugees is reinforced by international scrutiny—by other member states of the EC, by the media, and by nongovernmental organizations that monitor human rights performance and political extremism. Thus, neo-Nazi and skinhead attacks on refugees and Turks have been widely and thoroughly reported and criticized outside Germany. In early 1993 Chancellor Helmut Kohl's office took the unusual step of distributing to all German embassies and foreign correspondents a thick handbook that acknowledged the problem of antiforeigner attacks and summarized the government's efforts to deal with them. It also recognized Germany's special obligation in the statement that "there's no injustice in judging Germany more harshly

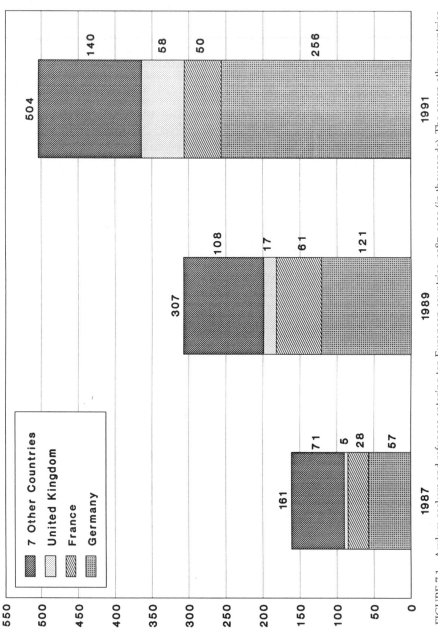

FIGURE 7.1   Asylum seekers and refugees entering ten European countries, 1987–1991 (in thousands). The seven other countries are Austria, Belgium, Denmark, the Netherlands, Norway, Sweden, and Switzerland. *Source: Continuous Reporting System on Migration, Trends in International Migration* (Paris: Organization for Economic Cooperation and Development, 1992).

and more emotionally than other states when it comes to the protection of democracy and human rights."[8]

German legislative proposals for slowing the influx of refugees have also been closely scrutinized, not the least by other European states that face similar pressures. The governments of neighboring Poland, Czechoslovakia, and Austria have criticized German plans because they fear asylum seekers who are turned back from Germany will become their responsibility.[9] Germany can move toward more restrictive policies if it coordinates its policies with those of other European states; however, Germany is expected to demonstrate its commitment to principles of equal treatment of minorities, which implies a more liberal citizenship law for Turks and other long-time non-German residents.

Regime Status and External Support

Germany has high international economic status; it ranks in the top 5 percent on all indicators of development, including per capita gross national product, capital formation, value of trade, levels of education, and so forth. Its political status, however, is lower than would be predicted based on economic status alone. Burdened by its Nazi past, the German government avoids involvement in international conflicts, especially those that might lead to military action. Its Basic Law, the equivalent of a constitution, prohibits German participation in military or peacekeeping actions, except to defend itself and its allies.

Turkish Status and External Support

The Turkish minority, by contrast, has little intrinsic international status. Since few of its members intend to resettle in Turkey, the Turkish government has less reason to be concerned with their welfare than it had in the past. Moreover, the Turkish government hopes to gain full membership in the EC and, thus, is reluctant to take positions that might antagonize one of that organization's leading members.

But the status of refugees and foreigners in Germany is widely recognized as one specific instance of a common European problem, one that cannot be resolved however the German government chooses. In 1993 the last restrictions were lifted on the movement of citizens of EC countries within the community; foreigners are still subject to checks, but many can and do take advantage of open borders. Hostility toward refugees and visible minorities has increased simultaneously throughout Europe. The greater the proportion of visible minorities and refugees in a country, the more antiforeign sentiment is likely to be a serious issue. As we suggested in Chapter 4, most European governments are moving on tracks parallel

TABLE 7.1 Summary of International Factors in Ethnic Mobilization for Four Groups

Variables	Kurds in Iraq	Miskitos	Chinese in Malaysia	Turks in Germany
External support for group	Limited and dependent upon shifts in regional and international alignments	Limited to political support from indigenous movement, U.S. support for insurgency	Very limited during 1950s insurgency, none since	Some diplomatic support from Turkish government, growing symbolic support from other EC countries
Status of regime				
Economic	Medium but badly weakened by Iran-Iraq War and Gulf War	Very low	Medium and rising because of exceptional economic growth	Very high but subject to EC constraints
Political	Low to medium before Gulf War, a pariah state after the war	Low because U.S. opposition outweighed support from socialist states	Medium and rising because of stability and economic growth	High
Status of ethnic challengers	Low before Gulf War, temporarily higher after the war because of strategic and humanitarian concerns	Very low before and after the contra war, higher during the war because of U.S. support	None because they are not recognized as challengers outside Malaysia	Low but slowly rising because of EC and international concerns

to Germany's: They are restricting new immigration and asylum seekers from outside Europe and are accelerating efforts to incorporate those who are already residents. But if these policies are not fully coordinated, one European country's solution can add to its neighbors' problems.

CONCLUSION

In conclusion, we summarize briefly how the international system affects each of the four groups and assess their current status with respect to governing regimes. It is evident that over time, the Kurds were drawn into the superpower contest in the Middle East, became pawns in regional realignments, participated indirectly in the Arab-Israeli conflict, played a part in the pan-Arab movement, and were subject to divisions among themselves. At present the Kurds enjoy limited support from the international community, but their future status is problematic. The ruling Baath Party under the leadership of Saddam Hussein is unlikely to formally recognize Kurdish autonomy. The 1993 thaw in Israeli-Palestinian relations has further relegated the Kurdish situation to the back burner among Mideast problems.

What are the prospects for communal tensions in Malaysia in the 1990s? We consider the anti-Chinese riots of 1969, in which a number of Chinese and Malays were killed, to be an aberration in an otherwise relatively stable democracy. At times the Malaysian quest for stability undermines the preservation of civil rights. Freedom of information is curtailed, and harsh punishments are meted out for those who advocate controversial views. Some sultans still hold immunity from prosecution, despite criminal assaults on employees. The political formula that guarantees preferential treatment to Malays in all government jobs, the military, and universities amounts to discrimination. However, the formula, which is commonly referred to as "positive discrimination," helps to hold the nation together. In Western states this formula exists in the form of quota systems for minorities, women, the handicapped, and other disadvantaged groups—for better or worse, it is a widely used strategy for improving the lot of those who have traditionally been disenfranchised and disadvantaged.

Because of Malaysia's continued high level of economic growth and relative stability, the country enjoys high international status. Typically, high-status countries are watched closely by the outside world and are scrutinized for impending internal troubles, if only to secure a stable investment climate. Susceptibility to world public opinion affects the way Malay politicians deal with the Chinese minority, especially since the Chinese still control a large share of Malaysia's finance and trade.

The Miskitos' conflict with the Nicaraguan state has largely been set-tled. By 1993 armed conflict had long since ended, although the regional councils of autonomous Yapti Tasba were still at odds with the Nicara-guan government over the control of resource development. What they need most is money, from either the government or international donors. The flood of international support that was supplied to the government, the contras, and the Miskitos during the 1980s has virtually dried up. Nei-ther the Managua government nor the Yapti Tasba councils have attracted sufficient public or private aid to meet the needs of the region.

The German government is not free to deal with its Turkish and other immigrant minorities as it wishes. The country's high economic perfor-mance is dependent upon a dense network of commercial and financial ties with other states; it has a high volume of foreign trade with a multi-tude of customers, and its economy is closely linked to the economies of the other EC states. Moreover, Germany depends heavily on imports of oil and other raw materials, which means it must maintain good relations with the oil-producing countries of the Middle East and with Third World sources of other primary products. Evidence of this sensitivity is seen in the fact that Germany ranks third among the world's foreign aid donors and allots 24 percent of its aid to the least developed countries.

We documented in Chapter 4 the existence in Germany of widespread negative attitudes toward immigrants and refugees. If these attitudes were translated directly into public policy, the status and prospects of the Turks and other visible minorities would not be good. There are two main guarantees of improved status for minorities in Germany. First are the po-litical and civil rights provided for all citizens in Germany's Basic Law (the equivalent of a constitution). Second are the international scrutiny and pressures focused on Germany, described previously, to which its policymakers are highly susceptible.

EIGHT

□ □ □

Ethnic Groups in the International System: State Sovereignty Versus Group Rights to Self-Determination

E thnic groups have become recognized independent actors in international politics. Some groups claim rights that negate other groups' rights, which leads to communal conflict or state repression. In some cases ethnic conflicts spill over to adjacent territories or contenders become embroiled in hegemonic struggles between external powers. Protracted communal conflicts pose a real threat to international security, often result in major humanitarian crises, and sometimes can be solved only through a resort to military force. Yet despite these dangers, ethnic groups have no special international legal status, and few are represented in the United Nations. We argue that legal recognition of ethnic groups allows for disputes to be settled in an orderly and civilized fashion. Mechanisms at the disposal of mediators in crisis situations between states could also be applied in dealing with ethnic strife. States and, to a lesser degree, individuals are subjects of international law. In this chapter we argue that it is necessary to recognize group rights under international law.

SEPARATISTS, PLURALISTS, AND ACTIVISTS

Ethnic groups can be divided into three distinct categories, based on and extending a distinction made in Chapter 2. *Separatists* include all groups that aspire to separate nationhood, in the form of either internal autonomy or independence. *Pluralists* are minorities who seek equal treatment under the law of an existing state plus other ascriptive and political groups that are targets of discrimination and persecution. This category includes some of the groups that are victims of genocide as well as all

139

those who are treated differentially by their governments but who do not seek autonomy. *Activists* are functional groups that have specific grievances against their governments. Membership in functional groups is not determined by ethnicity or political affiliation but is based on specific sets of grievances; thus, it usually cuts across ethnic, religious, and political lines.

Activists rarely threaten internal or international security, nor do they mobilize to the extent of pluralists and separatists. Their demands can more easily be satisfied by local or national authorities. Group members may withdraw support at any time and typically do so when their demands are met or when leadership fails to get results. Such groups do not require special international or legal attention. In contrast, both pluralists and separatists require special status under international law as well as special protection under municipal law, the domestic law of the states in which they live.

Why have groups been largely overlooked as important and independent actors in international relations? And what accounts for their neglect in international law? Persons belonging to national, ethnic, religious, and linguistic minorities who reside within sovereign states have always been subjects of municipal law. Thus, when communal groups fought each other without crossing state boundaries, they were engaged by definition in internal conflicts not subject to international law. Once conflict spilled over boundaries, however, the rules of war and peace could be applied to the warring factions. Only with the emergence of laws that granted individuals rights vis-à-vis their states (discussed in subsequent sections) has this invisible threshold of inviolable national boundaries been crossed to allow for third-party intervention. Simultaneously, the emergence of these laws has given rise to claims that groups seeking independence from existing states should be given special legal recognition.

Traditional international principles that deal with the right of secession or self-determination are inadequate to address the avalanche of new group claims to self-determination. In the past new states have come into existence through many routes: **formal recognition** (one of several indicators of statehood), the granting of independence from colonial powers, the dissolution of an empire, mutual consent of two independent states, seizure of independence, or de facto control of a territory. Self-declaration of independence does not automatically carry the right to statehood. One may argue that in such cases rebels could have been offered combatant or belligerent status, but, as Alexis Heraclides pointed out, "even though a number of insurgents have met the test, none have been accorded such status during the present century." Thus, in situations in which groups have ambitions to secede or to establish internal autonomy, few legal principles exist that could help them bolster their claims vis-à-vis a legally recognized state or, in the case of civil war, bolster one group's claim against that of another.[1]

In civil wars the situation is complicated by the absence of effective, legitimate authorities. These situations require outside observers to seek solutions that resolve competing group claims. The situations in Somalia and the former Yugoslavia may help to illustrate the emerging issues. In both cases the former state ceased to exist as a functioning, effective, legitimate, and legally recognized political entity.

Ethnic groups that we define as pluralist typically advance claims that do not include autonomy but that request the right to exercise their communal rights without discrimination. Such requests are habitually treated in international and municipal law as claims of individuals vis-à-vis the state; thus, group rights are not separately recognized. The collective rights are dealt with summarily as part of the principles that address self-determination of peoples and in the human rights **conventions,** which also stipulate obligations for states. These conventions give states the responsibility to uphold principles of equal treatment under the law and to guarantee bodily integrity, human dignity, freedom from persecution, and similar rights. Violations of such norms enable the international community to punish offenders.

However, at the forty-eighth session of the United Nations Commission on Human Rights on February 21, 1992, the commission approved a draft declaration on the "Rights of Persons Belonging to National or Ethnic, Religious and Linguistic Minorities," which for the first time attempts to give special status to groups under international law. The problem, however, is that the declaration only strengthens the role of the state, insofar as the state is the legal "person" responsible for protecting the rights of minorities. The declaration urges states to fulfill "the obligations and commitments they have assumed under international treaties and agreements to which they are parties." The treaties specifically named are the Universal Declaration of Human Rights, the Convention on the Prevention and Punishment of the Crime of Genocide, the International Convention on the Elimination of All Forms of Racial Discrimination, the International Covenant on Civil and Political Rights, the International Covenant on Economic, Social and Cultural Rights, the Declaration on the Elimination of All Forms of Intolerance and Discrimination Based on Religion or Belief, and the Convention on the Rights of the Child. States that are not signatories to these conventions theoretically could treat their citizens as they wish without fear of outside intervention. Minority groups, in turn, have few avenues by which to seek redress of their claims and can do so only as individuals seeking protection under existing human rights conventions.

THE UNITED NATIONS AS LAWMAKER

Although the United Nations is not officially endowed with the authority to make laws, as are national legislative authorities, it can convert **customary law** into **statutory law** through its ability to propose **multilateral** treaties that are open to ratification by all member states. Once a majority of member states have ratified a treaty, the provisions of the treaty are likely to be treated as general principles—namely, law. The importance of treaties as a source of international law, and the UN ability to promulgate conventions that specify mutual rights and obligations, has effectively granted the United Nations the role of lawmaker. In this role the United Nations has added significantly to the growing body of international law as it affects states in their relations with one another and has included in its **sphere of obligation** the protection of individual rights vis-à-vis the state. The UN Charter, which is essentially the constitution of the United Nations, has also prompted missions and activities that have set precedents that have added to international law. For example, the charter forbids the use of force as a means by which to settle disputes and emphasizes the obligation to settle disputes through peaceful means, such as negotiation, mediation, and similar methods. Although wars have not been abolished by declaring them to be illegal, warring states have sought to justify their actions in legal terms.

The United Nations has created new laws regarding the use of outer space, the oceans, and national waters; has made genocide a crime under international law; and has dealt with the rights of individuals vis-à-vis their states in the covenants on human rights cited previously. But UN efforts to promote international standards of human dignity and to define specific categories of rights have been significantly hampered by the existence of different legal systems that emphasize different rights. The cultural and ideological differences among the Communist-socialist states, non-Western states, and Western democracies in particular have blocked UN efforts to establish mutually acceptable human rights categories. For example, under Islamic law, in contrast to the **common law** tradition of the United States and Britain, women are treated differently. Muslim women have been granted extensive property rights at times when women in most Western societies had no such rights, but they have been denied the extensive civil and political rights granted as a matter of course to women in most twentieth-century democracies. Whereas socialist legal systems gave priority to economic and social rights, democracies have traditionally favored civil and political rights.

We may argue that at present only minimum standards of individual rights exist and are widely accepted—that is, have the character of law. Specific rights and obligations are spelled out in the treaties and covenants cited in the previous section. Although the language of the treaties is often vague, leaving some room for interpretation, this vagueness does not take away from the essential legal character of the documents. The essence of the treaties has been incorporated into many national legal documents, and violations of rights have prompted court decisions by national and international courts that have further amplified the stated principles. International law commissions and legal authorities have worked to eliminate ambiguities by offering legal opinions; moreover, writings on a variety of precedent-setting actions have helped to clarify the meaning of legal provisions.

What has emerged is a fairly specific body of norms that deal with the rights and obligations of individuals vis-à-vis existing states under international law. The real problem is determining how to deal with rights violations. There is no formal enforcement mechanism, and no punishments are attached to crimes committed against humanity. Recent efforts by UN policymakers have concentrated on addressing and remedying these glaring omissions. Since 1992 UN Secretary-General Boutros Boutros-Ghali has sought to extend the organization's traditional role as arbiter and mediator by adding policing and enforcement functions. UN actions in Cambodia, the peacekeeping and peace enforcement actions in Somalia, and the UN-sponsored **collective intervention** in the Gulf War may set the precedents necessary to provide the mechanisms by which minimum standards of human dignity can be guaranteed.

RECOGNIZING ETHNIC IDENTITY AND MINORITY RIGHTS IN THE INTERNATIONAL SYSTEM

We have previously pointed out that states are the traditional subjects of international law and that individuals enjoy some special rights but that, in contrast, groups are largely ignored and are more typically treated as extensions of the individual. Group rights are thus the aggregate of individual rights. The relationship that exists among individual consciousness, group identity, national identity, nationalism, and state-building has been explored to some degree by anthropologists and social scientists. But the literature tells us little about the nature of ethnic groups or the changes in their social organizations over time, which in some instances led to state-building or in others to ethnic disintegration or assimilation.

The Genocide Convention is one of the few international documents that specifically addresses group rights yet specifies their violations largely through reference to individuals. For example, in the original text, genocide includes the following: killing *members* of the group and causing serious bodily harm to *members* of the group. Another example of groups as subjects of international law is seen in the internationally recognized prohibition of terrorism, which identifies terrorists as members of identifiable groups.

None of the human rights conventions elaborates on group membership, with the notable exception of the UN draft declaration named in the section "Separatist, Pluralists, and Activists." Part of the problem undoubtedly lies in the identification of groups as a separate entity. Is group membership inherently fluid, and can it be changed at will? Or are groups coherent entities that exist in largely unaltered form for extended time periods? What really constitutes a group?

The Genocide Convention specifies four types of groups—national, racial, ethnic, and religious—but avoids any reference to political or gender groups. The UN draft declaration identifies national, ethnic, religious, and linguistic minorities and again avoids reference to gender and political groups. Of course, political groups typically have cross-cutting memberships and are more fluid than any of the other groups; thus, they are of lesser concern here for the reasons mentioned in the discussion of activist groups and because of the protection they enjoy under the covenant that deals with the protection of civil and political rights. By our definition, ethnic groups may share language, culture, religion, and race; nations are politicized ethnic groups. We conclude that existing conventions and the new draft declaration are inadequate in solving the problem of group rights vis-à-vis the rights of states to conduct their internal affairs without outside interference. The new declaration essentially endorses the sovereign rights of states and leaves it up to the conscience of respective policymakers to uphold obligations regarding their citizens.

THE CASE OF BOSNIA-HERZEGOVINA: INTERNATIONAL IMPLICATIONS OF GENOCIDAL COMMUNAL CONFLICT

The Bosnian case is an example of groups violating other groups' rights within contested national territories. Lack of international legal provisions that deal with group conflict during civil war make it difficult to respond effectively.

There are unquestionably major violations of human rights in Bosnia that constitute crimes under international law. The perpetrators are neither the legitimate authority nor the governing authority of a clearly specified territory. Essentially, the United Nations is asked to respond to an internal communal conflict that (1) has important international security implications because of its potential spillover or ripple effects, (2) is morally despicable in that it violates human rights laws, and (3) can probably be solved only by a resort to military force.

For their part, Bosnian Serbs claim they cannot live in a Muslim-dominated territory for fear of potential discrimination. Cynical nationalists have played on that fear to incite groups to commit the murder and ethnic cleansing of those "conspiring" to discriminate against Serbs. Of course, such claims are absurd in the absence of any evidence that gives us clues as to the intentions or potential behavior of the Muslim leadership. But UN authorities and national policymakers within this situation must deal essentially with one group's *claim rights,* which negate another group's rights. The Bosnian Serbs claim they can only live in a homogeneous territorial unit, whereas the Muslims are willing to share the national domain.

What we are witnessing in the case of Bosnia-Herzegovina may be only the beginning of an avalanche of similar claims and counterclaims that have been precipitated by the disintegration of the former Soviet Union and Yugoslavia into a multitude of national and subnational units. Given the tendency toward fragmentation of national units in the aftermath of the Cold War, ethnic group protection or the guarantee of rights to persons who belong to identifiable groups requires special attention. This is not to argue that the modern state will cease to function but instead is to suggest that other forms of social organization, such as the ethnic group, in some instances supersede, precede, or fragment state cohesion (this argument is more fully developed in the following section).

THEORETICAL CONSIDERATIONS: INDIVIDUALS, GROUPS, AND THE STATE

From a theoretical perspective one may argue that states have no independent existence beyond that of individuals; states exist for the express purpose of safeguarding the rights of individuals who have united under the banner of a common heritage, namely, the nation or ethnic group. Such reasoning ignores the role of the modern state, which, through an elaborate network of groups, institutions, and roles, protects its continued existence regardless of the wishes of individual citizens or a national people.

State leaders have frequently dealt with ethnic group demands through accommodation or, if that failed, through coercion. Many contemporary minority groups are gaining a higher level of group consciousness. They are less likely to accept assimilation with the dominant group, they seek special status simultaneously with nondiscriminatory treatment under the law, and in some cases they want to secede from the territorial state. Such demands are often incompatible with the idea of the nation-state as a heterogeneous social unit that promises equal protection for all its citizens under the law. The essential issue is that minority rights potentially conflict with the cohesion and continued existence of the multiethnic nation-state.

CONCLUSION

We have shown that the United Nations as lawmaker and supranational entity only implicitly recognizes specific group rights. Groups, thus, have no independent status apart from individuals or states, although there are some exceptions, such as the Palestine Liberation Organization.

Of course, we know that groups exist and take political actions that can lead to civil wars and humanitarian disasters on the scale of Bosnia-Herzegovina, events that affect the international community. Groups that seek independence or ask for internal autonomy from a sovereign state often come into conflict with other groups or with those who represent the legal authority of a sovereign state. When such groups commit atrocities against members of competing groups, we confront crises that require special legal attention and challenge policymakers. Groups that fight legal or de facto recognized authorities challenge the established world order. They have no legally recognized status apart from the nation-state, but they are responsible for many of the world's most protracted conflicts and are perpetrators and victims of many episodes of genocide and politicide that have occurred in the twentieth century. If such groups could attain legal status that details their rights as well as states' obligations to them, this would provide the objective basis on which policy decisions could be reached by outside actors.

NINE

□ □ □

Responding to International Crises

I n this concluding chapter we are concerned with how the international system can and should respond to ethnic conflicts, especially those that result in the loss of many lives. We deliberately become advocates rather than remaining objective observers, for we believe that giving national and ethnic groups "the right to determine their own destinies captures the essence of the argument for implementing basic human rights over and above the rights of states to conduct their own affairs"[1]—especially when a state chooses genocide or political mass murder to preserve its existing structure.

The new world order should emphasize collective responsibility and mutual cooperation and should lay the groundwork for an objective basis on which potential ethnopolitical conflicts can be settled in a manner that would satisfy the great majority of international actors.

EVOLVING DOCTRINES FOR ETHNOPOLITICAL CONFLICTS: LEGAL AND POLITICAL ISSUES

We showed in Chapter 1 that violent ethnic conflicts have increased steadily in frequency and intensity since the 1960s, sometimes accompanied by political mass murder and genocide. Episodes of politicides and genocides since 1945 have caused greater loss of life than all of the wars fought between states during the period between 1945 and the Iran-Iraq War. We think it is essential to demonstrate that such mass abuses violate the moral standards of global society and must lead with some certainty to sanctions that are proportional to the crime. From a strategic perspective, it is clear that the diffusion of future episodes of ethnic hatred, passion, and rebellion will eventually call for greater measures than a maximum collective show of force with a minimum use of weapons could have accomplished in Somalia. We know that serious ethnopolitical conflicts

147

rarely remain internal affairs; they often inflame irredentist passions and may politicize kindred groups. Failure to settle ethnic crises in an equitable manner, thus, may encourage authoritarian rulers to suppress ethnic demands by force.

In some cases international pressures and diplomacy may indeed forestall communal crises at an early stage, but too few diplomats are officially designated "ombudsmen" for national minority issues. A potentially important regional innovation was the creation in January 1993 of a high commissioner on national minorities for the Conference on Security and Cooperation in Europe (CSCE), who, with the help of a very small staff, is to "give an objective evaluation of brewing strife, as well as constructive recommendations for its resolution" to the European member states—a task clearly beyond the high commissioner's limited resources.[2]

Under the leadership of Boutros Boutros-Ghali, the United Nations is pressuring member states for greater commitment in terms of resources and political will to respond to ethnopolitical conflicts and flagrant human rights abuses. Typically, national policymakers have been reluctant to commit resources to crises that have no immediate national consequences; interventions are often costly in terms of material and manpower. The need for a more active UN role and for commitments by member states continues to be hampered by a lack of recognition that communal conflicts can indeed cause *threats to international security*. The Bosnian crisis has brought this point home to European and U.S. policymakers. The longer the delay in effective responses, the more difficult and costly peacekeeping and **peacebuilding** will be; the Cambodian effort described briefly in Chapter 1 (the most expensive UN effort since its creation) is a case in point.

International involvement in past conflicts typically meant unilateral meddling in the affairs of a sovereign state. Although they have been rare, collective interventions have taken place—for example, in the Korean War and, more recently, in Operation Desert Storm. The right to intervene in the affairs of a sovereign state has been severely curtailed under international law. Collective intervention, however, is allowed under Chapter VIII of the UN Charter, and article 34 empowers the Security Council to investigate disputes that cause international friction. A lawful government of a state can invite another state to intervene on its behalf; there are at least seven other circumstances under which states have a lawful right to intervene. Humanitarian causes are not included, despite clearly established norms that seek to protect basic rights of individuals vis-à-vis the rights of states. Thus, although intervention per se is illegal in principle, there are many exceptions. We maintain that humanitarian intervention should be included among the exceptions that allow intervention in the internal affairs of a sovereign state.

But thorny legal issues remain. States or international organizations that intend to intervene in ethnopolitical conflicts prefer to be on solid legal ground, for some interventions prolong conflicts rather than ending aggression, whereas others have resulted in continued occupation. Virtually any proactive response, such as sending a fact-finding mission and mediators or applying sanctions, can be construed as meddling in the internal affairs of a sovereign state. In the absence of legal norms that set clear standards regarding who should intervene and when and how they should do so, any form of intervention may be deemed illegal or unjust. Some legal authorities continue to claim that nonintervention should be the reigning principle; others argue for superiority of the protection of human rights, allowing for intervention in cases of massive abuses. In addition, past indiscriminate interventions by powerful states have victimized weaker states, increasing the sense among legal scholars, policymakers, and UN officials that humanitarian interventions should be evaluated on a case-by-case basis and as a moral issue but not a legal right. Such interpretations fail to consider that the *rights* to life and security of persons are explicitly protected in the Genocide Convention and the Universal Declaration of Human Rights. The Genocide Convention further forbids governments to take steps to destroy any ethnic, religious, or national group. We argue that *signatories to the convention are obliged to uphold its principles and that violations amount to breaches of contract.*

The current trend in international law is encouraging; the United Nations and the international legal community appear to be moving toward codification of principles and identification of appropriate conditions under which humanitarian imperatives will override national sovereignty.[3] This would mean essentially that when massive human rights violations are at stake, states' practices can be debated and condemned and recommendations to remedy the situation can be adopted by the United Nations. What is lacking, however, are (1) clear parameters identifying situations that warrant humanitarian intervention, (2) new laws that attach sanctions (punishment) to crimes committed, and (3) standards that identify what strategies should be applied to what kinds of violations.

Despite a few instances of unilateral or collective interventions in cases of massive human rights abuses, none has ever been undertaken for the sole purpose of correcting such violations. Motives were mixed in the few unilateral interventions that have been cited as precedent-setting humanitarian interventions. For example, in the case of Cambodia, Vietnam intervened in 1978, and Pol Pot went into exile—the killings stopped, the Vietnamese stayed. Tanzania intervened in Uganda in 1979, and Idi Amin went into exile—the killings stopped, but Tanzania never officially claimed it intervened to preserve lives and instead claimed self-defense. Had the Vietnamese left promptly and Tanzania asserted its right to inter-

United Nations notice. By Jeff Danziger in *The Christian Science Monitor*, October 15, 1992. © 1992 TCSPS. Reprinted by permission.

vene on humanitarian grounds, both interventions would probably be considered precedent-setting humanitarian interventions.

All unilateral interventions are beset with problems. If we are to allow unilateral intervention on humanitarian grounds, clear standards need to be set that identify which kinds of situations warrant what types of attention; otherwise, states could intervene on fabricated grounds, claiming humanitarian reasons. Although we do not argue for the necessity of extending the principles of humanitarian intervention to include *unilateral* interventions, a case can be made for its necessity, provided legal standards have been set. We are arguing for the provision of *standards* so humanitarian actions are not impeded and the United Nations can enforce its human rights provisions. Intervention should take place under the auspices of the United Nations but can be executed by regional organizations or, in rare cases, by individual states. Clear standards on when and how to intervene would, in principle, enable the United Nations to formulate appropriate responses.

Let us summarize our position. Two contradictory principles coexist under international law—the principles of territorial integrity and sovereignty versus the right to intervene in cases of violations of humanitarian principles. It is now widely accepted that the right to territorial integrity does not include the right to treat one's citizens as one pleases, such as starving people into submission, committing mass murder, or engaging in ethnic cleansing. States that are obliged to follow clearly specified rules in their relations with other states should be equally bound in their behavior toward their citizens. Violations of laws that deal with the external behavior of states often result in the violation of territorial integrity. States' internal behavior should be equally scrutinized, and violation of internationally recognized standards should have serious consequences.[4] The task is to identify the kinds of strategies that are appropriate for specific violations.

STRATEGIES FOR RESPONDING TO ETHNOPOLITICAL CRISES

The United Nations Agenda for Peace, formulated by Secretary-General Boutros Boutros-Ghali on June 17, 1992, outlines four kinds of responses to ethnic, religious, social, cultural, or linguistic strife: **preventive diplomacy, peacemaking,** peacekeeping, and postconflict peacebuilding. Peacebuilding refers to policies that address "the deepest causes of conflict: economic despair, social injustice and political oppression," whereas peacemaking includes any international action that may lead to a peaceful settlement of ongoing conflicts. Peacekeeping refers to the use of military personnel in noncombatant roles, such as monitoring cease-fires. Such activities require the consent of the warring parties. Ideally, peacekeepers are able to establish a lasting peace after the settlement of the immediate crisis or conflict. The Agenda for Peace makes no specific reference to peace enforcement, an option that would permit the use of force to compel belligerents to cease hostilities.[5]

Peacemaking and peacebuilding are of primary interest to us. Peacemakers need clearly defined policy goals, clear strategic objectives, and tactics that are suited to the desired end state of the involvement. Peacebuilders should be able to anticipate conflicts in order to apply proper measures to ensure peace. Peacekeepers must remain in place and be authorized to use whatever means are necessary to transfer authority to elected local leadership, as was done successfully in Cambodia under UN supervision.

We conclude this discussion by reviewing the measures that may enable policymakers to anticipate and restrain ethnopolitical conflicts. These include preventive diplomacy plus actions designed to respond to civil wars, repression, and anarchy that threaten the human rights and lives of large numbers of people. All of the measures discussed in the remainder of this section have been used selectively to remedy past violations or prevent major crises. Those discussed first are the lowest in cost and pose the least challenge to sovereignty; the last measure constitutes the revocation of a state's sovereignty.

1. Issue early-warning assessments of impending or escalating conflicts; send fact-finding missions and widely publicize results. Establish a UN-sponsored news bureau with instant access to satellite telecommunications to assure global distribution of news and reports (a CNN for peace). These policies are particularly appropriate for civil wars and repression in their early stages. Fact-finding reports issued after six months of deadly and widely publicized conflict, as occurred in Bosnia, are little more than empty gestures.

2. Call on governments and their opponents to seek accommodation; provide international mediation and arbitration; offer political and material incentives to encourage contenders to reach agreements. These actions are well suited for the early and middle stages of civil wars.

3. Condemn putative violations of international law; issue formal warnings of impending sanctions; set deadlines for corrective action by the perpetrators. Such responses may help to restrain states from committing gross human rights abuses. They are less likely to influence contenders in civil wars, especially those (like the Bosnian Serbs) whose moral and political ties to the international community are weak. More important, these symbolic acts help to set the legal and political stage for more forceful international action.

4. Withdraw diplomatic recognition; apply sanctions; embargo military goods, energy supplies, and other commodities that prolong fighting. These actions can be applied to all armed contenders in civil wars and against state perpetrators of gross human rights violations. Of these options, embargos are the most likely to be effective but are also the most difficult to enforce consistently. Their implementation is likely to require higher-order responses.

5. Use limited shows of force, such as overflights by military aircraft, the stationing of warships offshore, and the introduction of moderately armed peacekeeping forces with sufficient firepower to defend themselves when attacked. These actions convey strong messages to belligerents and position international forces to respond more forcefully if warnings are not heeded.

6. Begin selective applications of force, such as interdiction of military movements, air strikes on strategic targets, and the capture and disarming of combatants (individually or in small units). These actions require the international community to "take sides," which is politically feasible when one state or party is clearly the aggressor or perpetrator, as in Bosnia-Herzegovina, but which may be impossible in other civil war situa-

tions. Selective use of force also poses risks of escalation, which may worsen and prolong conflicts.

7. Use of collective military intervention with the objectives of separating forces, disarming contenders, protecting neutral areas, and establishing secure procedures and zones for delivering and distributing humanitarian aid. This is the most decisive and costly form of international response and seems to be the only one that might remedy situations that resemble those in Bosnia and Somalia. The key is to use all means necessary to establish secure and defensible zones in which civilians can be supplied and protected. This is an interim strategy that must be complemented with diplomatic and political initiatives aimed at bringing about a political settlement. We cannot deny the high-risk nature of such undertakings, but the consequences of inaction will ultimately lead to far greater cost and injustice.

8. Establish interim, internationally sponsored trusteeships; rebuild civil administration and basic services; provide material and technical assistance; supervise free elections. This form of wholesale intervention is equivalent to Allied policies in occupied Germany after 1945 and to UN actions in Cambodia. It requires a costly, long-term commitment. Military occupation and trusteeship are, or should be, the ultimate sanctions for states and local leaders who will not desist from mass killings. Intervenors must demonstrate necessity and proportionality: Military intervention must be shown to be imperative and should remain the last resort.[6]

THE SECESSIONISTS: A SPECIAL PROBLEM

The concern of traditionalists is that if ethnopolitical groups are given special legal status in international and domestic law, it could provide the impetus for innumerable claims and counterclaims, which would lead to protracted conflicts and leave few existing states intact, since most states are heterogeneous units. The answer to this concern is that potential conflicts could be circumvented or avoided by establishing clear standards under which groups have the claim-right to secede and, in cases of ongoing conflict, by designing specific international actions that would prevent further escalation and lead to peaceful settlements of conflicts.

There is real cause for concern: Among the 233 minorities we have surveyed in 127 countries, more than 80 supported autonomy movements at some time between 1945 and 1990. Of these, around 30 groups have fought protracted civil wars to attain autonomy. States with autocratic leadership are the quickest to suppress such challengers. Democratic states have often been able to accommodate nationalist and minority demands by granting equal treatment under the law or providing for special status and autonomy (see Chapter 4). Standards that would identify potential problem areas for minorities, such as discrimination or exploitation, and specify sets of criteria that would give groups legally sanctioned remedies for unwanted domination could only help to alleviate situations that reach levels of mutual intolerance. Regimes that respond within legal constraints have no reason to fear outside intervention. In contrast, oppressive regimes may have to face international consequences.

In the two most recent major cases of nationalist rebellions in Western democratic societies, those on behalf of Catholics in Northern Ireland and the Basques in Spain, claims either have been settled or have little validity. The Basques now enjoy regional autonomy within the Spanish state; the Irish Republican Army has declining public support and is widely rejected as a terrorist organization, even within the community it claims to represent. Violence continues in both regions because of die-hard militants, but it provides no grounds for international action. As proponents of the legalization of limited secessionist claims, we argue that few democratic governments or responsive autocracies have to fear the "Balkanization" of their territory.

INTERNATIONAL RESPONSES TO
FOUR ETHNOPOLITICAL CONFLICTS

We evaluate here international reactions to each of our four cases. They help to illustrate our argument that the lack of international standards, combined with uncertainty about which kinds of actions are appropriate and legal in cases of ethnopolitical conflict, may exacerbate existing conflicts.

The Malayan Emergency

International involvement during the Malayan Emergency in the 1950s was virtually nonexistent. The newly formed United Nations was not prepared to deal with colonial conflicts. Given the structure of the UN Security Council, in which the former imperial powers played and continue to play a larger role than other states, inaction was not surprising. France and Great Britain, two of the five countries that had veto power in the Security Council, had the two largest overseas colonial empires at the end of World War II. They would have vetoed any attempt to control their actions within their dependencies. In the immediate postwar period the United States seldom used its veto; the Soviet Union did so more often. Both countries did so largely to block each other and to control admittance of new UN members.

Although the General Assembly pushed the colonial powers toward accountability after 1946, it lacked the ability to pressure states to disclose information. Not until the 1960s did world public opinion and new UN members succeed in exerting pressures on colonial powers to account for and provide reports on the political and economic well-being of nonself-governing peoples. The Emergency occurred at a time when the United Nations was not yet able to play a role as arbiter between the last colonial powers and the emergent Third World. Moreover, the conflict was perceived as an internal Chinese problem in a country dominated by Malays. The Emergency had faded into obscurity by the 1960s, and by the 1980s there was no basis for international concern about the status of Malaysia's Chinese citizens.

The Miskitos in Nicaragua

The Miskito refugees in Honduras received extensive assistance that was organized by the UN High Commissioner for Refugees, which provides similar assistance to refugees throughout the world. Miskito leaders also benefited from regional and international pressures on the Sandinista regime to accommodate indigenous interests. The Reagan administration's support for the contras strengthened the Miskitos' bargaining position. The efforts of other governments in the region, called the Contadora group, eventually pushed the Sandinistas to accept settlement of the larger conflict. This is a situation in which regional players contributed to the resolution of an ethnopolitical conflict without any direct involvement of the United Nations.

Turks and Other Visible Minorities in Germany

The Turks in Germany pose a difficult challenge to the international community, especially to the other states of the European Community. Economic migrants who happen to share an ethnic identity resemble functional groups that want equal treatment under the laws of their host country. However, in most European states they are treated as ethnic minorities. The question remains, should Turks be given special minority status in Germany, as the Frisians, the Sorbs, and Danish minorities have received and as the Romas (as gypsies call themselves) are still fighting for? Or should they have a free choice to assimilate and simply be assured of equal treatment under the law? The problem became more acute after January 1, 1994, when all borders among European Community members became open to free movement of citizens. The foreign workers who do not have citizenship in any European state, as is the case with most Turks in Germany, have now become the objects of special scrutiny and controls to keep them from migrating to France, for example, in pursuit of economic opportunities. Many Europeans are deeply concerned about the implications of establishing a separate system of police controls over the movement of minorities within Europe.

The Kurds in Iraq

The Kurds in northern Iraq enjoyed Allied protection in the aftermath of the Gulf War, when safe havens were established under the protection of Allied air cover. But Allied leaders did not act until they were pressured by domestic and regional political considerations. Media coverage of atrocities mobilized public outrage in Western countries, and, in addition, the Turkish government expressed its concern about the destabilizing effect of the flood of Kurdish refugees. For many Iraqi Kurds the response came too late. This case highlights the need to organize responses at an early stage rather than wait for news about atrocities. Individual governments and the United Nations should have followed carrot-and-stick policies to encourage contenders to seek accommodation. By providing mediation and material incentives and simultaneously issuing formal warnings and condemning putative violations of international law, the international community might have prevented escalation.

CONCLUSION

Which case best exemplifies current dilemmas over how to respond to ethnic crises? The Kurds are typical of the fate that befalls ethnic rebels during times of changing global alliances and restructuring. Their self-proclaimed "federated state" in northern Iraq is experiencing economic crisis and is openly opposed by the Iraqi government. Their international support is weak, because there are as yet no consensual standards for dealing with ethnonational self-determination and because Iraq's treatment of minorities seems to be a lesser problem than more critical situations in Bosnia-Herzegovina, Somalia, Angola, and Burundi. Support for the Kurds in Iraq was and continues to be dependent upon the fickle fortunes of changing national interests and drifting international attention.

The Turkish situation in Germany exemplifies a different kind of dilemma. Settlement of such crises is particularly urgent, because at present we see a literal invasion of prosperous Western Europe by Eastern European economic refugees. Given current widespread recessions, no Western European country can effectively absorb millions of people from Africa, Asia, and Eastern Europe who are impoverished, are poorly trained, or have obsolete skills. Recently introduced measures designed to keep out some groups and accept others are troublesome, however. When Germany "exported" Roma (gypsies) back to Romania in 1993, one wonders whether their lack of marketable skills or their ethnic and cultural identity was the primary reason for their expulsion. What we may witness in Western Europe is the reemergence of xenophobia, or a fear of cultural dilution, that subordinates Europeanism to pan-Germanism, Francophilia, and British insularity.

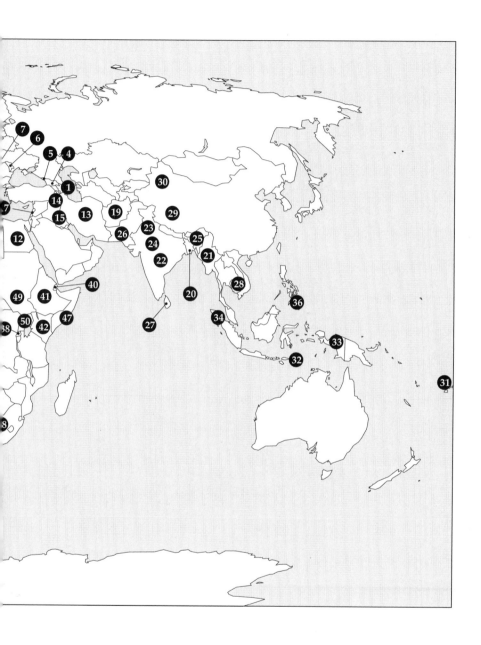

APPENDIX Serious and Emerging Ethnopolitical Conflicts in 1993

This is a list of all serious armed conflicts involving ethnopolitical groups in 1992 and 1993 plus a selection of lesser conflicts, like those in Germany (9), Jordan (16c), Fiji (31), and Ecuador (53), that were of serious concern to regional observers. The list does not include conflicts initiated by militant Islamicists against governments of Islamic countries such as Algeria and Egypt, because these do not meet our definition of ethnopolitical conflict.

Conflict Number and Country	Group(s) and Nature of Conflict	Group Type[1]	Conflict Type and Trend, 1993[2]	Lives Affected (in thousands)	
				Deaths[3]	Refugees[4]
EUROPE					
1 Azerbaijan	Armenians fighting for independence of Nagorno-Karabakh enclave since 1988	ETHNAT	War ++	3–7	767
2 Bosnia	Serbs and Croats fighting since 1991 to partition the country and "cleanse" their regions of Muslims	ETHNAT	War ++	200	1,700
3 Croatia	Serbians who fought for autonomy in 1991 and 1992 control one-third of Croatia	ETHNAT	LIC 0	50	690
4 Georgia	Russian-backed Abkhazians won independence in war that began in 1992	ETHNAT	War ++	3	132
5a Georgia	South Ossetians fighting for union with North Ossetians in Russia	ETHNAT	LIC 0	0.7	13
5b Russia	North Ossetians seek union with South Ossetians in Georgia	ETHNAT	LIC 0	0.3	—
6 Moldova	Slavic minority established trans-Dniestr republic with Russian help	ETHNAT	LIC 0	1	15
7 Serbia	Protest by autonomy-minded Kosovo Albanians repressed by Serbia	ETHNAT	REP +	0.2	—
8 France	Right-wing backlash against and attacks on immigrants from North Africa	ETHCLAS	DIS +	<0.1	—

(continues)

APPENDIX (*cont.*)

9	Germany	Right-wing attacks on refugees and immigrants from Third World	ETHCLAS	DIS +	>0.1	—
10	Northern Ireland	Catholic Irish Republican Army has fought against Protestant militants and for union with Republic of Ireland since 1969	COMCON	LIC N	3	—
11	Spain	Militant Basques have fought terror campaign for independence since 1960s	ETHNAT	LIC A	1	—

MIDDLE EAST AND NORTH AFRICA

12	Egypt	Islamic militants have attacked Copts (Egyptian Christians) since the mid-1980s	RELIG	DIS +	<0.1	—
13	Iran	Persecution of Baha'is has declined from its peak in early 1980s	RELIG	REP –	0.3	—
14a	Iran	Rebellion by Kurds for autonomy since 1980 has been suppressed	ETHNAT	DIS –	?	?
14b	Iraq	Rebel Kurds established autonomous region with Allied protection	ETHNAT	DIS 0	180–250	526
14c	Turkey	Terrorist campaign by Kurdish militants seeking independence	ETHNAT	LIC N	6–8	30
15	Iraq	Supporters of 1991 Shi'i rebellion continue to suffer reprisals	RELIG	REP – –	20	?
16a	Israel	Arab citizens have used protest to demand greater rights since 1980s	ETHCLAS	DIS 0	<0.1	—
16b	West Bank and Gaza	Palestinians used violent protest to seek autonomy in the period 1987–1993	ETHNAT	LIC N	1.7	965
16c	Jordan	Some Palestinians have opposed King Hussein's government since 1970s	COMCON	DIS 0	—	—

(*continues*)

APPENDIX (cont.)

17	Lebanon	Syrian intervention has ended a fifteen-year civil war among Muslim, Druze, and Christian communal contenders	COMCON	DIS 0	<1.0	—
18	Morocco	Western Sahara independence movement defeated by government, but UN referendum on independence is to be held	ETHNAT	LIC N	15	165

CENTRAL AND SOUTH ASIA

19	Afghanistan	Divided among warring factions including Pashtuns, Tajiks, Uzbeks, and others	COMCON	War +	?	?
20	Bangladesh	Chittagong hill peoples resisting settlers from lowlands, demanding autonomy	INDIG	LIC A	25	50
21	Burma	Guerrilla wars for autonomy conducted by Karen, Kachin, Shan, Mon, and other hill and tribal peoples since 1950s	INDIG/ ETHNAT	War –	130	1,333
22	India	Hindu nationalists provoking riotous clashes with Muslim minority	RELIG	LIC +	2	?
23	India	Pakistan-supported Kashmir rebels fighting for independence since 1990	ETHNAT	War +	12–20	?
24	India	Sikh rebels fighting for an independent Khalistan since early 1980s	RELIG	War +	20	—
25	India	Rebellions for autonomy in Assam conducted by Bodos, Tripuras, Nagas, others	INDIG	LIC 0	6	—
26	Pakistan	Small-scale rebellions in Sindh and Baluchistan	COMCON	DIS 0	9	—
27	Sri Lanka	Liberation Tigers fighting for an independent Tamil state since 1985	ETHNAT	War 0	50–100	181

(continues)

APPENDIX (cont.)

ASIA PACIFIC

28	Cambodia	Hate campaign and local massacres to drive out Vietnamese settlers seemed to have ended by 1993	ETHCLAS	LIC –	<0.1	?
29	China	Suppression of Tibetans who seek restoration of autonomy lost in 1951	ETHNAT	REP 0	100	128
30	China	Sporadic proautonomy activity among Muslim Uighurs and Kazakhs in Xinjiang	ETHNAT	DIS 0	1–2	—
31	Fiji	Fijian majority used military rule to repress East Indian minority	COMCON	LIC 0	—	—
32	Indonesia	Suppression of East Timor rebels fighting for independence since 1976	ETHNAT	REP 0	200	—
33	Indonesia	Suppression of West Irian (Papuan) natives resisting Indonesian control since 1963	INDIG	REP 0	5–32	—
34	Indonesia	Suppression of North Sumatra (Aceh) rebels seeking autonomy since 1970s	ETHNAT	REP — —	10–20	6
35	Papua–New Guinea	Rebellion for independence on Bougainville Island since late 1980s	ETHNAT	LIC 0	<1.0	—
36	Philippines	Minor insurgency by Moros (Muslims) who fought for independence in 1970s and gained limited autonomy in 1990	ETHNAT	DIS A	50	—

AFRICA SOUTH OF THE SAHARA

37	Angola	Mbundu-Ovimbundu rivalry underlies protracted civil war that resumed in 1992 after collapse of peace pact	COMCON	War +	500	1,300
38a	Burundi	Formerly dominant Tutsi minority in 1993 massacred supporters of newly elected Hutu regime	COMCON	War ++	25+	200+

(continues)

APPENDIX *(cont.)*

38b	Rwanda	Exiled Tutsi minority fighting a repressive Hutu regime	COMCON	War +	3.5	550
39	Chad	Current phase in protracted civil war involves fighting between Anakaza, who support the president, and Bideyet, who support the president ousted in 1991	COMCON	War 0	100	24
40	Djibouti	Civil war in 1993 as Afars challenged government dominated by Somalis	COMCON	War +	?	?
41	Ethiopia	Minor insurgency by Oromo and other groups that reject the revolutionary government that seized power in 1991	COMCON	LIC 0	?	?
42	Kenya	President Moi prompted his Kalenjin supporters to attack other peoples in the Rift Valley	COMCON	LIC +	1–2	45
43	Liberia	Ethnic rivalries fueled civil war now checked by West African peacekeeping force and 1993 peace accords	COMCON	War N	150	1,200
44	Mali and Niger	Insurgency by Tuareg nomads seeking autonomous region since 1990	INDIG	LIC –	<1.0	—
45	Nigeria	Deadly Moslem-Christian clashes in east-central region since 1980s	RELIG	LIC +	11	—
46	Senegal	Autonomy rebellion in Casamance region since late 1980s	ETHNAT	LIC 0	0.5	15
47	Somalia	Civil war since late 1980s; Isaaqs have led "independent" North Somalia since 1991, other clans still battle in south	COMCON	War –	350	2,900
48	South Africa	Despite four years of communal war between African National Congress and Zulu supporters, agreement was reached on a multiracial constitution in November 1993	COMCON	War 0	14	4,100

(continues)

APPENDIX (*cont.*)

49	Sudan	Muslim government in 1983 broke an agreement with Christian southerners, leading to renewal of Africa's most lethal civil war	ETHNAT	War – –	1,000–1,500	5,300
50	Uganda	Fighting between army (mostly from Baganda and Banyarwanda tribes) and northern Acholi and Langi rebels	COMCON	LIC 0	12	11

THE AMERICAS

51	Brazil	Sporadic clashes between Amazonian Indians and settlers and miners	INDIG	DIS 0	0.1	?
52	Canada	Secessionist movement in Quebec gaining political support	ETHNAT	DIS +	—	—
53	Ecuador	Countrywide indigenous rights protest in early 1990s led to government concessions	INDIG	DIS 0	—	—
54	Guatemala	Indigenous peoples continue to be victimized in government campaign against supporters of leftist insurgency that began in early 1960s	INDIG	REP –	150	200
55	Peru	Indigenous peoples have been forced to support leftist Sendero Luminoso guerrillas warring with government	INDIG	War –	30	500
56	United States	Tensions among urban ethnic groups lead to occasional rioting, as in Miami and Los Angeles	ETHCLAS	DIS 0	<0.1	—
57	United States	Sporadic terrorism since 1970s by supporters of Puerto Rican independence	ETHNAT	DIS 0	<0.1	—

(*continues*)

APPENDIX (*cont.*)

Notes

1. Type of ethnopolitical group(s) involved in conflict (see Chapter 2)

ETHNAT = ethnonationalists
INDIG = indigenous peoples
ETHCLAS = ethnoclasses
COMCON = communal contenders
RELIG = religious groups

2. Codes for type of conflict in 1993

War = major armed conflict
LIC = low-intensity conflict with significant violence, including armed clashes, terrorism, or deadly rioting
DIS = serious dispute with little violence but a potential for escalation
REP = serious conflict in which most violence is a consequence of state repression

Codes for trends in conflict during 1993

++ escalating conflict, ethnopolitical group close to military or political victory
+   escalating conflict, no end in sight
0   conflict continuing, no significant change in level
N   conflict low or fluctuating during cease-fires or negotiations
A   conflict low due to accommodations that satisfied most of the group
–   deescalating conflict, no end in sight
–– deescalating conflict, ethnopolitical group close to defeat or annihilation

3. Estimates of number of deaths, in thousands, attributed to the conflict, either directly through fighting or indirectly through starvation, disease, and displacement, from the beginning of its current phase through mid-1993. Most such estimates are very imprecise; some are shown as ranges. The symbol "<" means *less than*.

4. Estimates in thousands of the number of refugees from the conflict in need of international assistance plus number of people displaced by conflict within the country. International refugees can usually be counted accurately; only rough estimates can be made of internally displaced people.

Sources: The primary source of this information is an unpublished report by Albert J. Jongman and Alex P. Schmid, "Wars, Low-Intensity Conflicts and Serious Disputes: A Global Inventory of Current Confrontations," available from the Interdisciplinary Program of Research on Root Causes of Human Rights Violations (PIOOM), University of Leiden, the Netherlands. Supplemental information was taken from Peter Wallensteen and Karin Axell, "Armed Conflict 1989–92," *Journal of Peace Research* 30 (August 1993); Victor Kotowitz and Matt Moody, "A World of Civil Strife," *Los Angeles Times*, June 8, 1993; and the files of the Minorities at Risk project at the University of Maryland.

□ □ □

Discussion Questions

CHAPTER ONE

1. States are defined in international politics as territories that have a population and an effective government whose sovereignty is recognized by other states. What general definition can you suggest for politically active ethnic groups?

2. How important was ethnic conflict in world politics prior to the end of the Cold War?

3. In what ways has the end of the Cold War contributed to increases in ethnic conflict?

4. Under what circumstances are ethnic conflicts purely domestic matters of states, and under what circumstances do they have international implications?

5. What factors are pushing the international community (the United Nations, regional organizations, major powers) to take greater responsibility for ethnic conflict? What are the sources of resistance to change?

CHAPTER TWO

1. Three of the four types of politically active ethnic groups exist in the contemporary United States and its dependencies. Identify at least one of each type, and explain the basis for your categorization.

2. Which of the four types of ethnic groups, and in what regions of the world, are most likely to become involved in protracted communal conflicts?

3. Which types of ethnic groups are most likely to be linked to specific territories, and which are less likely to have such linkages? What implications does the difference have for the groups' political objectives and the kinds of conflicts in which they become involved?

4. What kinds of historical justifications do ethnonationalists use for their demands for autonomy or independence?

5. Ethnoclasses in Western societies were established as a result of what historical processes?

6. How do religious differences between groups affect the nature and intensity of ethnic conflict?

CHAPTER THREE

1. What accounts for the dispersal of the Kurds across many different countries? Does this weaken their claim to statehood?

2. When and under what circumstances did twentieth-century Kurds have a serious chance to attain separate statehood? Why did they fail?

3. Many Kurds believe they have been a distinct people since ancient times; some non-Kurdish observers think their identity was formed more recently. Does this kind of historical debate, which is echoed in debates over other ethnonational movements, have any relevance to the contemporary Kurdish struggle for independence?

4. How have Miskito culture and society changed over the past three centuries? Do these changes weaken Miskitos' claims to being a distinct indigenous people with special claims to the region they currently inhabit?

5. Why did some Miskitos ally first with the revolutionary Sandinista government and then switch to the U.S.-supported contra movement that sought to overthrow the Sandinistas?

CHAPTER FOUR

1. Why did the Malay Communists rebel in 1948? Did the rebellion have any lasting effect on the status of the Chinese in Malaysia?

2. Most former European colonies shifted toward socialist or autocratic governments following independence. Why do you think the Malaysian state retained its essentially democratic character?

3. Are the restrictions on the Chinese in Malaysia consistent with Western democratic principles and practices? To what extent do you think the restrictions are justified?

4. What kinds of groups, excepting foreign workers like the Turks, have moved to Germany in recent years? How has their arrival affected the situation of the Turks?

5. List all of the factors that seem to contribute to the current wave of antiforeigner attacks in Germany. Can you rank them in order of importance? Do you think they are caused in part by Germany's historical legacy of Nazism?

CHAPTER FIVE

1. To what extent are the various theoretical approaches that attempt to explain why ethnic groups mobilize compatible with one another; to what extent are they mutually exclusive?

2. Evaluate the argument that each ethnic conflict is specific to a particular historical and political context and, thus, that comparative generalizations are impossible.

3. Is it possible in principle to construct a general theory that can account for all aspects of ethnic conflict?

4. Why should social scientists develop and use models?

5. Are historians able to forecast when and under what circumstances ethnic groups will mobilize and fight?

Research Exercise. Use the model to assess the chances that conflict involving an ethnic group in country *x* is likely to increase.

Step 1: Study the historical and political circumstances under which the ethnic group has maintained its separate identity. Identify its objectives, grievances, and recent actions.

Step 2: Begin to collect information on each variable and indicator specified in the model during the past five years. The sources of current political and statistical information for indicators include:

The Europa World Year Book (London: Europa Publications, annual).

Arthur S. Banks, ed. *Political Handbook of the World* (Binghamton: CSA Publications, State University of New York, annual).

Appendix to T. R. Gurr, *Minorities at Risk: A Global View of Ethnopolitical Conflict* (Washington, D.C.: United States Institute of Peace Press, 1993).

Political Risk Year Book (New York: Frost and Sullivan, annual volumes for all world regions).

If no statistical data can be found, make informed judgments based on substantive information gathered in Step 1.

Step 3: Having collected information, evaluate how the group ranks on each variable in the model. On which indicators and variables does it have high rankings or scores? Are there variables that are not included in the model that seem especially important to gaining an understanding of the group's political actions?

Step 4: Assess the chances that conflict will increase by determining whether the group's rankings or scores on the independent variables and indicators have been increasing or decreasing.

CHAPTER SIX

Review the comparisons in Figure 6.1 as the first step in answering these questions.

1. Which kinds of discrimination seem to have the strongest and most consistent effects on the intensity of ethnic conflict?

2. Does conflict between an ethnic group and a government lead to stronger group identity and greater cohesion, as was proposed in Chapter 5? Are there circumstances in which these propositions do not hold?

3. We argued in Chapter 5 that increasing the severity of government force directed against an ethnic group is likely to increase the group's resistance, up to some threshold beyond which extreme force inhibits further opposition. Is the evidence from all four cases consistent with this proposition? Does it seem to hold in both democratic and autocratic political environments?

4. Do you think the Turks in Germany have more to gain from increased protest than the Chinese in Malaysia? Than other immigrant minorities in Western societies?

Research Exercise. The Kurds have been less successful than the Miskitos in gaining regional autonomy. Identify half a dozen general factors that explain the difference. Concentrate on factors that are strong or present in one case and weak or absent in the other: For example, there have been deep and persisting divisions among the Kurds but not among the Miskitos. Take into account international as well as internal factors.

CHAPTER SEVEN

Review the comparisons in Figure 7.1 as the first step in answering these questions.

1. What countries supported the Iraqi Kurds prior to 1991? How consistent was their support?

2. Iraq has committed gross human rights violations against civilians suspected of supporting Kurdish rebellions since the early 1970s. What was the pattern of international response prior to 1991? Why did it change?

3. How important was the U.S.-supported Contra war against the Sandinistas in helping the Miskitos achieve autonomy?

4. Can you foresee any circumstances, however unlikely, in which the Chinese Malaysians might attract more external support or concern?

5. Since Germany's international economic and political status is high, why should its policymakers be concerned about international reactions to attacks on Turks and other foreigners?

CHAPTER EIGHT

1. What are the international legal grounds for UN actions in support of individual rights?

2. What recent developments suggest that a stronger legal basis for international protection of the rights of ethnic groups is evolving?

3. What determines membership in functional groups, and why do they rarely require special international attention?

4. Evaluate the argument that states have no independent existence beyond that of individuals. Does this reasoning ignore the role of the modern state?

5. Why do serious abuses of human rights violate the moral standards of global society?

CHAPTER NINE

1. The right to intervene in cases of violations of humanitarian principles contradicts the principle of territorial integrity and sovereignty in international law. What is the current status of each principle among legal scholars?

2. Unilateral interventions are beset with problems. Why is this so?

3. Differentiate among preventive diplomacy, peacemaking, peacekeeping, and postconflict peacebuilding.

4. What should be the ultimate sanctions against states that engage in genocide? Who should have the responsibility to act?

5. Under which UN Charter provision is collective intervention allowed? Under what circumstances should regional organizations be allowed to intervene?

Notes

PREFACE

1. We have tabulated ethnopolitical wars and their casualties as reported for 1992 and 1993 by Albert J. Jongman and Alex P. Schmid, "Wars, Low-Intensity Conflicts and Serious Disputes: A Global Inventory of Current Confrontations," prepared by the Interdisciplinary Program of Research on Root Causes of Human Rights Violations (PIOOM), University of Leiden, the Netherlands. See the Appendix to the present book for information on these and other contemporary ethnic conflicts. *World Refugee Survey 1993* (Washington, D.C.: U.S. Committee for Refugees, 1993) estimates a world total of 26 million international refugees and internally displaced persons at the end of 1992; Jongman and Schmid attribute 23 million to ethnopolitical conflicts, to which we add estimates of additional refugees from the conflicts raging in the former Yugoslavia. By July 1993 these latter conflicts had generated a total of 4.2 million refugees and displaced persons, according to *Balkan War Report* no. 22 (October-November 1993), published by the Institute for War & Peace Reporting, 1 Auckland Street, London SE11 5HU. Thirteen UN peacekeeping operations are summarized in *Worldwide Peacekeeping Operations, 1993* (Washington, D.C.: Central Intelligence Agency, EUR 93-10008, May 1993).

CHAPTER 1

1. *"I am Timorese": Testimonies from East Timor* (London: Catholic Institute for International Relations, 1990), pp. 30–33.

2. Based on conversations with the authors in Kusadasi, Turkey, June 1990.

3. Five rules were used for enumerating these groups: (1) Only countries with populations greater than 1 million were analyzed; (2) only groups that numbered one hundred thousand or exceeded 1 percent of the population of a country were included; (3) ethnic groups that live in several adjoining countries were counted separately within each country; (4) divisions within an ethnic group in a country were not counted separately—for example, Native Americans in the United States were analyzed as one group, not as three hundred or more separate tribes; and (5) twenty-five minorities with political or economic advantages were included, because such minorities are often involved in conflict to protect or extend their advantages. Details of the study are described in Ted Robert Gurr, *Minorities at Risk:*

A Global View of Ethnopolitical Conflict (Washington, D.C.: United States Institute of Peace Press, 1993).

4. The authors' tabulation is from data in *World Refugee Survey 1993* (Washington, D.C.: U.S. Committee for Refugees, 1993), pp. 50–52. Information on internally displaced people is often guesswork.

5. Quoted in "Clinton Seeks Foreign Policy Bearings in Post Cold War Fog," *Washington Post*, October 17, 1993, p. A28.

6. George Klay Kieh, Jr., "Regional Peacekeeping Forces and Conflict Resolution in Africa," paper presented to the Annual Meeting of the International Studies Association, Acapulco, March 1993.

CHAPTER 2

1. The Mediterranean island of Corsica rebelled against rule by the Italian Republic of Genoa in 1730, which sought assistance from its French allies, who conquered and absorbed Corsica into the kingdom of France in the 1760s. The autonomous dukedom of Brittany was incorporated into revolutionary France in 1789.

2. Population figures are from the 1989 USSR census. The Soviet data on national peoples are approximately accurate, because all citizens were required to carry internal passports that specified their primary nationality. Estimates of the sizes of national and minority peoples in most Western societies are also relatively reliable. In Africa, the Middle East, and most of Asia and Latin America, the data are seldom more than estimates and are sometimes only guesses.

3. Information on developments in the indigenous people's movement is reported in the *Newsletter* and other publications of the International Work Group for Indigenous Affairs, which is based in Copenhagen, and in *Cultural Survival*, a quarterly journal published by the Cambridge (Mass.) organization of the same name. A detailed analysis of the movement is Franke Wilmer, *The Indigenous Voice in World Politics: Since Time Immemorial* (Newbury Park: Sage Publications, 1993). A new survey is *State of the Peoples: A Global Human Rights Report on Societies in Danger* (Cambridge: Cultural Survival, 1993).

4. See International Labor Conference (ILO), *Partial Revision of the Indigenous and Tribal Populations Convention, 1957 (no. 107)*. Report 6 (1 and 2), 75th Session (Geneva: International Labor Office, 1988). The new convention, no. 169, was adopted in 1989 but, like other ILO conventions, is not binding on member states. Rather, it sets a standard against which states' labor policies toward indigenous people are judged by the international community. This summary is based on an undergraduate research paper prepared for Ted Robert Gurr by Jean-Carlos Rivera.

5. The Chinese in Malaysia meet our definition of communal contenders; other Chinese communities in Southeast Asia are either restricted ethnoclasses (Indonesia) or have been largely assimilated (Thailand, the Philippines). Palestinians are a professional and commercial minority throughout the Middle East and also in Central America; on the latter, see Nancie Gonzalez, *Dollar, Dove and Eagle: 100 Years of Palestinian Emigration to Honduras* (Ann Arbor: University of Michigan Press, 1992).

CHAPTER 3

1. From "My Life," by Asir Shawkat, a fourteen-year-old Kurdish boy. In 1991 Shawkat was a student at London's Stockwell Park Kurdish School. His and other Kurdish refugee children's autobiographies are included in Rachel Warner, ed., *Voices from Kurdistan* (London: Minority Rights Group, December 1991), pp. 15–17.

2. An overview of these policies is provided by David McDowall, *The Kurds: A Nation Denied* (London: Minority Rights Publications, 1992), pp. 99–100, 108–110. More detailed accounts include P. W. Galbraith and C. Van Hollen, Jr., *Chemical Weapons in Kurdistan: Iraq's Final Offensive, A Staff Report* (Washington, D.C.: Committee on Foreign Relations, U.S. Senate, 1988); Kanan Makiya, "The Anfal: Uncovering an Iraqi Campaign to Exterminate the Kurds," *Harper's Magazine*, vol. 284, no. 1704 (May 1992): 53–61; *The Anfal Campaign in Iraqi Kurdistan: The Destruction of Koreme* (New York: Middle East Watch and Physicians for Human Rights, 1993); and *Report on the Situation of Human Rights in Iraq*, prepared by Max Van der Stoel, Special Rapporteur of the Commission on Human Rights (New York: United Nations, E/CN.4/1992/31). *Al-Anfal* is used in the Koran to refer to the spoils of a battle against the unbelievers in Mecca. The implication of the Iraqi government's use of the term is that the Kurds are unbelievers and that their lives and properties are forfeit.

3. The following sections draw mainly on three summary sources: Gerard Chaliand, ed., *People Without a Country: The Kurds and Kurdistan* (London: Zed Press, 1980); McDowall, *The Kurds;* and Stephen C. Pelletiere, *The Kurds: An Unstable Element in the Gulf* (Boulder: Westview Press, 1984). The account is updated with a collection of journalistic accounts, scholarly articles, and unpublished papers from the period 1990–1993. One of the most useful and best documented of the latter is Omar Sheikhmous, "The Kurdish Question: Conflict Resolution Strategies at the Regional Level" (Stockholm University: Centre for Research in International Migration and Ethnic Relations, July 1992). An excellent in-depth historical analysis is Martin van Bruinessen, *Agha, Shaikh, and State: The Social and Political Structures of Kurdistan* (1978, reissued London: Zed Press, 1991). The accounts also use summaries prepared for Ted Robert Gurr by Deina AbdelKader and Hossein Shabazi.

4. There are no precise and current census data on the Kurdish populations of any Middle Eastern country, and all estimates are subject to dispute. These are from Mehrdad R. Izady, *The Kurds: A Concise Handbook* (Washington, D.C.: Taylor and Francis, 1992), p. 117, and appear to be based on careful demographic analysis. They are higher than estimates given in most other sources. Some of these Kurds live outside their traditional homelands, for reasons explained in "Twentieth-Century Changes in Kurdish Society." Nearly half a million Kurds are also dispersed through the former republics of the USSR.

5. See Izady, *The Kurds*, for detailed accounts of Kurdish history, culture, religion, and society. His interpretations sometimes diverge from those of other authors. Izady thinks the Kurds have existed as a distinct people since ancient times, for example. He also interprets Alevism and Yazidism as indigenous, pre-Muslim

Kurdish faiths, which he collectively labels the "Cult of Angels" (in *The Kurds*, pp. 131–166), whereas some regard them as unorthodox forms of Shi'ism.

6. There are many names for traditional authorities in Kurdish society. *Aghas* are leaders of clans or extended families; some are very influential. *Mirs* and *begs* are the chiefs of tribal communities. *Shaiks* were the leaders of Sufi religious brotherhoods who played important roles in resolving disputes among Kurdish clans and tribes in the nineteenth and early twentieth centuries. *Pasha* and *Bey* were titles given to traditional leaders who the Ottomans appointed or confirmed in office as rulers or governors of Kurdish tribes and principalities. There are also alternative spellings for the names of Kurdish leaders. When possible, we follow the usage in Izady, *The Kurds*.

7. The Ottoman and Persian rulers in earlier centuries had also forcibly deported many Kurds to locations as distant as Baluchistan on the Indian Ocean and modern-day Bulgaria. Izady, *The Kurds*, pp. 99–107, provides a detailed summary of historical and contemporary Kurdish deportations and diaspora.

8. See Kemal Karpat, "The Ottoman Ethnic and Confessional Legacy in the Middle East," in Milton J. Esman and Itamar Rabinovich, eds., *Ethnicity, Pluralism, and the State in the Middle East* (Ithaca: Cornell University Press, 1988), pp. 35–53.

9. Quoted in McDowall, *The Kurds*, p. 32. A strong Armenian nationalist movement was already in existence. Kurdish and Armenian representatives quickly took advantage of the changed international situation and presented a memorandum on their common interest in independence to the 1919 Peace Conference in Paris. The boundaries proposed for the two new states are shown in Izady, *The Kurds*, p. 58.

10. A useful overview of Kurdish nationalism in the early twentieth century is Pelletiere, *The Kurds*, Chapter 3. For details on the Lausanne Treaty, see Chaliand, *People Without a Country*, pp. 41–44, 58–60, 158–163, 215. The treaty included provisions for the protection of the rights of non-Muslim minorities in the former Ottoman domain (e.g., Greeks and Armenians) but made no separate reference to Kurds. Minority rights were ignored in Turkey after 1924, but the separate status and rights of Kurds were respected in Iraq and French-mandated Syria until their independence in 1930 and 1946, respectively. Iran was not a signatory to the treaty.

11. The Kurdish minority in Syria was the target of discriminatory policies as part of an "Arabization" campaign from 1958 to the late 1970s. This campaign was inspired at first by the intense Arab nationalism of Gamal Abdel Nasser's Egypt; from 1958 to 1961 Syria and Egypt joined in the "United Arab Republic." It was also provoked by the beginning of political activism among Kurds in Syria. The Kurds in the former USSR are a small and widely dispersed minority. Neither group has taken significant political actions since the 1970s. See Chaliand, *People Without a Country*, Chapters 6 and 7; McDowall, *The Kurds*, Chapter 14; and Philip G. Kreyenbroek and Stefan Sperl, eds., *The Kurds: A Contemporary Overview* (London: Routledge, 1992), Chapters 8 and 10.

12. McDowall, *The Kurds*, p. 36.

13. This example comes from the memoirs of a Turkish governor of a Kurdish province, cited in Chaliand, *People Without a Country*, p. 83. Special government officials enforced the ban in urban Kurdish markets; the five-piaster fine was about one-tenth the market value of a sheep.

14. Written by a fourteen-year-old refugee in London; in Warner, *Voices from Kurdistan*, p. 11.

15. A useful journalistic account of the policy shift is Sam Cohen, "Turkey Lifts Language Restrictions on Its Kurdish Minority," *Christian Science Monitor*, February 7, 1991. The Diyarbakir incident is described in a release from the Kurdish Human Rights Watch (Fairfax, VA), "Report on Turkey," July 23, 1991. Participants in Aydin's funeral procession several days later clashed with police and army units, who shot and wounded four Labor Party deputies; a number of journalists and activists were arrested and reportedly beaten.

16. The history of the Kurds in contemporary Turkey is reviewed by Kendal (a pseudonym for a Kurdish scholar) in Chapter 2 of Chaliand, *People Without a Country*, and in Chapters 4 and 5 of McDowall, *The Kurds*. A contemporary political analysis is Michael M. Gunter, *The Kurds in Turkey: A Political Dilemma* (Boulder: Westview Press, 1990). Our account also makes use of extensive journalistic coverage for the period 1990–1993 and unpublished papers by A. Fuat Borovali and Suha Bolukbasi, Turkish scholars who have studied Kurdish issues.

17. An overview of the Kurds in Iran is provided by A. R. Ghassemlou in Chapter 3 of Chaliand, *People Without a Country*. An important English-language source on the Republic of Mahabad is William Eagleton, *The Kurdish Republic of 1946* (London: Oxford University Press, 1963). Kurdish resistance to the Islamic Republic is reviewed in McDowall, *The Kurds*, Chapter 9.

18. From documents captured in the 1991 Kurdish uprising; quoted by Aryeh Neier, "Putting Saddam Hussein on Trial," *New York Review*, September 23, 1993, p. 47.

19. This section draws mainly on Chaliand, *People Without a Country*, Chapter 5; McDowall, *The Kurds*, Chapters 10–13; and Pelletiere, *The Kurds*, Chapters 6–8. A detailed analysis of relations between the Baath governments and the Kurds is Edmund Ghareeb, *The Kurdish Question in Iraq* (Syracuse: Syracuse University Press, 1981).

20. For a news account of the agreement see *Washington Post*, September 19, 1989. The text of the agreement is contained in a letter dated September 22, 1989, from Jimmy Carter to Nicaraguan President Daniel Ortega. Copies of this and other documents on negotiations between the government and Miskito leaders were obtained from the files of the Indian Law Resource Center, Washington, D.C. In December 1992, Minister-Director Rivera was one of the principal speakers at the UN General Assembly's plenary session, which opened the International Year of Indigenous People.

21. Estimates of the Miskito population vary widely, because census information is inadequate and because there are no objective criteria for determining group membership. A 1981 Nicaraguan government report gives an impossibly precise "estimate" of 66,994 Miskitos in the Atlantic Coast region (in Carlos M. Vilas, *State, Class and Ethnicity in Nicaragua: Capitalist Modernization and Revolutionary Change on the Atlantic Coast* [Boulder: Lynne Rienner, 1989, p. 4]). Our 1990 figure, derived from expert estimates, is 126,000 in Nicaragua and 20,000 to 30,000 in Honduras.

22. Miskitos and Creoles have continued to intermarry with one another and with European, Chinese, and mestizo immigrants. To be considered an Indian or a Creole in this context, therefore, is mainly determined by where and how one lives

and what group one identifies with rather than by one's genetic makeup. Most Creoles live in coastal towns, especially in Bluefields and El Bluff, which are at the southern limit of Miskito lands. Both groups share a broader identity as Costeños, people of the coast, as distinct from the "Spaniards." But their interests are not identical: Armed opposition to the Sandinista government during the 1980s came mainly from the Miskitos, whereas most Creoles resigned themselves to Sandinista rule after a 1980 protest campaign failed.

23. There is a large and ideologically charged literature on the Miskitos. The principal sources for this section include a chronology prepared by Michael Hartman and Stephen Kurth for the Minorities at Risk project; Vilas, *State, Class and Ethnicity in Nicaragua,* a thoroughly researched account that is sympathetic to the Sandinista government; Roxanne Dunbar Ortiz, *The Miskito Indians of Nicaragua* (London: Minority Rights Group, Report no. 79, 1988); a series of articles in *Cultural Survival,* sources that favor the indigenous rights movement; and a first-hand journalistic account by Stephen Kinzer, *Blood of Brothers: Life and War in Nicaragua* (New York: Putnam, 1991), Chapter 16. A useful analytic account is Martin Diskin, "Revolution and Ethnic Identity: The Nicaraguan Case," in Nancie L. Gonzalez and Carolyn S. McCommon, eds., *Conflict, Migration, and the Expression of Ethnicity* (Boulder: Westview Press, 1989).

24. Little has been published about the Miskitos since the rebellion ended. This summary is based on "Nicaragua's Indians Find Little Peace," *Washington Post,* July 21, 1991; Bernard Nietschmann, "The Development of Autonomy in the Miskito Nation," *Fourth World Bulletin* 2 (February 1993): 1, 6–7, 15; and "Miskito Activists Draw the Line on Toxic Wastes," *Cultural Survival Quarterly* 17 (Fall 1993): 6–7.

CHAPTER 4

1. A more detailed account of the Emergency is given in the section entitled "The Emergency." Major sources include Richard L. Clutterbuck, *The Long War: Counterinsurgency in Malaya and Vietnam* (New York: Praeger, 1966); Edgar O'Ballance, *Malaya: The Communist Insurgent War, 1948–60* (Hamden, CT: Archon Books, 1966); Sir Robert Thompson, *Defeating Communist Insurgency: The Lessons of Malaya and Vietnam* (New York: Praeger, 1966); Anthony Short, *The Communist Insurrection in Malaya: 1948–1960* (New York: Crane, Russak, 1975); and Richard Stubbs, *Hearts and Minds in Guerrilla Warfare: The Malayan Emergency 1948–1960* (Boulder: Westview Press, 1989).

2. On Malaysian Chinese politics, see, for example, Chew Huat Hock, "Malaysian Chinese Politics and the 1982 General Election: Some Emerging Trends," *Asia Pacific Community* no. 18 (Fall 1982): 80–91; and Heng Pek Koon, *Chinese Politics in Malaysia: A History of the Malaysian Chinese Association* (Singapore: Oxford University Press, 1988).

3. On the historical origins of ethnic divisions in Malaya, see sources in note 1 to this chapter.

4. For general accounts of Malaysian politics, see Zakaria Haji Ahmad, ed., *Government and Politics of Malaysia* (Kuala Lumpur: Oxford University Press, 1987); and

Karl von Vorys, *Democracy Without Consensus: Communalism and Political Stability in Malaysia* (Princeton: Princeton University Press, 1975).

5. Quotation from Robert Klitgaard and Ruth Katz, "Overcoming Ethnic Inequalities: Lessons from Malaysia," *Journal of Policy Analysis and Management*, vol. 2, no. 3 (1983): 337. On post-1969 policies also see Milton Esman, *Administration and Development in Malaysia* (Ithaca: Cornell University Press, 1972); and Donald R. Snodgrass, *Inequality and Economic Development in Malaysia* (Kuala Lumpur: Oxford University Press, 1980).

6. Recent assessments of Malaysian politics include Zakaria Haji Ahmad, "Malaysia: Quasi Democracy in a Divided Society," in Larry Diamond, Juan J. Linz, and Seymour Martin Lipset, eds., *Democracy in Developing Countries: Asia* (Boulder: Lynne Rienner, 1991); and Gordon P. Means, *Malaysian Politics: The Second Generation* (Singapore: Oxford University Press, 1991).

7. German policies on immigration of guestworkers and data on their origins, numbers, and employment are described in Klaus J. Bade, ed., *Population, Labour and Migration in 19th- and 20th-Century Germany* (New York: St. Martin's Press, 1987), pp. 146–159; and Stephen Castles and Godula Kosak, *Immigrant Workers and Class Structure in Western Europe*, 2d ed. (Oxford: Oxford University Press, 1985), Chapters 2 and 3. Current statistical information on foreigners in Germany and other European countries is reported in *Trends in International Migration: Continuous Reporting on Migration* (Paris: Organisation for Economic Co-operation and Development, 1992). Other data for this section come from a special issue of *Zeitschrift für Kulturaustausch* on "Fremde in Deutschland," vol. 41, no. 1 (1991), published in Stuttgart by the Institut für Auslandsbeziehungen. There is no precise information on the numbers of migrants from Turkey who are ethnic Kurds.

8. Summarized by Castles and Kosak, *Immigrant Workers*, pp. 433–436.

9. See Stephen Castles, *Here for Good: Western Europe's New Ethnic Minorities* (London: Pluto Press, 1984), pp. 76–85. A comprehensive and up-to-date analysis is Klaus J. Bade, ed., *Deutsche im Ausland—Fremde in Deutschland: Migration in Geschichte und Gegenwart* (Munich: C. H. Beck, 1992).

10. Summarized in Bade, *Population, Labour and Migration*, pp. 159–160.

11. Reported by Castles, *Here for Good*, pp. 190–191. Chapter 7 in this source also documents the rise of antiforeign attitudes and politics in Germany and other West European countries in the 1970s and early 1980s.

12. Quotation from Bade, *Population, Labour and Migration*, p. 149. This and the following discussion of the current status of Turks in Germany use materials from recent journalistic accounts, including Joyce Mushaben, "Germany's Rising Nationalism: Everyone Deserves Some Blame," *Christian Science Monitor*, October 1992; Francine S. Kiefer, "German Violence Puts Turk Community on Edge," *Christian Science Monitor*, November 24, 1992; and Stephen Kinzer, "Bonn Plans Review of Citizen Law," *International Herald Tribune*, January 26, 1993. The educational status of foreigners in German schools is criticized by Castles, *Here for Good*, Chapter 6; recent evaluations by German scholars are more positive, for example, Bade, *Deutsche im Ausland*.

13. On the National Democratic Party see Castles, *Here for Good*, pp. 201–204. On the Republicans, see articles on Germany in Christian Soe, ed., *Comparative Politics 92/93* and *Comparative Politics 93/94* (Guilford, CT: Dushkin, annual editions).

14. "Time for German Action," *International Herald Tribune*, June 11, 1993, p. 6.

15. Political activism by Turkish immigrants in the 1970s is described by Mark J. Miller, *Foreign Workers in Western Europe: An Emerging Political Force* (New York: Praeger, 1981). Recent political developments are taken from news accounts and an unpublished "Chronology of Political Violence" for 1992, prepared by Albert Jongman of the Center for the Study of Social Conflicts, University of Leiden.

16. See Ronald Koven, "Muslim Immigrants and French Nationalists," *Society* 29 (May-June 1992): 25–33; and Eugene Robinson, "Racism Rising in Britain," *Washington Post*, October 25, 1993, pp. A1, A15.

CHAPTER 5

1. A critical survey of general theories is James B. Rule, *Theories of Civil Violence* (Berkeley: University of California Press, 1988). Theories of revolution are surveyed by Jack A. Goldstone, T. R. Gurr, and Farrokh Moshiri, eds., *Revolutions of the Late Twentieth Century* (Boulder: Westview Press, 1991), Chapters 2, 3, 14.

2. A classic work is Frederik Barth, ed., *Ethnic Groups and Boundaries: The Social Organization of Culture Difference* (London: Allen and Unwin, 1969). An important recent study is Nancie L. Gonzalez and Carolyn S. McCommon, eds., *Conflict, Migration, and the Expression of Ethnicity* (Boulder: Westview Press, 1989).

3. A recent review and synthesis is Susan Olzak, *The Dynamics of Ethnic Competition and Conflict* (Stanford: Stanford University Press, 1992).

4. The foundation of modernization theory was laid down by Karl Deutsch, *Nationalism and Social Communication* (Cambridge: MIT Press, 1953). A later statement is David E. Apter, *The Politics of Modernization* (Chicago: University of Chicago Press, 1965). Data on the upward trends in ethnopolitical conflict from 1945 to 1989 in each of the world regions are reported in Ted Robert Gurr, *Minorities at Risk: A Global View of Ethnopolitical Conflict* (Washington, D.C.: United States Institute of Peace Press, 1993), Chapter 4. A reappraisal of what modernization means for ethnic identities is Walker Connor, "Nation-Building or Nation-Destroying?" *World Politics* 26 (April 1972): 319–355.

5. Influential theorists who assume the fundamental importance of ethnic identity and solidarity include Connor, "Nation-Building"; Donald L. Horowitz, *Ethnic Groups in Conflict* (Berkeley: University of California Press, 1985); Anthony D. Smith, *The Ethnic Revival in the Modern World* (New York: Cambridge University Press, 1981); and Pierre L. van den Berghe, *The Ethnic Phenomenon* (New York: Elsevier, 1981).

6. Charles Tilly interprets all civil conflicts as resulting from the instrumental pursuit of group interests in response to changing opportunities; see *From Mobilization to Revolution* (Reading, MA: Addison-Wesley, 1978). The internal colonialism theory was first developed by Michael Hechter, *Internal Colonialism: The Celtic Fringe in British National Development* (Berkeley: University of California Press, 1975).

7. For a review and synthesis of theories of secession, see Alexis Heraclides, *The Self-Determination of Minorities in International Politics* (London: Frank Cass, 1991),

Chapter 1, Appendix 2. He tests his arguments with case studies of separatist movements, including the Kurds in Iraq.

8. See Susan Olzak, *The Dynamics of Ethnic Competition and Conflict* (Stanford: Stanford University Press, 1992), Chapters 1 and 2. Her theoretical argument is more complex than this sketch and is concerned mainly with Western societies; on ethnic stratification, competition, and conflict in African and Asian societies see Horowitz, *Ethnic Groups in Conflict*.

9. A review of theories and evidence about genocide is Helen Fein, "Genocide: A Sociological Perspective," *Current Sociology* 38 (Spring 1990): 1–126.

10. This preliminary theory is the work of Barbara Harff, as developed in "The Etiology of Genocides," in Isidor Wallimann and Michael N. Dobkowski, eds., *Genocide and the Modern Age: Etiology and Case Studies of Mass Death* (Westport, CT: Greenwood Press, 1987), pp. 41–59; and in Barbara Harff and Ted Robert Gurr, "Victims of the State: Genocides, Politicides and Group Repression Since 1945," *International Review of Victimology*, vol. 1, no. 1 (1989): 23–41. A general explanation for elites' use of violence against their citizens is Ted Robert Gurr, "The Political Origins of State Violence and Terror," in Michael Stohl and George A. Lopez, eds., *Government Violence and Repression: An Agenda for Research* (Westport, CT: Greenwood Press, 1986), pp. 45–71.

CHAPTER 6

1. Studies of the settlement of protracted ethnic conflicts include I. William Zartman, *Ripe for Resolution: Conflict and Intervention in Africa* (New Haven: Yale University Press, 1989); Joseph V. Montville, ed., *Conflict and Peacemaking in Multiethnic Societies* (Lexington, MA: Lexington Books, 1990); and Roy Licklider, ed., *Stopping the Killing: How Civil Wars End* (New York: New York University Press, 1993).

2. The uses of detention powers are critically analyzed in Jomo Kwame Sundaram, "Malaysia: Economic Recession, Ethnic Relations and Political Freedom," *Cultural Survival Quarterly*, vol. 12, no. 3 (1988): 55–63. On deportation and citizenship status of immigrants in Malaysia, see Minority Rights Group, *The Chinese of South-East Asia* (London: Minority Rights Group, Report 92/6), pp. 6–7; in Germany, see Stephen Castles, *Here for Good: Western Europe's New Ethnic Minorities* (London: Pluto Press, 1984), pp. 82–84.

3. This section is based on a more detailed analysis of the accommodation of ethnopolitical conflicts in Ted Robert Gurr, *Minorities at Risk: A Global View of Ethnopolitical Conflict* (Washington, D.C.: United States Institute of Peace Press, 1993), Chapter 10.

CHAPTER 7

1. Recent studies on this general topic include Hurst Hannum, *Autonomy, Sovereignty, and Self-Determination: The Accommodation of Conflicting Rights* (Philadelphia: University of Pennsylvania Press, 1990); Manus I. Midlarsky, ed., *The International-*

ization of Communal Strife (London: Routledge, 1992); and "Ethnic Conflict and International Security," special issue of *Survival*, vol. 35, no. 1 (Spring 1993).

2. David McDowall, *The Kurds: A Nation Denied* (London: Minority Rights Publications, 1992), p. 129.

3. Data for this and similar comparisons can be found in United Nations, *World Development Report* (New York: United Nations, 1992).

4. CIA assistance probably began in the early 1960s, but the first agreement for significant aid was reached in 1969. On U.S. and other sources of aid for the KDP, see Edmund Ghareeb, *The Kurdish Question in Iraq* (Syracuse: Syracuse University Press, 1981), Chapter 7; and Stephen C. Pelletiere, *The Kurds: An Unstable Element in the Gulf* (Boulder: Westview Press, 1984), Chapter 8.

5. For an elaboration of the reasons for the settlement of Iraq's claim, see McDowall, *The Kurds*, p. 98; and Ghareeb, *The Kurdish Question*, Chapter 8.

6. Two documents on the case are reprinted in Gary E. McCuen, *The Nicaraguan Revolution* (Hudson, WI: GEM Publications, 1986), Chapter 4.

7. The regional peace process was very complex, because it involved other states in the region and aimed at resolving other regional conflicts as well. For accounts of the role of international actors in the Nicaraguan conflict, see Devora Grynspan, "Nicaragua: A New Model for Popular Revolution in Latin America," in Jack Goldstone, Ted Robert Gurr, and Farrokh Moshiri, eds., *Revolutions of the Late Twentieth Century* (Boulder: Westview Press, 1991), pp. 108–109; Martin Diskin, "Revolution and Ethnic Identity: The Nicaraguan Case," in Nancie L. Gonzalez and Carolyn S. McCommon, eds., *Conflict, Migration, and the Expression of Ethnicity* (Boulder: Westvew Press, 1989), pp. 12–17; and Carlos M. Vilas, *State, Class and Ethnicity in Nicaragua: Capitalist Modernization and Revolutionary Change on the Atlantic Coast* (Boulder: Lynne Rienner, 1989), Chapter 5.

8. "Germany Now Telling Its Officials to Acknowledge Neo-Nazi Problem," *Washington Post*, March 19, 1993, p. A54.

9. "Germany's Neighbors Resist a Revision of Its Asylum Law," *Christian Science Monitor*, March 5, 1993, p. 6.

CHAPTER 8

1. For an extended discussion of the etiology of secession see Alexis Heraclides, *The Self-Determination of Minorities in International Politics* (London: Frank Cass, 1991); also see John Chipman, "Managing the Politics of Parochialism," *Survival: The IISS Quarterly*, vol. 35, no. 1 (Spring 1993): 143–170. The quotation is from Heraclides, p. 25.

CHAPTER 9

1. From Barbara Harff, *Genocide and Human Rights: International Legal and Political Issues* (Denver: University of Denver Monograph Series in World Affairs, vol. 20, book 3, 1984), p. 78.

2. Quote from Konrad J. Huber, "Preventing Ethnic Conflict in the New Europe: The CSCE High Commissioner on National Minorities," in *Minority Rights and Re-*

sponsibilities: Challenges in the New Europe (New York: Institute on East-West Studies, forthcoming).

3. See Jarat Chopra and Thomas G. Weiss, "Sovereignty Is No Longer Sacrosanct: Codifying Humanitarian Intervention," *Ethics & International Affairs* 6 (1992): 95–117.

4. The doctrine of humanitarian intervention is discussed in Harff, *Genocide and Human Rights,* and in Chopra and Weiss, "Sovereignty Is No Longer Sacrosanct." A comprehensive annotated bibliography is Barbara Harff and David Kader, "Bibliography of Law and Genocide," in Israel W. Charny, ed., *Genocide: A Critical Bibliographic Review, Vol. II* (New York: Facts on File, 1990).

5. Boutros Boutros-Ghali, *An Agenda for Peace: Preventive Diplomacy, Peacemaking, and Peace-Keeping* (New York: United Nations, 1992), quotation from paragraph 11.

6. These eight points are taken from Barbara Harff, "Bosnia and Somalia: Strategic, Legal, and Moral Dimensions of Humanitarian Intervention," *Report from the Institute for Philosophy and Public Policy,* vol. 12, no. 3/4 (Summer/Fall 1992): 5–7. An interesting recent collection of articles on intervention is Elizabeth Ferris, ed., *The Challenge to Intervene: A New Role for the United Nations?* (Uppsala, Sweden: Life and Peace Institute, 1992).

□ □ □

Suggested Readings

ON ETHNICITY AND ETHNOPOLITICAL CONFLICT

See issues of the journals *Ethnicity* and *Racial and Ethnic Studies*, both published since the 1970s; the magazine *Cultural Survival*; reports issued by the Minority Rights Group (379 Brixton Road, London SW9 7DE, UK); and the publications of the International Work Group for Indigenous Affairs (Fiolstraede 10, Copenhagen K, Denmark).

Barth, Frederik. 1969. *Ethnic Groups and Boundaries: The Social Organization of Culture Difference*. London: Allen and Unwin.

Brass, Paul R., ed. 1985. *Ethnic Groups and the State*. Totowa, NJ: Barnes and Noble.

——. 1991. *Ethnicity and Nationalism: Theory and Comparison*. New Delhi: Sage Publications.

Cultural Survival. 1993. *State of the Peoples: A Global Human Rights Report on Societies in Danger*. Cambridge: Cultural Survival.

Esman, Milton J., and Itamar Rabinovich, eds. 1988. *Ethnicity, Pluralism, and the State in the Middle East*. Ithaca: Cornell University Press.

Fein, Helen. 1993. "Accounting for Genocide After 1945: Theories and Some Findings." *International Journal on Group Rights* 1: 79–106.

——. 1993. *Genocide: A Sociological Perspective*. London: Sage Publications.

Gonzalez, Nancie L., and Carolyn S. McCommon, eds. 1989. *Conflict, Migration, and the Expression of Ethnicity*. Boulder: Westview Press.

Gottlieb, Gidon. 1993. *Nation Against State: A New Approach to Ethnic Conflicts, the Decline of Sovereignty, and the Dilemmas of Collective Security*. New York: Council on Foreign Relations.

Gurr, Ted Robert. 1993. *Minorities at Risk: A Global View of Ethnopolitical Conflict*. Washington, D.C.: United States Institute of Peace Press.

——. 1993. "Why Minorities Rebel: A Global Analysis of Communal Mobilization and Conflict Since 1945." *International Political Science Review* 14, no. 2: 161–201.

Harff, Barbara. 1987. "The Etiology of Genocides." In *Genocide and the Modern Age: Etiology and Case Studies of Mass Death*, edited by Isidor Wallimann and Michael N. Dobkowski. Westport, CT: Greenwood Press.

Harff, Barbara, and Ted Robert Gurr. 1989. "Victims of the State: Genocides, Politicides and Group Repression Since 1945." *International Review of Victimology* 1, no. 1: 23–41.

Horowitz, Donald L. 1985. *Ethnic Groups in Conflict*. Berkeley: University of California Press.

Lijphart, Arend. 1977. *Democracy in Plural Societies*. New Haven: Yale University Press.

McMullen, Ronald K. 1993. "Ethnic Conflict in Russia: Implications for the United States." *Studies in Conflict and Terrorism* 16: 201–218.

McGarry, John, and Brendan O'Leary, eds. 1993. *The Politics of Ethnic Conflict Regulation*. London: Routledge.

Mikesell, Marvin W., and Alexander B. Murphy. 1991. "A Framework for Comparative Study of Minority-Group Aspirations." *Annals of the Association of American Geographers* 81, no. 4: 581–604.

Minority Rights Group. 1990. *World Directory of Minorities*. Chicago: St. James Press.

Montville, Joseph V., ed. 1990. *Conflict and Peacemaking in Multiethnic Societies*. Lexington, MA: Lexington Books.

Motyl, Alexander. 1987. *Will the Non-Russians Rebel? State, Ethnicity, and Stability in the USSR*. Ithaca: Cornell University Press.

Ringer, Benjamin R., and Elinor R. Lawless. 1989. *Race-Ethnicity and Society*. New York: Routledge.

Rupesinghe, Kumar, Peter King, and Olga Vorkunova, eds. 1992. *Ethnicity and Conflict in a Post-Communist World*. New York: St. Martin's Press.

Samarasinghe, S.W.R. de A., and Reed Couglan, eds. 1991. *Economic Dimensions of Ethnic Conflict*. London: Pinter Publishers.

Smith, Anthony D. 1986. *The Ethnic Origins of Nations*. Oxford: Basil Blackwell.

———. 1993. *National Identity*. Reno: University of Nevada Press.

Tiryakian, Edward A., and Ronald Rogowski, eds. 1985. *New Nationalisms of the Developed West: Toward Explanation*. Boston: Allen and Unwin.

Watson, Michael, ed. 1990. *Contemporary Minority Nationalism*. New York: Routledge.

Wilmer, Franke. 1993. *The Indigenous Voice in World Politics: Since Time Immemorial*. Newbury Park: Sage Publications.

ON THE KURDS

Chaliand, Gerard, ed. 1980. *People Without a Country: The Kurds and Kurdistan*. London: Zed Press.

Ghareeb, Edmund. 1981. *The Kurdish Question in Iraq*. Syracuse: Syracuse University Press.

Gunter, Michael M. 1990. *The Kurds in Turkey: A Political Dilemma*. Boulder: Westview Press.

Izady, Mehrdad R. 1992. *The Kurds: A Concise Handbook*. Washington, D.C.: Taylor and Francis.

Kreyenbroek, Philip G., and Stefan Sperl, eds. 1992. *The Kurds: A Contemporary Overview*. London: Routledge.

Makiya, Kanan. 1992. "The Anfal: Uncovering an Iraqi Campaign to Exterminate the Kurds." *Harper's Magazine* 284, no. 1704 (May): 53–61.

_____. 1992. *Cruelty and Silence: War, Tyranny, Uprising, and the Arab World.* New York: Norton.

McDowall, David. 1992. *The Kurds: A Nation Denied.* London: Minority Rights Publications.

Middle East Watch. 1990. *Human Rights in Iraq.* New Haven: Yale University Press.

_____. 1993. *The Anfal Campaign in Iraqi Kurdistan: The Destruction of Koreme.* New York: Middle East Watch and Physicians for Human Rights.

Pelletiere, Stephen C. 1984. *The Kurds: An Unstable Element in the Gulf.* Boulder: Westview Press.

van Bruinessen, Martin. 1991. *Agha, Shaikh, and State: The Social and Political Structures of Kurdistan* (1st ed. 1978). London: Zed Press.

ON THE MISKITOS

Americas Watch. 1987. *The Sumus in Nicaragua and Honduras: An Endangered People.* New York: Americas Watch.

Dennis, Philip A. 1981. "The Costeños and the Revolution in Nicaragua." *Journal of Interamerican Studies and World Affairs* 23 (August): 271–296.

Diskin, Martin. 1989. "Revolution and Ethnic Identity: The Nicaraguan Case." In *Conflict, Migration, and the Expression of Ethnicity,* edited by Nancie L. Gonzalez and Carolyn S. McCommon. Boulder: Westview Press.

Dunbar Ortiz, Roxanne. 1988. *The Miskito Indians of Nicaragua.* London: Minority Rights Group, Report no. 79.

Kinzer, Stephen. 1991. *Blood of Brothers: Life and War in Nicaragua.* New York: Putnam. See especially Chapter 16.

Nietschmann, Bernard. 1993. "The Development of Autonomy in the Miskito Nation." *Fourth World Bulletin* 2 (February): 1–16.

Ohland, Klaudine, and Robin Schneider. 1983. *National Revolution and Indigenous Identity: The Conflict Between Sandinistas and Miskito Indians on Nicaragua's Atlantic Coast.* Copenhagen: International Working Group on Indigenous Affairs, Document no. 47.

Reyes, Reynaldo, and J. K. Wilson. 1993. *Ráfaga: The Life Story of a Nicaraguan Miskito Comandante.* Norman: University of Oklahoma Press.

Vilas, Carlos M. 1989. *State, Class and Ethnicity in Nicaragua: Capitalist Modernization and Revolutionary Change on the Atlantic Coast.* Boulder: Lynne Rienner.

ON THE CHINESE IN MALAYSIA

Ahmad, Zakaria Haji, ed. 1987. *Government and Politics of Malaysia.* Kuala Lumpur: Oxford University Press.

Ali, S. Husin. 1991. "Development, Social Stratifications and Ethnic Relations: The Malaysian Case." In *Economic Dimensions of Ethnic Conflict,* edited by S.W.R. de A. Samarasinghe and Reed Couglan. London: Pinter Publishers.

Coppel, Charles A., with Hugh Mabbett and Ping-Ching Mabbett. 1982. *The Chinese in Indonesia, The Philippines and Malaysia.* London: Minority Rights Group Report no. 10, revised ed.

Koon, Heng Pek. 1988. *Chinese Politics in Malaysia: A History of the Malaysian Chinese Association.* Singapore: Oxford University Press.

Means, Gordon P. 1991. *Malaysian Politics: The Second Generation.* Singapore: Oxford University Press.

Minority Rights Group. 1992. *The Chinese of South-East Asia.* London: Minority Rights Group, Report 92/6.

Mutalib, Hussin. 1990. *Islam and Ethnicity in Malay Politics.* Singapore: Oxford University Press.

O'Ballance, Edgar. 1966. *Malaya: The Communist Insurgent War, 1948–60.* Hamden, CT: Archon Books.

Short, Anthony. 1975. *The Communist Insurrection in Malaya: 1948–1960.* New York: Crane, Russak.

Snodgrass, Donald R. 1980. *Inequality and Economic Development in Malaysia.* Kuala Lumpur: Oxford University Press.

Stubbs, Richard. 1989. *Hearts and Minds in Guerrilla Warfare: The Malayan Emergency 1948–1960.* Boulder: Westview Press.

von Vorys, Karl. 1975. *Democracy Without Consensus: Communalism and Political Stability in Malaysia.* Princeton: Princeton University Press.

ON IMMIGRANT MINORITIES IN EUROPE

Bade, Klaus J., ed. 1987. *Population, Labour and Migration in 19th- and 20th-Century Germany.* New York: St. Martin's Press.

Castles, Stephen. 1984. *Here for Good: Western Europe's New Ethnic Minorities.* London: Pluto Press.

Castles, Stephen, and Godula Kosak. 1985. *Immigrant Workers and Class Structure in Western Europe,* 2d edition. Oxford: Oxford University Press.

Miller, Mark J. 1981. *Foreign Workers in Western Europe: An Emerging Political Force.* New York: Praeger.

Power, Jonathan, with Anna Hardman. 1984. *Western Europe's Migrant Workers.* London: Minority Rights Group, Report no. 28, 2d revised edition.

Solomos, John, and John Wrench, eds. 1993. *Racism and Migration in Contemporary Europe.* Oxford: Berg Publishers.

Waever, Ole, Barry Buzan, Morten Kelstrup, Pierre Lemaitre, and others. 1993. *Identity, Migration and the New Security Agenda in Europe.* London: Pinter Publishers.

INTERNATIONAL DIMENSIONS OF ETHNIC CONFLICT

Boutros-Ghali, Boutros. 1992. *An Agenda for Peace: Preventive Diplomacy, Peacemaking, and Peace-Keeping.* New York: United Nations.

Cahill, Kevin M., ed. 1993. *A Framework for Survival: Health, Human Rights, and Humanitarian Assistance in Conflicts and Disasters.* New York: Basic Books and Council on Foreign Relations.

Chopra, Jarat, and Thomas G. Weiss. 1992. "Sovereignty Is No Longer Sacrosanct: Codifying Humanitarian Intervention." *Ethics & International Affairs* 6: 95–117.

Damrosch, Lori Fisler, ed. 1993. *Enforcing Restraint: Collective Intervention in Internal Conflicts*. New York: Council on Foreign Relations.

de Silva, K. M., and R. J. May, eds. 1991. *Internationalization of Ethnic Conflict*. New York: St. Martin's Press.

Doyle, Michael W. 1994. *UN Peacekeeping in Cambodia: UNTAC's Civilian Mandate*. Boulder: Lynne Rienner.

Ehrlich, Thomas, and Mary Ellen O'Connell. 1993. *International Law and the Use of Force*. Boston: Little, Brown.

"Ethnic Conflict and International Security." 1993. Special issue of *Survival: The IISS Quarterly* 35, no. 1 (Spring): 3–170.

Hannum, Hurst. 1990. *Autonomy, Sovereignty, and Self-Determination: The Accommodation of Conflicting Rights*. Philadelphia: University of Pennsylvania Press.

Harff, Barbara. 1984. *Genocide and Human Rights: International Legal and Political Issues*. Denver: University of Denver Monograph Series in World Affairs, vol. 20, book 3.

———. 1991. "Cambodia: Revolution, Genocide, Intervention." In *Revolutions of the Late Twentieth Century*, edited by Jack A. Goldstone, Ted Robert Gurr, and Farrokh Moshiri. Boulder: Westview Press.

———. 1991. "Humanitarian Intervention in Genocidal Situations." In *Genocide: A Critical Bibliographic Review, Vol. II*, edited by Israel W. Charny. New York: Facts on File.

———. 1992. "Bosnia and Somalia: Strategic, Legal, and Moral Dimensions of Humanitarian Intervention." *Report from the Institute for Philosophy and Public Policy* (University of Maryland, College Park) 12, no. 3/4 (Summer/Fall): 1–7.

Heraclides, Alexis. 1991. *The Self-Determination of Minorities in International Politics*. London: Frank Cass.

Licklider, Roy, ed. 1993. *Stopping the Killing: How Civil Wars End*. New York: New York University Press.

Makinda, Samuel M. 1993. *Seeking Peace from Chaos: Humanitarian Intervention in Somalia*. Boulder: Lynne Rienner.

Midlarsky, Manus I., ed. 1992. *The Internationalization of Communal Strife*. London: Routledge.

Ramcharan, B. G. 1991. *The International Law and Practice of Early-Warning and Preventive Diplomacy: The Emerging Global Watch*. Dordrecht: Martinus Nijhoff.

Rupesinghe, Kumar, and Michiko Kuroda, eds. 1992. *Early Warning and Conflict Resolution*. New York: St. Martin's Press.

Ryan, Stephen. 1990. "Ethnic Conflict and the United Nations." *Ethnic and Racial Studies* 13 (1990): 25–49.

Weiss, Thomas G., and Larry Minear, eds. 1993. *Humanitarianism Across Borders: Sustaining Civilians in Times of War*. Boulder: Lynne Rienner.

Zartman, I. William. 1989. *Ripe for Resolution: Conflict and Intervention in Africa*. New Haven: Yale University Press.

□   □   □

Glossary

Assimilation is a strategy for accommodating ethnic minorities that gives individual members incentives and opportunities to subordinate their identities to the language, values, and lifeways of the dominant group. Also see the definitions of **pluralism** and **power-sharing.**

Autocracies sharply restrict civil rights and political participation, concentrate most or all political power in the executive, and distribute and transfer political power within a small political elite.

Autonomy is a political arrangement in which an ethnic group has some control over its own territory, people, and resources but does not have independence as a sovereign state. The specifics of autonomy arrangements vary widely. **Ethnonationalists** who fight **wars of secession** are often ready to accept autonomy rather than independence.

Baathists—Baath Party was founded in the 1940s in Syria. Originally, it combined a secular blend of pan-Arabism with non-Marxist socialism. During the 1970s Baathist power was concentrated within ethnoreligious minorities in Syria (Alawis) and Iraq (Sunnis who were largely from the Tikrit region).

Civil war—see **Wars of secession.**

Collective intervention is the interference by a group of states in another country's internal or territorial affairs.

Communal contenders are culturally distinct peoples, tribes, or clans in heterogeneous societies who seek a larger share of state power. Most African states are made up of numerous communal contenders and are governed by coalitions of these groups.

Contagion is the intentional transmittal of models of political action from one country to another.

Containment became a major theme in U.S. foreign policy after World War II and refers to policies aimed at halting the spread of communism.

Contras are opponents of the Sandinistas who included members of the defeated Somoza National Guard plus disillusioned former supporters of the Sandinistas.

A **convention** in international law is a formal written agreement between states that creates legal obligations for the parties involved.

Democracies guarantee political and civil rights for all citizens, have constitutional limitations on the power of the executive, have multiple parties that compete for office, and transfer power by constitutionally prescribed means.

189

Discrimination refers to deliberately maintained inequalities in ethnic group members' material well-being (**economic discrimination**) or political access (**political discrimination**) in comparison with those of other social groups.

Dominant minorities are numerically small ethnic groups that exercise a preponderance of both political and economic power within a society. Contemporary examples include South Africans of European descent and the Alawis of Syria.

Empirical generalizations are conclusions about a substantial number of cases based on observation, experience, and data.

Ethnic cleansing is the systematic elimination of ethnic minorities from a given territory using such means as terror, expulsion, and murder.

Ethnic groups are composed of people who share a distinctive and enduring collective identity based on shared experiences and cultural traits. They may define themselves, and may be defined by others, in terms of any or all of the following traits: lifeways, religious beliefs, language, physical appearance, region of residence, traditional occupations, and a history of conquest and repression by culturally different peoples. Ethnic groups are also called **communal groups, identity groups,** and **minorities.** The term **minorities** can be misleading, because some people so labeled, like Black South Africans and Shi'i Muslims in Iraq, constitute numerical majorities.

Ethnoclasses are ethnically or culturally distinct peoples, usually descended from slaves or immigrants, who have special economic roles. Examples from Western societies, like the Turks in Germany and African Americans in the United States, are usually of low status. Asian examples, like the Chinese in Malaysia and Indonesia, are often economically advantaged but politically restricted.

Ethnonationalists are large, regionally concentrated groups of people with a history of political independence or autonomy who seek to reestablish their independence or extend their autonomy. Those who want complete independence are called **separatists.**

Ethnopolitical groups are ethnic groups that have organized to promote their common interests. When their actions bring them into open conflict with states, the result is **ethnopolitical conflict.**

Formal recognition in international law and practice refers to the establishment of relations between two countries exemplified by the accreditation of ambassadors.

Genocide is mass murder carried out by or with the complicity of political authorities and directed at distinct communally defined groups. See also **politicide.**

Hegemony refers to the domination of the world or of a region by one state and also to the preponderance of a state's power within the international system.

Humanitarian intervention (see also **intervention**) is reliance on force for the justifiable purpose of protecting the inhabitants of another state from treatment that is arbitrary and persistently abusive.

A **hypothesis** is a testable proposition (one that includes an if-then statement) that can be verified or disproved.

Indigenous peoples are conquered descendants of original inhabitants of a region who usually live in peripheral regions, practice subsistence agriculture or herding, and have cultures that are clearly distinct from those of dominant groups.

Instrumental explanations of ethnic conflict attribute it mainly to the use or manipulation of ethnic identity in the pursuit of material and political objectives; see also **primordial.**

Insurgency refers to guerrilla wars fought by Marxist-inspired revolutionaries. Strategies designed by military planners during the Cold War to fight such challengers were called **counterinsurgency.**

International law refers to the body of rules that govern primarily relations between states; it is derived primarily from custom and treaties. An important distinction is made between **common** or **customary law,** which is based on those practices that through repeated usage have been widely accepted as binding rules by states, and **statutory law,** which is enacted by the legislative branch of governments or by an international body and is intended as a permanent rule.

Intervention means the dictatorial interference by one state in the affairs of another state for the purpose of either maintaining or changing the existing order of things, rather than mere interference per se.

Islamic fundamentalism is a movement that stresses the literal adherence to basic principles as written in the Quran, the Hadiths, and the Sharia (Islamic law), and its five schools of legal interpretation. There are four Sunni schools (Hanafi, Maliki, Shafii, Hanbali) and one Shi'i school (Ja'fari).

Legitimacy refers to the perception that a government, its leaders, and its policies are just and worthy of support.

Levels of analysis refers to the factors thought to influence the decisionmaking process; they range from individual preferences to roles, societal input, regime characteristics, regional relations, and traits of the world system.

Mestizo is a term used in Latin America to refer to people of mixed Spanish and Indian descent.

Micronationalism is the demand for independent statehood by small communal groups.

Mobilization is the process by which leaders organize the energies and resources of their followers to pursue common political objectives.

A **model** is a simplified image of reality that describes the causes of any given phenomenon.

Modernization refers to the process by which people break away from primordial ties and develop loyalties to larger associations, a nation, or a state. The term was formerly used to refer to the process by which non-Western peoples adopt Western economic and political institutions, but it is now widely recognized that people can modernize without following Western models.

Multiculturalism is a synonym for **pluralism.**

Multilateral means actions that involve several countries, as distinct from **unilateral,** which describes actions initiated by one country.

Operationalization refers to the process of defining concepts in a hypothesis so they can be measured in real quantities.

Pan-Arabism is a doctrine that stresses the unity of all Arabs, favors social reform and economic development, and opposes imperialism and Zionism. It was especially influential in Middle Eastern politics during the 1950s and 1960s.

Peacebuilding refers to the ability to anticipate conflict in order to apply proper measures to create the conditions for peace.

Peacekeeping refers to the use of military personnel in noncombatant roles, such as monitoring cease-fires. Such activities require the consent of the warring parties.

Peacemaking (or peace enforcement) enables peacekeeping forces not only to monitor a cease-fire but also to enforce it if it breaks down. Control over deployment and operation is exercised by the UN Security Council or can be delegated to a regional organization.

A **plebiscite** is a vote in which the people of an entire region express their preference for or against a proposal, such as choice of government.

Plural societies consist of a number of ethnic groups, each with a distinct collective identity and interests, who are not ranked or **stratified** in relationship to one another. See also **stratified societies.**

Pluralism is a strategy for accommodating ethnic minorities that recognizes their individual and collective right to preserve their language, values, and lifeways in coexistence with those of the dominant group. Also see **assimilation** and **power-sharing.**

Politicide is mass murder carried out by or with the complicity of governing authorities (as in **genocide**), but victims are targeted primarily because of their political affiliation.

Populist states are weakly institutionalized political systems that are in a transitional state to either democracy or increased autocracy. Political power is usually transferred through military coups or popular uprisings short of revolution.

Power-sharing is a strategy for accommodating ethnic minorities based on the assumption that ethnic identities and organizations are the basic elements of society. Political power is exercised jointly by these groups, each of which is represented in government and each of which has veto power over policies that adversely affect group members. Also see **assimilation** and **pluralism.**

Preventive diplomacy refers to nonmilitary options used to prevent escalation of crisis into open conflict, such as sending fact-finding missions, providing for mediation and arbitration, issuing formal warnings of impending sanctions, and offering political or material incentives.

Primordial explanations of ethnic conflict attribute it mainly to the desire to protect a people's identity and culture; see also **instrumental.**

Probability statements in social science research indicate that there exists a partial or tentative relationship between x (cause) and y (effect). That is, there is a tendency for x to be associated with y, but the relationship is not exact.

Propositions are untested statements or ideas about a specific kind of causal relationship.

Protracted communal conflicts are conflicts between ethnic groups and governments over fundamental issues of group rights and identity that persist for generations unless and until the underlying issues are resolved. They usually involve recurring episodes of intense violence.

Sanctions are agreements among states to stop trade with violators of international law completely or in one particular commodity, such as military goods.

Shi'i Muslims are the minority that follows basic tenets of Islam but that regards Ali and his heirs as the only legitimate successors to the prophet Muhammad.

Socialist states use the doctrines of Marx and Lenin to justify concentration of power in a single party that is used by the elite to mobilize mass support for the regime, encourage political participation only within the party, and transfer power through competition within the party.

The **sphere of obligation** refers to who or what enjoys the protection of principles of identifiable norms or laws.

The **state system** is the political organization of the world into a set of territorial-based states with governments whose sovereignty is recognized by other states.

In **stratified societies,** status, power, and wealth are unequally distributed among groups according to their ethnicity. The socially maintained distinctions among groups in stratified societies are called **cleavages.** Also see **plural societies.**

Sunni Muslims are the orthodox majority of Islam who accept the teachings of the Quran, the Hadith, and the four schools of jurisprudence (identified under **Islamic fundamentalism**), and who also accept the Sunna and the historic succession of caliphs.

Variables are measurable properties of concepts.

Visible minorities is a fairly recent term used in European and North American societies to refer collectively to resident minorities of African, Asian, and indigenous origins. It is replacing the older term *people of color.*

Wars of secession are violent conflicts in which a regionally based ethnic group attempts to secede from an existing state. They are different from **revolutions,** in which rebels who may or may not have a common ethnic identity seek to seize power in an existing state. **Civil war** is often used as a generic term to refer to these and other kinds of intense conflicts within states.

□ □ □

About the Book and Authors

As hot spots from Bosnia to the Caucasus to the Horn of Africa clearly signal, the end of the Cold War does not mean an end to regional conflict but rather the early phase of a new era in world history. This book is an introduction to this new era of ethnic challenges to world order and security.

From Africa's post-colonial rebellions in the 1960s and 1970s to the anti-immigrant violence in the 1990s, *Ethnic Conflict in World Politics* surveys the historical, geographic, and cultural diversity of ethnopolitical conflict. Using an analytical model to elucidate four well-chosen case studies—the Kurds, the Miskitos, the Chinese in Malaysia, and the Turks in Germany—the authors give students tools for analyzing emerging conflicts based on the demands of nationalists, indigenous peoples, and immigrant minorities throughout the world. The international community is challenged to respond more constructively to these conflicts than it has in divided Yugoslavia, by using the emerging doctrines of peacekeeping and peacemaking that are detailed in this book.

The text is liberally illustrated with maps, tables, and figures to enhance students' understanding of the quest of unfamiliar peoples for autonomy and rights, putting it into the context of international politics. An appendix surveying over fifty of the most serious ethnopolitical conflicts in the world today—keyed to a global map and identifying the groups and issues as well as counting the number of lives affected—shows the enormous geopolitical and cultural reach of this issue.

Ted Robert Gurr is professor of government and politics and Distinguished Scholar at the Center for International Development and Conflict Management, University of Maryland at College Park. **Barbara Harff** is associate professor of political science at the U.S. Naval Academy in Annapolis.

BOOKS IN THIS SERIES

Kenneth W. Grundy
**South Africa: Domestic Crisis
and Global Challenge**
□ □ □
Gareth Porter and Janet Welsh Brown
Global Environmental Politics
□ □ □
Davis S. Mason
**Revolution in East-Central Europe
and World Politics**
□ □ □
Georg Sørensen
**Democracy and Democratization:
Processes and Prospects in a Changing World**
□ □ □
Steve Chan
**East Asian Dynamism: Growth, Order, and
Security in the Pacific Region, second edition**
□ □ □
Barry B. Hughes
**International Futures: Choices in
the Creation of a New World Order**
□ □ □
Jack Donnelly
International Human Rights
□ □ □
V. Spike Peterson and Anne Sisson Runyan
Global Gender Issues
□ □ □
Sarah J. Tisch and Michael B. Wallace
**Dilemmas of Development Assistance:
The What, Why, and Who of Foreign Aid**
□ □ □
Frederic S. Pearson
**The Global Spread of Arms:
Political Economy of International Security**

Index